MEET ME AT 10

BOOK 2

VICKY JONES
CLAIRE HACKNEY

Copyright © 2019 by Vicky Jones and Claire Hackney.

All rights reserved.

No part of this book may be reproduced in any form or by any electronic or mechanical means, including information storage and retrieval systems, without written permission from the author, except for the use of brief quotations in a book review.

GRAB YOUR FREE BOOK NOW

Chloe - A prequel to Meet Me at 10

What if a life-shattering family tragedy forces you to completely rethink your future? Destined for a different path in life, twenty-year-old Chloe Bruce's world is shattered after a tragic accident on her father's plantation in Alabama.

Ok, so how do I get my FREE book?

EASY! See the next page

GRAB YOUR FREE BOOK NOW

Instructions:

1. Open the camera or the QR reader application on your smartphone.
2. Point your camera at the QR code to scan the QR code.
3. A notification will pop-up on screen.
4. Click on the notification to open the website link

GRAB YOUR FREE BOOK NOW

Instructions:

1. Open the scanner or the QR code Application on your smartphone.
2. Point the camera at the QR code & scan the QR code.
3. A notification will pop up on screen.
4. Click on the notification to open the exclusive link.

SCAN ME

JOIN IN!

If you would like to receive regular behind-the-scenes updates, get beta reading opportunities, enter giveaways and much, much more, simply visit the site below:

http://hackneyandjones.com

CONTENTS

About Vicky Jones — xiii
About Claire Hackney — xv
The Shona Jackson series — xvii
The Shona Jackson series — xix
Grab the Shona Jackson series HERE — xxi

Chapter 1	1
Chapter 2	7
Chapter 3	10
Chapter 4	13
Chapter 5	15
Chapter 6	18
Chapter 7	20
Chapter 8	22
Chapter 9	26
Chapter 10	28
Chapter 11	38
Chapter 12	41
Chapter 13	44
Chapter 14	47
Chapter 15	49
Chapter 16	54
Chapter 17	57
Chapter 18	63
Chapter 19	65
Chapter 20	68
Chapter 21	71
Chapter 22	74
Chapter 23	80
Chapter 24	83
Chapter 25	86
Chapter 26	91
Chapter 27	95
Chapter 28	99

Chapter 29	102
Chapter 30	107
Chapter 31	113
Chapter 32	118
Chapter 33	123
Chapter 34	128
Chapter 35	135
Chapter 36	138
Chapter 37	141
Chapter 38	143
Chapter 39	149
Chapter 40	152
Chapter 41	156
Chapter 42	161
Chapter 43	167
Chapter 44	174
Chapter 45	182
Chapter 46	188
Chapter 47	191
Chapter 48	195
Chapter 49	198
Chapter 50	201
Chapter 51	206
Chapter 52	212
Chapter 53	216
Chapter 54	227
Chapter 55	237
Chapter 56	242
Chapter 57	245
Chapter 58	250
Chapter 59	259
Chapter 60	268
Chapter 61	275
Chapter 62	279
Chapter 63	288
Chapter 64	298
Chapter 65	304
Chapter 66	307
Chapter 67	309

Chapter 68	315
Chapter 69	321
Chapter 70	330
Chapter 71	333
Chapter 72	342
Chapter 73	344
Chapter 74	347
Chapter 75	355
Chapter 76	358
Chapter 77	365
Chapter 78	374
Chapter 79	379
Chapter 80	391
Chapter 81	402
Chapter 82	404
Chapter 83	414
Chapter 84	418
Feedback	423
The Beach House	425
PART 1: AUGUST 1958	429
Chapter 1	431
Chapter 2	441
Join in!	445
Acknowledgments	447
Our Team	449

ABOUT VICKY JONES

Vicky Jones was born in Essex, England. She is an author and singer-songwriter, with numerous examples of her work on iTunes and YouTube. At 20 years old she entered the Royal Navy. After leaving the Navy realising she was drifting through life with no sense of direction, she wrote a bucket list of 300 things to achieve which took her traveling, facing her fears and going for her dreams. At the time of printing, she is two-thirds of the way through her bucket list.

One item on her list was to write a song for a cause. Her anti-bullying track called "House of Cards" is now on iTunes to download.

Writing a novel was on her bucket list, and through a chance writing competition at her local writing group, the idea for *Meet Me At 10* was born. Vicky hopes she can change hearts and minds due to some of the gritty themes of the book.

Vicky is a keen traveler, stemming from her days traveling the world in the Royal Navy, and has visited around 50 countries so far. She has also graduated from The Open University after studying part time for her degree in psychology and criminology—another bucket list tick! She is currently writing a book series about her bucket list adventures, the first of which is entitled *'Project Me, Project You'*, alongside planning and writing more fiction books and book marketing guides for self-published authors.

Also in the pipeline is a writing course, put together to help aspiring authors plan and write their first novel.

She now lives in Cheshire, splitting her time between there and visiting her family and friends back in Essex.

For more information on upcoming book releases, to tell us what you think of the books, or just to say hi, visit the sites below.

facebook.com/VickyJonesWriter

twitter.com/vickyjones7

instagram.com/vickytjones

ABOUT CLAIRE HACKNEY

Claire Hackney is a former English Literature, Drama and Media Studies teacher who, after attending a local writing group with Vicky and writing several of her own short stories over the years, has now decided to focus her career on full-time novel writing.

She is an avid historian and has thoroughly enjoyed researching different aspects of the 1950s for the 'Shona Jackson' trilogy of novels.

Claire is very much looking forward getting started on the many future writing projects she and Vicky have in the pipeline, including the 'DI Rachel Morrison' thriller series and several standalone novels.

For more information on upcoming book releases, to tell us what you think of the books, or just to say hi, visit the sites below:

facebook.com/ClaireHackneyAuthor
twitter.com/clairehac
instagram.com/clairehackneyauthor

THE SHONA JACKSON SERIES

Shona: Book 1 - A prequel to Meet Me at 10

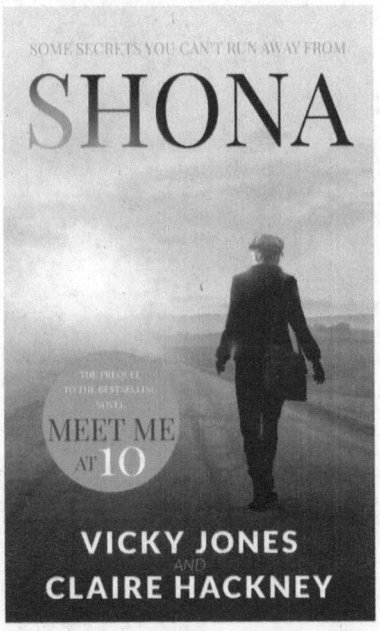

Everyone has a secret. Hers could get her killed... Mississippi, 1956. Shona Jackson knows two things—how to repair cars and that her dark childhood secret must stay buried. On the run from Louisiana, she finds shelter in the home of a kindly old lady and a job as a mechanic. But a woman working a man's job can't avoid notice in a small town. And attention is dangerous...

THE SHONA JACKSON SERIES

The Beach House: Book 3

New town. New life. Old enemies. With the past and present colliding and threatening their future together, can Shona protect her new life and the lives of those closest to her?

GRAB THE SHONA JACKSON SERIES HERE

Instructions:

1. Open the camera or the QR reader application on your smartphone.

2. Point your camera at the QR code to scan the QR code.

3. A notification will pop-up on screen.

4. Click on the notification to open the website link

CRACKTHE SHONA JACKSON SERIES HERE

Instructions:

1. Open the camera on the QR code or application on your smartphone.
2. Hold the camera up to QR code to scan the QR code, a link icon will popup on screen.
3. Click on the pop-up icon to open the series link.

MEET ME AT 10

Chapter 1

Trudging along the seemingly endless straight road, Shona Jackson shivered as she felt the temperature in the air around her starting to fall. Jagged hills on both sides of the road loomed over her, their interweaving faces sliding down into plush greenery. The emerging crescent moon brought with it fears of being stranded in its wake, surrounded by darkness with her path ahead illuminated only by the occasional glare of speeding truck headlights. Hunger pangs groaning within her reminded Shona that she had little choice but to push onwards in search of civilization.

Running a dry tongue over her parched lips in a vain attempt to lubricate them, she wrapped her coat around her body to keep out the icy chill as the roar of a truck engine sounded in the short distance behind her. She stepped to the side of the road, safely out of the truck's path. She held a hand to her eyes, preparing herself for the expected whoosh from its heavy tires and for the cloud of dust that would no doubt be kicked up by them to choke and blind her temporarily. But there was neither a whoosh nor a dust cloud.

The truck was slowing down.

Its headlights remained on as the truck creaked to a halt,

the driver's hulking silhouette darkly framed by the windshield.

Edging forward, Shona pulled her crumpled cap down to just above her eyebrows and tucked her short blonde hair safely behind her small ears. Nervously, she hooked her thumbs underneath her coat collar, folding it up around the soft skin of her neck and pinching it against her chin.

"Need a lift?" shouted a gravelly voice from the driver's side.

"Um–" she replied in her deepest voice, looking from side to side as she assessed her predicament.

"Look, I ain't got all night, son."

"Sure, thanks."

Stifling a relieved grin at his assumption, Shona reached up for the door handle, climbed up the three steps into the cab and slammed the door. She sat on the passenger seat furthest away from the driver, his malodorous stink making this a necessity if nothing else.

"Where you headin', boy?"

The driver was easier to see now under the cab's overhead strip light. Shona discreetly grimaced as she noticed his pudgy white belly overhanging a pair of ripped jeans, the waistband of which had long since given up the fight. His straggly brown beard appeared to have yesterday's food still clinging to it and dark, grubby sweat patches adorned the armpits of his grimy red t-shirt, completing his stomach-churningly feculent look.

"Just the next town, sir." She lowered her chin as she spoke, hugging her battered old brown satchel close to her chest.

"Well, that ain't no five-minute journey, boy. What the hell y'doin' out here at this time?"

Shona cast a surreptitious glance at the driver's watch. It was 10:55 p.m.

"My ride bailed."

He peered over the bridge of his blotchy red nose at his passenger, an air of suspicion crossing his eyes. He grunted, then returned his attention to the pitch-dark road up ahead. Hoping he wouldn't pry too much, Shona tucked her satchel underneath her weary head and leaned against the door, then pulled her cap down over her eyes. The fingers on her right hand traced along the doorframe until she found the handle as the motion of the truck began to rock her into a deep, well-needed sleep.

∼

After what only felt like five minutes to Shona, the truck hit a massive pothole in the road. The driver's subsequent swerve jolted her awake. She rubbed her tired, red eyes and squinted into the bright lights of the oncoming cars, shaking her head a few times to clear it after being snatched from her dream. It was then she looked up at the driver's staring eyes and recoiled in horror when she realized her cap had fallen backward, revealing her heart-shaped face and high cheekbones. Her satchel pillow now lay in the footwell, having dropped from underneath her head after the sharp swerve. Her coat had slipped open, revealing her delicate neck through the open top buttons of her checked shirt, and the thin straps of her bra peeking beyond. Shona, realizing her cover had been blown, buttoned up her shirt as quick as she could and pointlessly straightened her cap.

"You're a *broad*?"

The driver's face contorted with confusion, his nicotine-stained fingers gripping the truck steering wheel as he fought to control the swerve.

"Please, sir, I'm sorry. I didn't intend to trick you. I just wanted to get to the next town, and when you thought I was a guy, I guess I just went along with it." She shrugged.

"What game you playin'? You tryin' to make me look like an idiot?" he growled.

"I didn't mean to. I understand if you don't wanna take me any further." Shona looked through the windshield into the darkness with no way of guessing where in the hell they were. She hunched her knees into her chest and curled up into a ball, shrinking into the darkest corner of the cab.

The driver sat with his eyes fixed on the road ahead, his gray teeth grinding as he shook his head with embarrassment at his earlier assumption. After a few minutes his indignation appeared to fade as he chewed on his bottom lip, seemingly deep in thought.

It wasn't noise this time but silence that woke Shona again that night. Still dark out, the truck was now parked in the middle of nowhere, with no sign of civilization or any kind of landmark. She turned her head left in the hope of gleaning an explanation from the driver, but as she did so her eyes widened with revulsion, the dim light of the cab revealing a sight that turned her stomach.

"What the hell y'doin'?" Shona stared in horror.

The driver had fixed his black beady eyes on her, his body reclined into a more *comfortable* position. His pants were wide open, exposing his fat, hairy thighs. The cab window had misted up from his hot breath as he steadily rocked his hand backward and forward inside his stained underwear.

"There's one way you could earn your ride," he drawled.

Shona kept her eyes on the driver as she tried to plan her next move.

"I'm sorry. I don't want *that*." Holding her left hand up, she reached down to the footwell with the other, feeling around for the strap of her satchel.

"Come over here, help me out, darlin'. You're a real pretty

girl and I've had a long journey." His eyes rolled back in his head.

Scrabbling along the surface of the door, Shona's shaking fingers finally located the metal handle. At that same moment, the driver lunged towards her and dug his dirty nails into her neck, forcing her downwards onto him. Gagging from the stench of his body odor, she struggled with all her might to keep her face out of his lap as he squeezed her throat tightly. She spread her arms out wide, her right hand gripping the dashboard, her left clinging desperately onto the seat next to him as she fought to stop him entering her mouth.

"No!" she squealed.

As the driver's arousal reached fever pitch, his grip began to increase in pressure around the back of her thin neck. With a frustrated grunt and a fistful of Shona's messy blonde hair, he jolted her head fiercely, causing her sweaty hand to slip from the dashboard. Shona's head fell forward, but instead of falling onto his lap, she found herself met with the top of his chubby thigh. Instinctively, she bit down on it so hard that within seconds the rancid taste of blood oozed into her mouth. Yelping in white-hot agony, the driver lashed out, punching her square on the right side of her jaw. Flying back into her seat, she slammed her head against the door window, cracking the thick glass. Through blurred vision, she watched the driver grimace as he tucked himself away, inspected his injured thigh, then wiped his bloody hands on his grubby jeans.

With the driver distracted, Shona grabbed her satchel and wrapped her fingers around the door handle. Her heart pounded as she took a final look across at the driver, who was now staring murderously at her as he tried to stem the blood flowing freely from his bitten thigh. His face twisted in pain as he buttoned up his jeans, then bent forward and reached into the glove box. Panicking, she pressed heavily against the door, relieved to hear its hinges groan as it opened behind her, sending bitingly cold air rushing into the stuffy cab. She stumbled down the steps, landing in a crumpled heap on the ground. With a tight hold on her satchel, Shona sprinted away as fast as her trembling legs could carry her.

Running in a zigzag formation, she ducked as the crack of a gunshot pierced the silent night air and whizzed inches past her ear. Then another. Then a third. She dropped to her knees behind a mound of fallen rocks to catch her breath, listening for any further shots. In the distance, she heard the truck's engine restarting and then the whoosh of wheel-spinning tires as it skidded away, its headlight beams disappearing into the bitterly cold night.

A few hours and several miles later, Shona sighed with relief as the dawn finally began to break. Tentatively, she touched the back of her throbbing head with her fingers, groaning when she saw the dark red blood that had coated them.

Just as her exhaustion threatened to overwhelm her, she spotted a river in the distance. Knowing it had to lead into a town somewhere, she headed towards it. With the sun beginning to pour its light into the sky, landmarks that the darkness had hidden were now illuminated. She could see a shed-like building on the horizon and began to make her way over to it, treading cautiously over uneven rocks littering her path. Approaching the shack with caution, she reached out for the latch on the wooden door, hearing a welcome click as it bore no resistance. Over in the far corner, a small pile of hay looked as good a place as any to snuggle down and get some longed-for rest. She lay down, placed her satchel underneath her pounding head and instantly fell sound asleep.

Chapter 2

"**W**ho the hell are you?"

Shona jolted awake as the metal barrel of a shotgun cast its long shadow over her.

"What? Oh, I'm sorry, sir. I was dog-tired last night. I've been traveling and I found this place. I'll move on, I'm sorry–" she sat upright and reached for her satchel.

"Don't you move, not one inch. You plannin' on stealing my animals?" He edged closer, the shadow of his gun now crossing the beam of sunlight that had been burning her dry eyes. An old man, with tousled white hair and weathered skin, stood glaring at her.

"No way, sir, I just needed to rest."

She held her hands up in surrender for the second time in less than six hours.

"Get up." He gestured with his gun, keeping his suspicious eyes fixed on the young blonde girl he'd found on his property. Shona rose, wobbling slightly from the ache still thundering around the back of her head. He lowered his gun a little and backed up until he was almost outside the shack. In the dawn light, his sharp gray eyes softened when he saw the girl he was pointing his shotgun at was injured.

"You been in a fight or something?" He furrowed his brow, noticing the angry bruise on her right cheek.

"Some jerk tried to attack me. I ran, and I been hiding out here to rest until I move on, sir." Her bright blue eyes pleaded with him for mercy.

He lowered his rifle, his aggression towards her waning. "Well, you won't get much rest out here. The cows are gon' want that bale of hay you're lyin' on for their breakfast soon. Come back to the house. M'wife can make you some food for your journey. I'm Tom, Tom Bird, and you are?" He unloaded the cartridges from his shotgun, placed them in his top shirt pocket and slung the open gun over his forearm.

"Shona Jackson, sir."

~

"Would you like some more sweet tea?"

Ruby Bird's smile had straight away put Shona at ease after Tom returned to the house for his breakfast with a stray in tow. She put down the jug in front of her guest, readjusted the handmade shawl that was draped around her neck and smoothed back a lock of graying hair into the bun on top of her head as she busied herself in the kitchen, ensuring there was plenty of food on the table.

"Thank you, Mrs. Bird."

"Please, call me Ruby," she said, tapping Shona's forearm.

"So, Shona...heck, that's a strange name for these parts. How'd you end up with that one?" Tom chuckled as he buttered his toast.

"Well, sir, my momma had some real good friends when she was a girl, called Shane and Fiona. They came over from Ireland, y'see, to start a new life. So, I guess when I came along she just decided to honor them by namin' me *Shona*. Heck, I guess y'could say I'm all mixed up!" She grinned back at Tom, who nodded his head and took a huge bite of his toast.

"So, what's next for you, lil' lady? What are your plans?"

"Not sure really, sir. Just keep on movin' on until I figure somethin' out." Her voice tailed off. She had no idea where the hell she was.

"Tom, call me Tom. I'm not one for formalities," he said.

Shona smiled. "OK, Tom. I don't have any exact plans. It was just to find a job, somewhere to sleep. Live the simple life, y'know?" She leaned forward to take another bite of her toast, her elbows planted firmly on the table.

"Can you sew?" Ruby asked as she sipped her coffee.

"Pardon me, ma'am?" Shona spluttered.

"Can you mend clothes?" she elaborated.

"I'm sorry, no ... but I can mend vehicles, any kind you put in front of me! I may be a girl, only twenny-four, but I know more about trucks than any man. I can ride too, tame any damn horse you give me, I swear I can." Her keen eyes shone.

Looking at each other, Ruby and Tom chuckled at her enthusiasm, overlooking the fact that she was chewing her toast heartily with no regard for table manners.

"Where you from, Shona?" Ruby asked, clearing the breakfast plates off the red and white gingham tablecloth.

"Claybank, Louisiana, ma'am."

"Never heard of it." Tom took another bite of his toast.

"Nobody has." Shona chuckled. "It's a small town. I worked on a farm with my father until I was sixteen."

"Why'd you leave?" Ruby asked, sitting back down to face her.

"Yeah, and how the hell did y'end up all the way out here in Alabama?" Tom added.

Shona's smile faded. "See now, that's a long story."

Chapter 3

"Linda!" Larry Bruce bellowed at the top of his voice in the direction of his secretary, who was working away at her desk.

"Yes, Mr. Bruce." She raced over to his office and cowered in the doorway, peering at him over the top of her narrow-framed glasses.

"Linda, get the sheriff on the phone right now! Tell him to come straight over here," he growled, eyeballing the three terrified men standing in front of him.

"Right away, Mr. Bruce," she squeaked, adjusting her glasses to write down a quick note on her miniature notepad, then hopping back to her office.

Bruce's mustache bristled with anger as he glared at the men in front of him. One had beads of sweat on his forehead which slithered down his nose, his eyes wild with panic.

"Sir ... please, may I speak?" he begged.

"Shut your damn filthy mouth, you son'bitch," Bruce spat. "Y'go crawling to Ellis for a job, knowing he's the easy touch when it comes to you coloreds, then have the audacity to thieve wallets from the good, honest white folk here?"

Bruce erupted out of his chair and glared at the petrified

man. "I hope they rip your ass apart in prison where you belong, all chained up!"

"Mr. Bruce, I swear to Almighty God, I don't know about no wallets. Ain't seen 'em, none of us have!" The sweating black man fell to his knees.

"Get your sorry ass up." Bruce flicked his booted foot at him.

In desperation, the man dragged himself upright and stood next to the two others. The elder of the three looked towards Larry Bruce but dared not make eye contact. Instead, he focused on a large, elegantly framed photograph of a smiling young man on the wall above Bruce's head.

"Mr. Bruce, sir, I promise on my own dead son's grave. We ain't taken those wallets. Search us, search our bags, search our lockers."

Larry Bruce smirked.

Ten minutes later, Linda's voice rang out again from just outside the door.

"Mr. Bruce, sir, the sheriff's here."

Sheriff Landon's intimidating figure almost filled the doorway as he entered Bruce's office, flanked by his scrawny-looking deputy.

"Y'know what to do, sheriff. I'll leave this matter in your ... capable hands." Bruce winked at Landon who responded with a tip of his hat. He unclasped the small leather strap holding his revolver in its holster and motioned to his deputy to slap the iron handcuffs onto the black men, so weak with dread that they didn't struggle as they were led off.

"Anything else, Mr. Bruce?" Linda asked, about to return to her desk.

"No, thank you. Close the door behind you," Bruce replied, opening his desk drawer to retrieve his ever-present bottle of whiskey. Underneath the bottle, three black leather wallets he'd arranged that morning to be taken from the lockers of his workers nestled snugly underneath. Pouring himself a large measure, he slouched back in his chair and swigged it down in one deep gulp, smiling to himself in satisfaction at an excellent afternoon's work. It was his mission to rid his business of colored workers.

His plan had been a success so far.

Chapter 4

"This is Storm."

Tom patted the neck of the feisty chestnut-colored mare stomping her hooves on the ground next to her stable as if she were about to be let loose in a race. He and Shona were standing in the back field behind the farmhouse, a stunning expanse stretching as far as the eye could see. Their shadows lengthened as the afternoon sun lowered in the clear sky.

"Storm?" her eyebrows raised.

"Yep, every time we let her out, she moves like a damn whirlwind. This beast really is untamable." Tom held on tightly to the reins as Storm bucked at him, proving his point.

Shona laughed and patted the animal who threw her head to the side in response, almost taking Shona's arm out its socket. She back-kicked the wall of her stable door several times, sending loud thuds echoing across the flat ground.

"Yeah, I can see that," Shona grinned.

She scanned her eyes over the landscape that surrounded her. It headed down towards the Weaver, a fast-flowing river with gorgeous Cahaba lilies and wildflowers blooming on its banks. The Birds' land was used for growing crops and grazing their farm animals, generating most of their stable but meager income. Tom smiled as he left her lost in her faraway thoughts.

When she returned to the farmhouse a while later, she sensed she'd interrupted Tom and Ruby talking in the kitchen. She turned on her heel to head back outside.

"Shona, wait!" Ruby gestured towards her. "Tom and I have just spoken, and we wanted to ask if you would like to stay here a night or two, just until you find yourself somewhere more permanent, I mean. We'll have to clear some space in the barn across the way, but it's warm."

"Really?" Shona couldn't contain her excitement long enough to even allow Ruby to complete her offer. "My God, yes, please! I'll help with the animals for my keep. I don't have no money yet, but–"

"That's OK. Ruby and I would just appreciate any help you can give on the farm. We're not getting any younger!" Tom glanced over at his wife, a cheeky smile sweeping over his kindly face.

"Speak for yourself, Bird!" Ruby jabbed a finger into his belly.

"I'd like that. I surely would. Thank y'all so much!" Shona beamed, leaping at Tom and Ruby and wrapping them both in a tight hug.

Chapter 5

"Mr. Bruce, sir! What an honor to be chosen to work alongside a fine gentleman such as yourself, who I respect and, quite frankly, am in awe of."

The dashingly handsome Kyle Chambers ran a hand over his perfectly coiffed jet black hair and flashed a well-rehearsed smile exposing his bright white teeth as he extended his muscular arm to shake Larry Bruce's hand. He wore his best gray flannel suit, white button-down collar shirt and tapered, pleatless pants. Aiming to impress his new boss, Kyle's outfit was completed by a striped tie and shiny black leather wing-tipped shoes. At thirty-four years old, he knew he was finally onto a good thing as he glanced eagerly around Bruce's lavishly decorated office.

"I'm sure you'll do well here, Kyle. I like the way y'think. Hell, you remind me of myself at your age," Bruce replied, walking around the back of his desk.

"Thank you, sir." Kyle felt the swell of confidence grow larger in his belly.

"Great. I'll ask Linda to give you details of when you'll start work. By then, my daughter Chloe will be home from college. She's gon' be my number two, but y'know, we'll see how you do and who knows," Bruce said, pouring a celebratory drink for the two of them. "I'll be training her to help run this place once I retire, but I need a man to, y'know, take this company forward. I mean, who in the hell heard of a woman being in charge? Investors would run a mile. But she's my only child to pass my half of this place on to after my son died five years ago. Just twenty-three years old he was."

Bruce paused for a moment, remembering the tragic day he'd found his son lying dead in a pool of blood, his arm ripped clean off by the threshing machine a colored worker was trapped in. He'd never come to terms with the fact that the colored man had lived and his son hadn't.

"I won't let you down, sir!" Kyle assured him.

Ruby joined Tom and Shona in the sparsely furnished barn, her arms laden with cotton towels and thick flowery blankets to make the place feel more like home. A weary-looking single mattress lay on top of some wooden pallets, keeping it off the hay-strewn floor. It wasn't much, but it was more than Shona had had in a long time.

Perfect, she thought.

"Shona, do you wear dresses at all?" Ruby asked, trying to be as tactful as she could.

"Dresses? No, ma'am, I don't. I guess I dress like I do 'cos I travel around so much. That way, guys don't give me no trouble, y'know?" Her cheeks flushed bright red.

"I was only asking as I could fix you a few new things to wear if you like? I saw you only had a little bag, so–"

Ruby gestured towards the battered-looking satchel lying on the floor next to Shona's new bed.

"Well, Shona, until Ruby here can make you some other kinda clothes, I'll lend you some pants, shirts, overalls and stuff.

Will that make you feel more comfortable?" Tom smiled, sensing her embarrassment.

"I'd really like that, thank you," she replied.

Clearing space and tidying the area, they smiled at each other as they created a little haven for Shona and basked in the warm glow of the longed-for family feeling that was enveloping the three of them.

Chapter 6

"Larry? What can I do for you?"

Jeffrey Ellis poured himself a glass of his finest red wine from a crystal decanter, relaxing in his chair in the palatial home he shared with his wife Marjory, who was resting upstairs after another bout of illness. Holding the phone to his ear, he sipped his wine, savoring its flavor.

"I've had to get rid of those damn coloreds you sent my way. They've been thievin'." Bruce tried hard to sound disappointed.

"What?" Ellis lowered his glass. "I heard good things from the guy they came from. You sure?"

"Oh, yeah, I turned them over to the sheriff like the last ones. You can't change 'em. They don't appreciate what you're tryin' to do for them, Jeffrey," Bruce continued in feigned dismay.

Ellis reclined back in his chair, deciding, as usual, to give Bruce the benefit of the heavy doubt.

"Fine. Got anything else for me?"

"You know about us taking on Kyle Chambers. I think he'll do well. Other than that, the numbers are looking good. There is one thing; I'm looking to buy some replacement machinery. Damn tractors keep breaking down, so I'll need to buy new parts. We can't keep up with the orders if things ain't working right!"

"Sure, go ahead. I dropped some cash off on my last visit. There should be plenty in the safe."

"That's great, Jeffrey. Oh, and say hi to Marj for me. I hope she's feeling better soon."

"OK, Larry, see you when I'm next in the office."

Ellis put the phone down and drained the last of his wine. Bruce sat back in his chair, a satisfied smile creeping over his face.

Chapter 7

"D'you know anywhere I could find work 'round these parts?" Shona asked, glancing up from the hearty breakfast Ruby had prepared the following morning.

"Tom?" Ruby aimed her spatula in his direction as she heated up the pan to fry more eggs.

"Daynes is a tough town, Shona. I mean, opinions have changed a little since the war ended, but it's still pretty much unheard of having a woman working with trucks, even one as hardworking as you. I know your old place back in Mississippi let you, but that's rare. There are some bone-idle people in this town, but they'd rather die than let a slip of a girl show 'em how to do their job properly! But we're only a coupla years away from the '60s so who knows, maybe things'll change."

"Want some more?" Ruby put the freshly fried eggs in the serving dish next to Shona's plate as if to offer some crumb of comfort.

Tom put down his knife and fork and wiped his mouth with his napkin. "Well now, see, there's this one place over the other side of town, coupla miles from here. I mean, I ain't worked there or nothin', but I've heard from people. They got trucks, tractors, you name it coming and going. It's a cotton plantation with a workshop on the side doing repairs and stuff. All depends if you get the chance to speak to the *nice* guy."

"Nice guy?" Shona said.

"Yeah, his name's Jeffrey Ellis. He co-owns the business but lets that no-good Larry Bruce run it day-to-day. It's Ellis you need to find. Don't bother speaking to Bruce. The things I've heard about that man would make your hair curl! He runs the whole of Daynes through fear alone. Me and Ruby try to stay away from town as much as we can nowadays, away from that son'bitch's influence. Ruby used to be the town's nurse until about five years ago, but then Bruce made the place feel so damn dangerous for her to be out at night on call. Nah, it's Ellis you want. I hear that even coloreds get a job after speaking to him–"

"Ellis tries to give 'em a chance first, y'know?" Ruby chipped in, trying to sound optimistic.

Shona leaned forward, drinking in every word. Her keen blue eyes widened at the prospect of getting a job that would help her to stay longer with Tom and Ruby and allow her to save some money to figure out her next move. After a few moments of contemplation, she raised her eyes to Tom and Ruby.

"Where can I find this Jeffrey Ellis?"

Chapter 8

"Hayward, what the hell's in your glass? You're talkin' like you're drunk already."

Henry Conway stubbed out his ever-present cigar in the ash tray next to him later that evening as he laughed at another ridiculous idea coming from James Hayward, a man notorious for his harebrained schemes to make even more money for himself. The two men frequented the Copperpot Inn weekly to meet with Jeffrey Ellis and discuss their numerous investment deals. It was a high-end establishment, known for its select clientele and innate respect for privacy. Hayward and Conway were Ellis's business acquaintances, but he'd over the years tried to distance himself from their vacuous *double-your-money* scams and instead build a business he could be proud of.

"Can I help you ... *Miss*?" The immaculately presented woman at the front of the house pursed her lips as she eyed the visitor up and down. Shona flicked her floppy blonde bangs out of her eyes and stood up straight, pulling at her clothes to try and make herself look more presentable. She was grateful that Ruby had expertly altered one of Tom's shirts for her.

"Hello ma'am, I'd like to talk to Mr. Ellis, please." She flashed a bright smile.

"Does he know you?" The woman raised a perfectly-shaped eyebrow in disgust.

Shona took in a calming breath. "I just need a minute of his time, ma'am."

"This is an *exclusive* members' bar that is men-only. Mr. Ellis is our most valued customer and we won't see him being disturbed by the likes of ... you."

"Ma'am, I just need to talk to him."

"I will have you removed if you do not leave!"

This last interaction stopped the group of men mid-conversation. One of them, Brian Carson, went over to see what the problem was.

"Hey Gracie, you OK? She causin' you trouble?" He nodded his head towards Shona.

"Sir, I just need to speak to Mr. Ellis."

"What could the likes of you possibly want with Mr. Ellis?" Carson replied, curling his lip.

Ellis's name being spoken made his ears prick up. "What's going on over there?"

"Nothing, sir, it's all under control." He turned his head away from Shona, who, at that moment, saw her opportunity.

In one fluid motion, she ducked and headed straight for Ellis. Carson awkwardly rotated his body, reaching out to grab a fistful of Shona's shirt as she passed, but she wriggled free before he could wrap his arm around her. In two seconds, she was at Ellis's table, a swirling mixture of eagerness, nerves and adrenaline pulsating through her body. Carson raced after her, red-faced with frustration for not containing the menace that Shona had become.

"Sir, Mr. Ellis–" Shona gasped. As she opened her mouth to continue, Carson wrestled her into a headlock.

"Get off me!" she shrieked.

"Let her go. She's a woman, for Christ's sake." Ellis stood up sharply.

He snarled as he shoved Shona loose, almost knocking her into the empty glasses on the table.

"Thank you," she panted, rubbing her reddened neck. "I didn't mean to disturb you, sir. I just heard that you're a real nice guy and you've given people chances to work–" she looked intently at him.

"All this and you're looking for a *job*?" Ellis sat back down, his inquisitive eyes fixed on her.

"Yessir. I am." Shona set her jaw.

"The thing is–" Ellis rolled his hand, prompting her for her name.

"Shona."

"The thing is, Shona, I already have a wonderful secretary. I just don't have a job for you," he shrugged.

"No, sir, you don't understand, I can work on your trucks! I can repair any vehicle you put in front of me! I can work in the fields picking the cotton like I used to do with my father. I'll be the hardest worker you've ever had." She punched her fist into her other hand, ignoring the derisory sniggers around her.

"*Trucks*? I must be drunk hearing this trash." Hayward took another swig of his spirit.

"I'm serious, sir. I wouldn't let you down," she continued.

The tables' gaze switched from Shona to Ellis. After a lengthy pause, he finally spoke.

"I give chances to people who won't waste 'em, young lady. I can show 'em through the door, but then it's up to them. If they steal, they're out. They don't show up for work one day, they're out. If they're late, they're out. They refuse *any* kind of work given to 'em, Mr. Bruce has my blessing to toss them out. It's tough in there."

"I can handle it, sir," Shona assured him. "I've worked with men before. They'll see how hard I work. I just need the chance...please?"

Ellis's fingers were interlocked, his elbows planted on the

table, the tips of his two index fingers resting against his pursed lip. He admired the courage of this young girl, who had fought her way to stand in front of him. "Shona, I'm gon' give you a chance. It's up to you from here. I'll arrange for somebody to let Mr. Bruce know. You can start Monday morning. Report at the front desk at 6:30, OK? Don't you be late!"

Her face erupted into a huge grin. "Mr. Ellis, I swear I won't let you down, sir ... I promise! Thank you!" She tried to contain her excitement but it was impossible. Turning to leave, she grinned even wider as she passed the astonished front of house assistant at the door.

"You do realize, Jeffrey, you've just fed that lil' girl to a pack of damn wolves. God help her!" Hayward whispered to Ellis who silently watched Shona exit the Copperpot.

Chapter 9

"**G**et that son of a bitch!"

That same evening, the elder of the three huntsmen led through the open fields of Daynes, three miles from the Ellis and Bruce site. They were closing in on their target, but he was too fast. He needed to be. He was dead if they caught him.

Stopping for a moment, he looked frantically from side to side. Panting and sweating profusely, he placed his hands on his knees as panic raged through his exhausted body. The three men had split up and strategically blocked off his exit, closing in around him and pushing him closer to the edge of the rushing Weaver. In the distance, the escaping man could hear the unmistakable sound of ferocious barking.

"Let him go, boy!"

Turning around, he watched in horror as a bloodthirsty canine headed straight for him, baring its razor-sharp teeth. On the last dregs of adrenaline, the man raced towards the end of the field straight ahead, his lungs perilously close to giving up on him.

"Stop him before he gets to the river, boys!"

With fatigue finally overpowering him, he fell to the

ground, causing a cloud of dust to billow up from his crashing boots and give away his position. The men shined their flashlight in his direction, dustcloud particles catching in the beams. Dragging himself up, the target hopped forward a few more steps. Mercifully, he saw he'd reached the riverbank.

He was almost safe.

Suddenly, a searing pain flooded through the back of his right thigh. In agony, he looked behind him, his wide eyes meeting those of a massive Alsatian hound hell-bent on stripping the flesh clean from his leg. Its ferocious teeth glinted in the half-light, its mouth frothing as it locked its jaws on the man's bleeding thigh.

With no choice, he tore his leg out of the jaws of the beast, screaming as he did so. He jumped off the bank three feet down into the river heading to God knows where, but it had to be better than here. Keeping his head underwater for as long as he could, he fought against the strong current, trying to avoid getting knocked out by the rocks as it swept him downstream.

Giving up their pursuit, the three men and barking hound melted away into the evening. The target of their sport waited until it was completely silent before emerging from the cool waters of the Weaver, immediately feeling the intense sting rushing through his mangled leg as he continued on through the brush to find a safe place to sleep.

He was one of the lucky ones.

Chapter 10

"S'cuse me, I start work here today?"

Shona spoke loudly in the direction of the office behind the front desk that Monday morning. Through the half-open door she heard muffled voices, the occasional laugh and bad language, but she didn't care.

"Well, look what we got here," one of the voices eventually emerged. The man it belonged to leered at Shona, a sly grin breaking out over his unshaven face as he chewed a mouthful of tobacco.

"Mr. Ellis told me to report here and that somebody would show me around so I can get straight to work on the trucks," Shona said brightly.

"Did he now? Good ol' Mr. Ellis, he's really lost his mind this time! Boys, get out here, you gotta see this."

Two other guys appeared and stared open-mouthed at the slim, blonde-haired, pretty young woman. She wore baggy blue mechanic's overalls, which on anyone else would look grungy, but Shona's perfect figure wore them well. One of the men had no shame in ogling her, his greasy black hair flopping over his seedy eyes as he mentally undressed her.

"What can we do for you, sweetheart?"

"I'm here to work on the trucks? If you show me where I need to go, I'll start straight away," Shona replied, trying hard to mask her disgust.

"Well, I'll be damned. I thought you were our new cleaning lady! Hey Paul, you gotta see this!" All three laughed loudly.

"Mr. Ellis said I could," Shona said, straightening her back.

"Oh, did he now? You and Mr. Ellis *good* friends, then?" The first man leaned over the counter.

"I just came to work. I don't want no trouble." She raised her voice, bored with being a figure of fun now.

"What's goin' on out there? Who are you?" Paul, the workforce deputy, pushed open the door of the office behind the counter.

"I'm Shona Jackson, sir. Mr. Ellis told me to report here at 6:30 and I'd be working on the vehicles or in the fields?"

Deputy Paul's cold eyes narrowed as he rested his hand on his hip.

"Yeah, I heard about you. I don't know what game you're playing, lil' lady. This ain't no place for a broad. But Ellis is the boss and orders are orders. Come with me," he sighed.

~

"This is where you'll get changed."

Deputy Paul opened a small room containing brooms, buckets and old equipment. It was dark and damp with broken cupboards and shelves that were chipped and falling down. Later, he ended the tour just outside a messy tool room. "Wait in here." He pointed to a cluttered bench and, as Shona stepped inside, he disappeared.

Alone, she looked up at the clock on the wall. It was already 7:25 a.m. *Where was everybody?*

Almost gagging from the musty odors in the room, she opened the metal back door leading to the fields behind the site to let the fresh air in. Bored, Shona began to tidy, almost jumping out of her skin when a loud buzzer sounded at 10 o'clock. She stopped cleaning down the benches when she heard the sound of upbeat voices passing by outside the tool room door, which could only mean one thing in a place like this – break time!

Thinking that this would be the best time to find someone who knew what was going on, Shona yanked the handle of the rickety metal door back towards her to secure the room. As she did so, a strange noise outside caught her attention. It came from behind a large mound of used tires beside the doorway.

"Hello?" She paused as she glimpsed the worn-out boots of someone who seemed desperate to remain out of sight.

"You OK?" Shona asked. The feet quickly disappeared from view. She raised her eyebrows, then edged closer. It was then that she saw the pitiful shape of a man cowering.

He didn't get up, but just sat with his head bowed. He was reluctant to make eye contact, his dark brown face wet with fresh tears.

"Who are you?" Shona asked, wearing her sternest face. She was mindful not to get too close.

"Cuban–" He sniffed. "My name is Cuban, ma'am. I just wanted to get some water from this faucet. I don't want no trouble."

He shifted positions on the gravel, wincing as he exposed the dark red blood pool underneath his right thigh.

"You're bleedin'," she noticed, her eyes softening.

"I got chased. I managed to outrun 'em but then I got bit by the goddamn dirty dog they set on me. I'm lucky, I got away. Lord only knows how but I did." He coughed and winced again.

"Who's out there?" a scratchy old voice called out from inside the tool room. Both Shona and Cuban froze.

"It's just me–" Shona shouted back, her eyes still fixed on the colored man below her.

The half-open metal back door to the tool room groaned on its rusty hinges as an elderly man stepped outside. His wispy white hair peeked out from underneath his tatty gray cap, and his eyebrows raised in surprise at Shona.

"Who are you?"

"I'm Shona. I start work here today."

Open mouthed, he looked down at her clothes.

"Workin' here? Doin' what?"

"I can repair trucks," Shona replied brightly.

He paused, staring at her. "Who's this?" His eyes diverted as he motioned his leathery hand downwards.

"I'm Cuban, sir."

He struggled to his feet, limping on his injured leg. As he stood up, Shona realized how tall this man was, well over six feet even with his back arched in discomfort. His hands had obviously not shirked hard work in the past. Thick, calloused fingers rested on his blood-drenched pant leg, his open-necked work shirt revealing a necklace with a small crucifix on it. She could sense the sadness within him but she was not ready yet to trust this stranger.

"I'm Elbie. You, young lady, must have really sweet-talked Mr. Ellis to get in here." He smiled at Shona, then turned to Cuban with a much graver look on his weathered face.

"See you bleedin' quite badly there. I can help fix you up but that'll be the least of your problems. Thugs 'round these parts huntin' black folks like you for sport. You should keep movin' on," Elbie warned.

Cuban shifted his weight, looking uncomfortable from the throbbing pain in his thigh.

"I know what it's like 'round here, sir, don't need no lecture. I seen this town for what it is. No one need tell me what I got to lose!"

Elbie and Shona listened in silence, Cuban's words piercing the heart of their uncertainty.

"Let's have a look at that leg, get you patched up. Shona, take his arm."

Together, they half-dragged Cuban inside the tool room and sat him on a stool.

"Hand me that box over there, will you," Elbie pointed to the shelf in the corner of the room. Shona returned with the first aid box, still not wanting to engage too much with the colored man. She'd always been told by her father they were never to be trusted, but Shona never knew which of his drunken tales to believe. She was on her guard, though, just in case he was right on this one.

Elbie finished cleaning and dressing Cuban's wounded leg, using up half of the first aid box's supplies to stem the bleeding. He knew the man needed stitches but judging by how quickly Cuban pulled his pants up and thanked Elbie for his trouble, he knew he wasn't willing to go to the hospital.

"Alright, now that we got that dealt with, I'd like to know who the hell's been moving things around in this tool room, huh?" Elbie frowned.

Shona held her breath.

"Well, I guess that was me, sir." She ran her hand through her hair, sweeping it out of her eyes. "You see, they left me here to wait for my orders and I don't like to be idle. I was just tryin' to clean the place up a bit–" Shona was rambling now.

"Whoa there–" Elbie held his hands up. "I was just gon' say thanks, it looks good! Folks normally treat this room like a dump. Just one thing, though, I don't want you goin' in the workshop back there, 'cos that's *my* space, got it?" the old man warned as he hooked his thumb over his shoulder.

Minutes later, the conversation paused as the three of them turned their heads to the doorway where Deputy Paul appeared.

"You got visitors, Jackson!" He flashed his dirty gray teeth in mock pleasure, tipping his head towards the voices behind him.

It was Larry Bruce and Jeffrey Ellis.

"Ah, there she is! Just wanted to see how my new girl was doing on her first day." Ellis approached Shona, followed closely by Bruce. Shona turned her head to smile her response but, as she did so, a colored face was revealed behind her.

"What the *fuck* is that?" Bruce snapped.

Before she realized what she was doing, Shona intervened.

"He just wanted to speak to Mr. Ellis about a job, sir."

Cuban held his breath but Shona continued, mesmerizing him with her bravery.

"Instead of sitting 'round doin' nothing, sir, I watched him clean the whole tool room! Look, see–" Shona held her arms out wide. She had no idea why she was speaking up for him, but she couldn't unsee the look of dread that was etched on Cuban's face when Bruce had spotted him.

"Shona, you not been put to work yet?" Ellis frowned.

"No, sir, I was told to wait here."

Ellis switched his attention to Deputy Paul.

"We can get her cleanin', scrubbin'–" Deputy Paul shrugged.

"Trucks," Ellis interrupted. "I want her on trucks. Let's see what she can do."

Bruce glared at Ellis.

"That one just come in?" Ellis pointed out of the tool room window at a white truck being winched off a low-loader, then dropped to the ground outside. Outwardly, it looked reasonably sound but the fact that it hadn't driven itself there didn't bode well for it. Three mechanics surrounded the stricken vehicle, scratching their heads. One stubbed out his cigarette, took out his wrench and motioned to the other two to pop the hood.

Deputy Paul nodded. "Yessir."

"See if you can get it goin'," Ellis smiled at Shona.

"Jeffrey, you lost your mind?" Bruce said in a low voice.

The group walked outside towards the truck. The mechanics attending it looked perplexed as to why the truck was resisting all their best efforts to spark it into life. The engine's problem seemed a bit of an enigma, but this didn't faze Shona. She approached Deputy Paul and gestured for the keys, his stare burning a hole in her head as he dropped them into her hand. Bruce smirked as they waited for her embarrassment to commence. Ellis exhaled, hoping she wouldn't disappoint him.

"This vehicle's expensive, y'understand?" Deputy Paul snarled.

Ellis folded his arms as Shona got to work. She stuck her head under the hood and tinkered about. Clanks and clonks sounded from the engine bay as she investigated the manifolds, sprockets and gaskets. Little grunts and groans emitted from her as she tightened her wrench around the bolts and metal tubes.

Five long minutes passed.

Shona was done. She climbed up into the driver's seat and slid the key into the ignition as everyone in the group held their breath. The engine coughed for a few seconds and then spluttered into life, black smoke billowing from the exhaust. Before long, the truck was purring like a kitten.

"Well, I'll be *damned*," Ellis blew out his cheeks.

Closing his eyes, Bruce shook his head.

"So what? Pull a few wires, flick a few switches? That's the easiest damn job you coulda given her!" He was furious.

His attention, however, soon moved away from her and, like a searchlight in the darkness, landed on Cuban who was smiling at Shona's success. He'd enjoyed the few brief moments of blending in with the crowd, but it couldn't last. Cuban met Bruce's fiery eyes, panic fizzing in the pit of his stomach.

"Let's get this bastard off our land!" Bruce snarled. "Paul, grab his arms–"

"Wait!" Shona jumped out of the truck and in front of

Cuban. He didn't stand a chance out there judging by the state he'd arrived in.

"Get out the way!" Deputy Paul growled.

"Mr. Ellis, please give Cuban a chance. Look at the difference he's made to the tool room already, and that's without being paid!" she begged.

"Paul, wait," Ellis waved his hands for Deputy Paul to cease manhandling Cuban. "Elbie, the tool room is normally your domain, right?"

Elbie nodded.

"This man here, y'think he's done a good job?" Ellis continued.

"Sir, that room–" Elbie paused. "I ain't seen it no better in a long time, do say so m'self. You could eat your dinner off that floor!" He caught Shona and Cuban's relieved faces in the corner of his eye.

Deputy Paul and Bruce put their hands on their hips. Ellis approached Cuban and spoke in a low voice.

"You got one chance. You mess it up, I ain't gon' help you. I'll leave Shona to explain my rules. If you break 'em, I'm behind Larry all the way. Understand?"

Tears glistening in the corner of his eyes, Cuban managed to croak out his thanks.

"Come on, gentlemen." Ellis turned to walk around the side of the building and back to his office. Shona noticed him limping slightly.

Waiting until Ellis was out of earshot, Deputy Paul strode over to Shona, Cuban and Elbie.

"Mr. Bruce told me to let you know that if you pull another stunt like that you won't be *able* to work, y'hear?" he growled. He stepped closer to Shona and traced down the side of her smooth face with his dirty fingernail. She stood motionless, regarding him with an icy stare. Not receiving the satisfaction of a rise out of her, he cackled as he left them and ran to catch up with Ellis and Bruce.

"So, what now?" Cuban asked.

"Don't know about you two," said Shona, "but I need to wash that dirty bastard's stink outta my face!"

Shona walked over to the faucet outside the mechanics' shed. Feelings rushed around her body like a kaleidoscope as she splashed the cool water on her face. *Humiliating one of your bosses isn't the most ideal way to start a new job,* she thought. Turning to look over at her two new friends, she saw them toeing the dust and attempting to make small talk. She smiled as she walked back over to them, her hands in her pockets.

"You're quite the brave lil' lady," Elbie said.

"Yeah, thank you. You didn't have to do that," Cuban added.

"You're welcome. It looks like we need each other 'round here?" Shona said as they made their way back to the tool room.

"You're damn right. This place, it's awful. Didn't used to be." Elbie's eyes saddened.

"What changed?" Shona asked.

"Larry Bruce, that's what! This place was run by Mr. Ellis for twenty years and he did a damn fine job of it too. But he needed to spend more time with his sick wife, so he got *Bruce the Brute* on board to take care of the day-to-day running around five years ago and then–" Elbie fiddled with his cap. "It got real dark 'round here."

"What d'you mean?" Cuban asked.

"People just came and went. If you disagreed with the bosses, well, your days were numbered. Good people with consciences left or were made to leave." Elbie's face dropped.

"Well, we got each other, right?" Shona affirmed.

"I could tell you some stories, alright. I write everything down in my diary. I started writing it when my wife passed. I made a promise I would talk to her every day." Elbie licked his lips as his emotions began to engulf him. "I write about everything that goes on here but my damn hands tremble with age now, so I have to keep it short."

The same loud buzzer from earlier sounded again.

"What's that?" Cuban asked.

"We've been summoned." Elbie's face blanched.

Chapter 11

The three of them were the last to reach the canteen, where all staff briefings were routinely held. In the far right corner was a wrought iron spiral staircase leading up to the management offices on the balcony above. As soon as the trio walked in, there was an ominous silence when the crowd of workers caught sight of Cuban. As looks of disgust were thrown in his direction, whispers, jeers and growls from the hostile crowd began to ring out.

"Another fuckin' colored."

"Lock up your stuff, boys."

Men spat at Cuban's feet but it wasn't the first time that had happened to him. Shona was stunned by the savagery of the crowd, which seconds later turned on her.

"What the *fuck* have we got here, boys?"

"I'll bet you five bucks she's screwin' somebody within the week."

From above, a man's voice bellowed, followed by a whistle and then a hammering on the iron bars of the balcony.

"Alright, everybody, hush now!" Deputy Paul hit the balcony bars with his wooden stick, his face maroon with the exertion of trying to silence the mob. "We have a couple of new additions we'd like to present to you and I'm sure they'll get your usual warm welcome. I'll hand it over to Mr. Bruce."

Bruce's intimidating stare held the attention of the crowd. He appeared at the edge of the balcony in his expensive three-piece suit, showing the glint of a gold watch that would take these workers a year to save up for. His bass tones growled as he addressed the workforce.

"It's no secret I'm always looking to advance the company, but Mr. Ellis and I won't be around forever." Bruce glanced towards Ellis.

"*I* plan to be," Ellis lightened the mood.

"It's a good time to invest," Bruce continued. "The market's expanding, which is exciting for all of us. We're doing more business further afield so we need some fresh young blood to keep up with it. I've sat down with a few guys and I've picked one. Somebody who's from great stock, has good energy and thinks the way I do."

"That ain't no good thing, let me tell you," Elbie whispered.

"I'd like to welcome...Kyle Chambers."

Bruce gestured towards Kyle, who swaggered forward in a made to measure gray flannel suit. His highly polished Oxford shoes echoed on the metal platform of the balcony as he made his entrance to the crowd's applause. He muttered something to Bruce and then beamed his winning smile down at the canteen floor, giving a wave to indicate that he was ready to speak.

"It's an honor to be given a chance to lead such a fine-looking workforce. I'm sure we can do great things together."

After five long minutes of grins and smug mutual backslapping from Bruce and Kyle, the sound of shuffling feet and bored grunts began floating around the assembled workforce. Sensing they'd dragged on for too long, Bruce quickly concluded.

"I got one more thing to announce–" Bruce pointed at the crowd below him. "My daughter Chloe is finally home where she belongs. She's been studying business at college these last five years, so she can help run things when I'm gone." He went back into the management office, then returned holding his daughter's hand.

"Everybody, meet Chloe."

The applause was initially polite, but when all eyes focused on her properly, a few low whistles and murmurs of admiration followed.

Chloe Bruce shone a beaming smile at the crowd, her chocolate-brown eyes radiating warmth as she acknowledged some of the more well-mannered comments with a dainty wave. She wore a bright red fitted jacket, a red and white polka-dot blouse and a smart black pencil skirt, showing off her perfectly toned legs and significantly distracting the men standing below. She cleared her throat as her father raised his hands to hush the crowd for her.

"Well, I didn't expect *that*. Thank you, I'll keep it brief. I just want to learn the business, help the company grow, and I especially can't wait to come around and meet every single one of you."

The workforce below cheered more rapturously this time as Chloe stared down at them. She flicked her light brown mid-length hair out of her eyes as she continued to melt the crowd with her effortless charm.

But not everybody in the crowd was cheering.

Chapter 12

"Shona, you in here?"

Elbie called out to her as he returned to the tool room with Cuban. Walking quickly over to the back door to investigate why it was wide open, he found her outside hunched over, trying desperately to control the wave of retching that had consumed her. Embarrassed, she wiped her mouth on her sleeve and walked back into the tool room, brushing past Elbie and taking a seat on one of the stools.

"Why'd you take off like that?" he asked.

"I just needed to get out of there. I didn't feel so good. This was where I was told to wait," Shona mumbled as she wrapped her arms around herself. Elbie looked at her, his eyes full of concern.

"It's gon' be tough here," Cuban sighed, wincing as a fresh stab of pain rippled through his thigh.

"We just gotta keep our heads down, work hard for our money and get the hell out of here as soon as goddamn possible," Shona said into space, her mind somewhere else entirely.

Deputy Paul swaggered into the tool room ten minutes later, a sly grin draping itself over his greasy face. He strode over to Shona who was gradually recovering, helped by a small tot of the brandy that Elbie kept in his drawer for emergencies.

"Let's get one thing crystal clear, lady. You ain't gon' work on no trucks, y'hear? I don't give a *fuck* what magic you pulled from your ass out there, you ain't touching 'em from now on, get it?" He pressed his face inches from Shona's. "You'll clean the trucks when the ones for repair are ready to go, you scrub the canteen, the floors and anything else I wipe my feet on. *That's* what you do. As for you, boy, you'll get changed in a different place to us. I don't want your dirty fucking diseases or you being 'round my things thievin' 'em, you hear me? You'll take a shit in a hole if you have to but you stay the fuck away from us." Deputy Paul finished his brief by pointing in Cuban's face, then stormed off.

Cuban took a seat at a work bench, unsurprised by Deputy Paul's hostility.

"This is bullshit! Why we gettin' treated this way? I got a job fair and square. I fixed the damn truck in front of their eyes," Shona ranted.

"This is the work of *Bruce the Brute*, I'm telling you," Elbie reflected quietly.

~

That afternoon, as the three of them had completed their list of jobs, they sat down to take a well-earned five-minute break. Just as they did so, their peace was interrupted.

"Elbie!"

All three heads swung to face the door. It was Deputy Paul again and he wasn't alone. The kitchen staff he'd brought with him looked menacing in their chef whites and blue work pants, laden with large pots and deep bowls. The deputy hung back by the doorway as his cronies stomped into the tool room.

"You said to us the tool room was so shiny, so clean—" he taunted. "A man could even eat his dinner off that floor! So—"

Elbie's face hardened. He knew what was coming next.

"Let 'em have it, boys!"

On Deputy Paul's command, they tipped what seemed like gallons of sludgy brown liquid, mashed up food and waste all over the spotless floor, splashing it all over Elbie, Cuban and Shona. The kitchen staff marched out on orders, leaving Deputy Paul unscathed and grinning in the doorway.

"You should know better than to side with a colored. That's almost worse than being one. Get this mess cleaned up. Now!" He barked and then sauntered out. Elbie straightened his cap and stared at the dirty floor.

"This was a bad idea, you helpin' me," Cuban said shaking his head

"Don't you say that!" Shona said as anger raged inside her at Deputy Paul's cruel actions. She went to get a mop and some rags to start cleaning up.

"I shoulda retired years ago. Biggest mistake o'my life. I hope you two don't end up like me, where the only safe place you can speak your thoughts is in a damn diary." He shook his head, still staring at the floor as he clenched his fists.

Shona looked around, quietly assessing the mess. Food waste was everywhere. It'd splashed on the walls, all over the tools and had even found its way inside the workbench drawers. Her attention was momentarily drawn back to Elbie who seemed to be deep in thought. He leaned heavily on the workbench, his watery red eyes staring at her.

"I think we just rattled the cage of a goddamn monster," Elbie warned.

Chapter 13

Shona walked the two miles home that evening after work thinking over the events of the day–Deputy Paul's cruel stunt, Cuban's situation, Elbie's diary and Bruce's speech to the workers.

And Chloe.

So many conflicting thoughts tumbled over themselves in her mind, but right now she was walking back to a place of pure happiness and looking forward to the simplicity of sitting around the table with two genuinely kind-hearted people whose only agenda was to make sure she had enough wholesome food in her belly. Her route home took her along the long driveway of the Ellis and Bruce site, up to the crossroads, past the town gas station on the corner, then across the road and into town. As she passed the gas station, two oily-looking men whistled at her, then pointed down suggestively to their private parts.

"In your dreams, jerks," Shona muttered in repulsion, injecting a faster pace into her stride.

The town of Daynes was only five minutes' walk from the gas station. On either side of the main road were the typical small-town shops—a grocery store, a butcher's, a drugstore, the town's Methodist church and a few small eateries. She noticed one building in particular, a small, ornate-looking fabric shop with the assistant outside closing down the hatches for the day. He was exceptionally well dressed, his gray hair combed meticulously into a perfect side part, his small round glasses delicately perched on the end of his nose. He wore an elegant navy plaid suit jacket with a yellow tie and neatly pressed pants. Shona looked down at her own dirty, stained overalls and sighed with envy at this man's obviously less messy day.

The light was fading as Tom and Ruby's house came into view half a mile further on. It wasn't huge, but it was their home. The sight of it filled her with warmth, not least as it was Ruby's mouthwatering roast chicken, biscuits and gravy for dinner. Shona could almost taste the cornbread as she walked with a spring in her step up to the front door.

"Hi, only me," she called out as she bounded into the kitchen.

"Hey, Shona, how was your first day?" Ruby's soft voice immediately made her feel at home.

"It was ... different," she replied with a lopsided grin.

Tom walked into the kitchen minutes later and kissed his wife on the cheek.

"You two must be famished," Ruby said as she placed a steaming roast chicken on the table and invited them to sit down. Shona didn't need to be asked twice and jumped into her seat. Warm biscuits and a jug of thick gravy joined the chicken in front of her, but when Ruby motioned to her to wash her hands before she was allowed to tuck in, Shona's face dropped. Within seconds her hands were the cleanest they had ever been and she was back at the table clutching her knife and fork.

Tom and Ruby chuckled at Shona's lack of social etiquette as she shoveled food into her mouth, not letting the novel idea of swallowing slow her down.

Happiness engulfed the three of them as they talked and

laughed over dinner and long into the evening as the Alabama sun sank slowly below the horizon.

Chapter 14

With a jolt, Shona woke, then froze. The familiar dread of those footsteps coming down the stairs and entering the poorly lit, cold basement where she had been forced to sleep was overwhelming. Her heart thumped.

They seemed to take forever, as if prolonging the torture. There were no windows and no exits apart from the door that was about to be opened. The doorknob groaned. Shona instinctively curled into a ball.

A shard of light stabbed through the darkness as the door creaked open. Shona squinted. Launching at her, the men took advantage of her temporary blindness. They were rough as always.

"Noooooo ... Get off me, please—"

"Shona ... SHONA! Wake up!" Tom's shadow loomed over her, his strong hands gripping her trembling shoulders. Shona blinked open her tear-filled eyes and sat bolt upright.

"What? ... I was just dreamin'," she mumbled, her head pounding.

"Dreamin'? Sounded like a goddamn nightmare," he replied, his own eyes laced with concern.

"I ... I'm sorry!"

Tom reached out to try and comfort her. Without meaning to, she shrank away from him and pulled the blanket up around her shoulders. She lay back down, her gaze not shifting from the thin halo of moonlight that ran around the edges of the barn door.

He sighed as he sat down on the edge of her bed. Silently, he watched over her for the next hour until Shona, slowly but surely, felt safe enough to fall back to sleep.

Chapter 15

"Larry, you seen this?"

Kyle Chambers held out the tabloid to Bruce who was gazing out of his window early on Monday morning, a week later.

"Seen what?" Bruce turned, half listening.

"Damn colored college burned down," said Kyle. "For the best, I say. I mean, you can't teach' 'em nothin' so what's the point in trying?"

Bruce took the newspaper and started reading the story.

"Trouble is–" he began, leaning back into his expensive chair. "They're gettin' everywhere! You got do-gooders representin' 'em. You wait until people start getting their damn money stolen, their sons murdered and their daughters raped. Then come back and tell me it's good to give 'em a voice."

"Why does Ellis do what he does, then?" Kyle asked, leaning back in his own chair.

"Long story, goin' way back. He's a damn fool." Bruce clicked his silver lighter and held his cigar to the flame. "Thing is, Kyle, that new colored, Cuban or whatever the fuck his name is, is getting way too comfortable here. He and that broad have been here a week now and still no sign of them quittin' yet. I can't afford for him to think he's the same as us. My daughter's here now. Is she safe? I don't like it, but whatever I get Paul to give to both of 'em, they just keep comin' back for more!"

"What you want me to do, Larry?" Kyle leaned forward.

"Just make life a little more *unwelcoming*. If they both leave of their own accord, it's nice and tidy."

∽

The canteen was its usual hive of activity at the 10 o'clock break time that Monday—mostly abusive comments hurled at anyone who was deemed weak. Cuban entered the melee and, as usual, it was the same greeting.

"You know where you need to be."

Cuban knew his place: the back of the queue. Even when he reached the front, men would play tricks on him after they'd eaten and keep going up for seconds. On a few occasions the buzzer sounded before Cuban could get any food at all.

"Could I have some of that, please?" Cuban asked as he finally reached the counter. He thought better than to make eye contact with head chef Lou who chewed slowly, looking Cuban up and down and screwing his face up.

"Gimme your plate." Lou forced his rough face into a fake smile.

Cuban handed Lou his plate, then turned around to see Shona eating on her own at the end of a long bench, with six men at the other end making no attempt to talk to her. While his head was turned, Lou poured dark slop onto his plate from a height so it splashed everywhere, including over Cuban. He looked back to see Lou grinning at him.

"Here's some bread. You need to keep your strength up."

Lou gripped a slice of bread in each of his grubby hands and rubbed them up and down his chef jacket, smudging the grayish, pitted bread into congealed meat juices, tea and sweat stains. Smirking, he spat on one slice, then squashed it into the other to make a sandwich which he dropped on top of Cuban's plate of slop.

"Lemme help you there! Coffee?" Deputy Paul appeared over Cuban's shoulder and tipped his half-empty mug over his bread-topped plate, making it an even soggier mess. He lifted the tray off the counter, then dropped it.

The clatter ensured all eyes were on the situation now.

"Oh, I'm sorry, Cuban, how clumsy am I?" Deputy Paul mashed up the food with his boots, then grabbed a large serving spoon and scooped up the rancid gloop onto another plate. "Thing is, I'm told that when you clean floors you can eat your dinner off 'em. So, *eat!*" Deputy Paul picked up a dirty spoon from someone else's leftovers and dipped it in Cuban's *lunch*. "Come on, boy. You must be hungry!" he snarled.

The canteen ground to a halt. Workers began shouting their encouragements to Cuban, who stared in disgust at the spoon hovering in front of him.

"Come on, Cuban, you can't go back to work on an empty stomach! Lou here assures me that this food is full of highly nutritious goodness!" He smirked at Lou who sniggered back.

Thoughts raced through Cuban's brain. He needed this job. The money would go towards his ticket to New York, a place he'd dreamed of going to all his life. They were more tolerant there. His dream was to play in the jazz clubs and make a life for himself. But that didn't come cheap. It had to work this time. It wouldn't have to be long, just until he could afford his ticket.

Cuban knew he had no choice. He took his first bite.

"More. More. More. More." The chanting resonated louder. Snarling men banged their knives and forks on the table, enjoying every second of Cuban's humiliation. His retching made it even more fun to watch.

Shona couldn't bear it any longer. She pushed her way

through the crowd as bits of food were thrown at Cuban who didn't dare retaliate.

"Get outta my way ... *MOVE!*" Shona yelled, but another female voice eclipsed her own and instantly hushed the baying mob.

"Stop! What on earth's going on here?" Eyes shifted up from Cuban's plight to the balcony. Shona looked too, her gaze passing up over the smart black heels, business skirt and scarlet red jacket.

Shona stared in silence. Gripping the handrail, Chloe Bruce descended the steps leading onto the canteen floor, looking disgusted.

"You say anything, boy, and you won't be able to take a shit for a month, y'hear?" Deputy Paul whispered to Cuban before disappearing in the opposite direction to where Chloe was approaching from. The hustle and bustle resumed as the crowd nonchalantly returned to their food and conversations. Trying hard to control his shaking hands, Cuban bent down to clean up the mess.

"You OK, Cuban?" Elbie appeared holding a mop.

"I'm fine," he lied.

"What the fuck? This is some messed up shit," Shona snarled as she watched the workers finish their food. She put her hand down on Cuban's shoulder. He shrugged it off in frustration.

"You can have some of my food if you like?" she offered, kneeling to help clean the mess up with some paper towels.

"Are you OK?" A voice sounded behind them. Elbie, Shona and Cuban looked up.

"Yessum," Cuban replied.

"What happened here? I heard a lot of noise," Chloe asked, concern lacing her soft voice. Cuban and Elbie stood but Shona continued to scrub the floor.

"Just guys being guys, ma'am," Cuban replied half smiling.

Elbie looked down at the now-shiny floor and shook his head in disgust.

"All done. I'm goin' back to work," Shona jumped up and left.

"Who was that?" Chloe asked, staring at the back of the departing worker.

"Who, that? That's Shona," Elbie replied as he watched her stride away.

Chapter 16

"You heard about me letting that colored know where he stands earlier?"

Deputy Paul hovered over Kyle who was busy writing at his desk. He paused to look up and flashed a lopsided grin at Cuban's tormentor.

"I did. Chloe came in saying she thought the guys were being mean. I pretended to care."

Deputy Paul snorted. "Not sure what it'll take to show him he ain't welcome, boss. The men are goin' nuts that he's still here thinking he can hide under Ellis's fuckin' protection wing!"

Kyle fiddled with his silver cartridge pen. "Leave it with me, Paul. Get him to work even later tonight."

"You got it, boss!" Deputy Paul replied, a glint of menace in his cold eyes.

∽

"I thought you were a little rude towards Miss Chloe before, Shona," Elbie said as he emptied out his bucket of dirty, soapy water onto the dry dust of the garage forecourt. Shona was cleaning the outside of one of the trucks.

"I don't trust any of 'em, Elbie. All the same, all assholes," she replied, scrubbing hard enough to rip the paint from the hood.

"Not Miss Chloe, she's genuine enough. Didn't you notice how she was with Cuban? Real nice!" Elbie reasoned.

"So?" Shona threw her sponge into her soapy water and rested her hand on the hood. "Deserves a medal, does she? She's probably a spy, finding out about us. Like I said, I don't trust any of 'em."

Shona's tirade was interrupted as Cuban trudged by.

"Hey."

"You OK?" she asked, standing up straight.

"Deputy Paul told me I have to work late. He wants everywhere spotless." Cuban looked deflated. Shona's heart went out to him, but at the moment it was all about survival.

For both of them.

It was nine thirty, three hours after Cuban should have gone home, and he was exhausted. A small group of men were in Deputy Paul's office drinking, smoking and playing cards, judging from the muffled conversation and joviality emanating from inside. He put the mop away in the cleaning cupboard after leaving the canteen spotless and ready for inspection.

"What an *amazing* job you've done," Deputy Paul said sarcastically as he walked around the canteen admiring the shiny pots and pans.

"Thank you, sir," Cuban replied.

"Well now, I think you should run along home and get some rest." Deputy Paul looked Cuban dead in his eyes.

"Thanks. I will." Cuban grabbed his satchel and left.

Three men from Deputy Paul's office emerged just as

Cuban closed the door to the canteen on his way out. Poised, they awaited their instructions.

"Get to work, boys!" he drawled as the men began to trash the perfectly cleaned kitchen.

Chapter 17

"**G**ET ME THAT FUCKING NIGGER!"
Chef Lou hurled to the floor what remained intact of the canteen's crockery. He'd arrived at work on Tuesday morning to find his precious kitchen turned over: dishes smashed, food splashed everywhere and cooking pots strewn indiscriminately all over the counters.

"Wait, Lou, calm down. Think! You go and beat him in front of everybody and you'll have Ellis on your back saying you're being unkind to one of his *protected* little birds. You gotta be smarter."

Deputy Paul held Lou back.

"I'm gon' take a shit and make him eat it. He's wrecked my kitchen, Paul. I swear I wanna kill him."

Lou spat as he spoke.

"He'll pay, Lou. I'll see to it," Deputy Paul assured.

"You know, I can't wait to see the West Coast. To feel free, go to the beach. That's what I'm saving for, you?" Shona asked Elbie as they were painstakingly cleaning old oil and grease from inside the rivets of engine parts.

"Me? I wanna see my daughter and granddaughter in Tennessee before I get too old to travel. I retire in a few months so as soon as I get my pension I'm gon' go visit them! It's been three years now."

"Wow, you write them?" Shona asked.

"Yeah, but you know how life is. My daughter's busy so she doesn't write that much. I just feel bad I can't be there for her but she moved away and started a family. I couldn't leave the house I lived in with my wife all those years. It's where I feel closest to her. Couldn't stand living in a busy town where my girl lives either. I'm an old country boy at heart," Elbie smiled, tipping his cap.

"How about you?" Shona gestured to Cuban as he walked in and sat down next to them.

"I jus' wan' make it to New York to see some of my friends who've made it there already," he sighed.

"Cuban, you're wanted. Now." Deputy Paul's flat, emotionless voice bounced off the concrete walls as he strolled into the tool room.

Cuban put down his cleaning cloth and took in a calming breath. He followed Deputy Paul through the corridor, with Shona and Elbie walking behind.

The entire workforce was present, staring at him as he entered the canteen. Not a single plate, cup or any item of cutlery was present on the tables.

It was deathly silent.

Cuban was led over to the serving hatch. Chef Lou was already standing there, his face blotchy with anger.

"What's goin' on?" Cuban asked, his dry mouth barely able to frame the words.

"You did this!" Lou pointed at the mess.

Cuban frowned. "Me?"

"You're fucking lyin'! I don't believe a single word that comes out of that dirty black mouth of yours." Lou clenched his teeth.

"Deputy Paul asked me to clean the kitchen so I did. He checked it and said I done a good job, then I went home. That's the truth."

"You blamin' me, boy?" Deputy Paul stepped forward.

"Just sayin' what happened is all."

"But that's *not* what happened, is it?" Deputy Paul raised his eyebrows at Cuban."You were the last to leave! Wasn't like this when I saw it," he lied.

"There were guys. I don't know how many. I heard 'em in your office," Cuban protested.

"Please tell me you're not accusing my guys of committing this atrocious act?"

Deputy Paul stepped towards Cuban.

"I didn't do it."

"So, you're happy to accuse others, are you?"

A new voice joined in from the far left. Larry Bruce had descended the metal staircase from his office, bodies parting to let him through.

"Am I right in thinking there was an incident in here yesterday?" he continued.

"Yessir," Cuban replied.

"Am I also right in thinking that maybe Chef Lou took things a little far?" Bruce almost appeared sympathetic as Cuban nodded again.

"So, Cuban, you'd be justifiably angry at what happened to you in here yesterday, wouldn't you?"

Tears began to well up in Cuban's eyes as he realized the trap that Bruce was setting for him.

"The best form of revenge is to hit somebody where it hurts, right?" Bruce nodded, looking at the faces in the crowd. "You were working late last night and everybody had gone home, is that correct?"

"Yessir." Cuban looked at his feet.

"And now Lou finds it in this state?"

"Yessir." He knew he was defeated.

"How's that look to *you*?" Bruce squared up to Cuban.

"Like I did it." Cuban wiped his dripping nose on the back of his hand.

"*Like*? *Like* you did it?"

Cuban closed his eyes.

"He wouldn't have done this. He's been set up," Shona shouted, fighting her way through the crowd who then flipped their attention to her.

"Stay outta this," Deputy Paul barked at her.

"This ain't fair. Can nobody see? Why'd he make it so obvious if it was revenge?" Shona yelled.

"You'll sit the *fuck* down and shut the *fuck* up if you still wanna keep your job! I wonder what Mr. Ellis would say about you talkin' back to the boss?" Bruce screwed his face up.

Elbie shuffled next to Shona, resting a cautious hand on her shoulder.

"Now," said Bruce, "you'll apologize to *all* these men. They couldn't have any food this morning. Then you'll grovel to Lou to ask for forgiveness, y'hear me? And then you'll clean up the mess. Because if you don't, that's refusing work and Ellis will back me when I fire your ass. D'you understand me, boy?"

Cuban nodded.

"Well, now's a good time," Bruce snarled.

Cuban scanned the angry faces in the crowd.

"Get on with it." Deputy Paul shoved Cuban.

"I'm–" He swallowed his tears back. "I'm real sorry for you goin' without food–"

"And what you did," Bruce interrupted.

Shona shook her head in disgust.

"And what I did."

The baying crowd shouted their rejections of his apology, their unforgiving mood not helped by their empty stomachs.

"Now apologize to Lou," Bruce taunted.

Cuban turned towards Lou, who came from behind the counter to face him.

"Say it. Fucking say it," Lou snapped.

"I apologize–"

"Kneel down. Fucking beg!" Lou interrupted.

Deputy Paul and Bruce glanced at each other and smirked.

Cuban dropped to his knees in front of the head chef. He cast his mind forward to the day he made it to New York and pictured himself standing in a jazz bar holding a Manhattan and tapping his foot to the beat. He'd imagined that scene every time. Swallowing the lump in his throat, he straightened his back and looked up at Lou.

"I beg for your forgiveness." Cuban felt the wetness on his face double as Lou spat in it.

"Fuck you!" Lou raged as he stormed out.

"Anything for me?" Chloe asked Bonnie on the front desk as she returned from her meeting in town.

"No, ma'am."

"Seems quiet?" she said, looking around her.

"They're all in the canteen, Miss Chloe."

Curious, she headed over there, confused when she saw Cuban on his knees and objects being thrown at him. Alarmed that nobody seemed to be doing anything about it, she made a beeline for her father.

"Daddy, what's goin' on?"

"You're back early," Bruce replied, surprised to see her.

"We made good progress. What's going on? Why's Cuban on his knees? Is he OK?"

"Honey, it's nothing. Just guys being guys."

Chloe headed towards Cuban who was being picked up off the floor by the blonde girl she'd seen rush away after her introduction to the workforce. Catching sight of her approaching, Shona quickly brushed Cuban down and dragged him out of the horror towards the relative safety of the tool room before Chloe could make it over to them through the dense crowd.

Chapter 18

"We all set?" Kyle appeared on the balcony that Tuesday afternoon flanked by three smartly dressed men. He'd arranged a meeting with local investors to discuss his future vision for the company. The group sidled into the meeting room, taking their seats around the boardroom table. Kyle remained standing, puffing out his chest, ready to give his performance.

"Gentlemen, thank you for joining us," he began. "Jeffrey couldn't make it today, probably in the Copperpot–" Kyle's sly questioning of Ellis's integrity drew a sharp intake of breath from around the table. "But I'm sure we'll manage." He paused, drinking in the attention he was getting from these wealthy men.

"Now, I haven't been here long but Larry's allowed me to hit the ground running with ideas and to let me focus my attention on driving the company forward."

The investors nodded at each other in agreement. Kyle ran a hand through his jet black hair, smoothing it down at the back as he continued his pitch. "We have a good name – a *great* name – but that's because we're forward thinkers. The market's changing and companies are investing. *We* need to invest!" He leaned over and tapped his index finger on the table to emphasize his point. "Larry's spoken to Jeffrey, who's signed off the capital to buy more trucks and equipment which I believe will put us ahead of a market that's becoming crowded. We need to remain the best so *this* is the time to keep investing into Ellis and Bruce, not hold back!" His speech ended with the investors clapping their approval.

Bruce smiled. His protégé was doing very nicely indeed.

∼

"I wonder what crap they talking 'bout up there." Elbie looked upwards to the balcony.

"They need somebody around here to speak the truth to those investors," Shona huffed, scrubbing down one of the walls in the canteen.

Cuban remained in the melancholic state he'd been in all morning.

"Hey Cuban, are you any good at building benches? Think I'm gon' make some and maybe sell 'em in town for some extra dough, what d'you think?" Shona said, trying to lighten the mood.

He nodded impassively.

"Shona, you got wood for 'em? Sometimes on weekends I get a little cash for picking up bits from farms. I either use it or sell it cheap, depends on what it is. Got some good pieces at home that would suit a bench, if y'want?" Elbie offered.

"That'd be great, Elbie, thank you. I'll cut you in on the money too. Then we can all get outta here!"

Cuban, for the first time that day, showed the faintest glimmer of a smile.

Chapter 19

An eerie silence enveloped Daynes that Tuesday at nightfall, a bird flapping its wings frantically the only sound. Around 10:30, a weary-looking black man emerged from the front door of the elementary school after finally finishing his cleaning shift there. An equally exhausted-looking black woman followed him out. Pulling shut the thick wooden front door, he fiddled with the lock to secure it up for the night. Wiping his brow as he struggled, he cursed the uncooperative key.

"You want me to help with that?" the woman asked lightly.

"No, I can do it, damn thing!" he cursed again as he fought in vain to pull the door and turn the key simultaneously. He sighed. "Alright!" The man stepped aside.

"Let me work my magic." Blowing on her fingertips, she gave the man a knowing smile as she got to work. Seconds later, the key turned effortlessly and the lock slid home with an unhindered clunk.

"You done it?" he leaned over her and pushed on the tightly-closed door. "Well–" He blew his cheeks out in admiration. "That's the Lord's truth why I married you."

"Of course it is," she joked back. "You knew you were on to a good thing, Mister! Now let's go home, I'm beat." The wife kissed her husband on the nose. They both turned around to head for their car when headlights blasted onto them.

A dark green Ford pickup truck was parked in front of them, blocking their path. Slowly, the driver's side door creaked open and a shadowy figure emerged. He placed his heavy boots onto the tarmac below with a clump, then crunched a cigarette into the ground beneath them. He looked older than the second man who moments later stepped out of the passenger side. They both stood in silence, staring at the black couple. The man and his wife squinted into the blinding light and held their hands to their faces trying to see who the men were, but they were impossible to identify with the glow of the headlights forming a haze around their imposing figures. As one man passed the front of the truck to whisper something to the second man, his body crossed and bent the front left beam, redirecting it onto a third man who was now visible in the back seat. He looked noticeably smaller than the other two and not particularly keen to step out of the vehicle. The fourth silhouette that the black man saw through the refracted light was the one that struck terror in his heart – two pointed ears and clouds of hot breath rising from its muzzle in excitement.

"Baby, what's happening?" The woman gripped her husband's hand as he squeezed it back.

"Just stay behind me," he said under his breath. "We don't want any trouble," he called out to the shadows by the truck.

Gripping her husband with both hands, the woman froze with fear as the muffled noise of barking rang out.

"Please don't hurt us–" The black man started to tremble. "OK, baby, listen," he whispered sideways to his wife. "I want you to run to Mr. Robinson's place. He always leaves the yard gate unlocked. Wait for me there. I'll be right behind you, OK? Baby, you ready?"

"I don't wanna leave you, I can't–" his wife sobbed.

Their voices stirred the men on either side of the truck, who then muttered their own instructions to each other.

"You can. I'm right behind you. I'll stall 'em. Ready? One, two, three. GO!" He threw her hand out of his own and shoved her away from him.

She ran down the steps but one of the men gave chase and caught her easily. Her husband leaped down the steps, grabbed his wife's aggressor and unlocked the young man's arms from around her. In a fit of blind rage, the black man punched him in the head, knocking him to the brink of unconsciousness. His wife sprinted into the night wailing. The truck driver raced over the instant he saw his partner in crime crash to the floor. Turning his head back to the truck, he shouted his instruction to the person in the back holding the leash.

"Let him go, boy!"

Excited paws scrabbled out of the truck as the beast ran off down the street in pursuit of the fleeing woman.

The driver strode over to the shell-shocked target of their night's sport and pummelled him to the ground.

The sound of screaming and barking echoed along the street and far off into the darkness beyond. The gate to Mr. Robinson's yard clattered open under the weight of the woman falling through it. She slammed it shut as the Alsatian's bared teeth snapped at her. Sinking to the ground, she sobbed through strangled breaths in the relative safety of Robinson's yard.

Chapter 20

"Jeffrey, there you are."

Kyle, drink in hand, made his way over that Tuesday evening to Ellis's table at the Copperpot Inn. Ellis loved the finer things in life—he'd certainly worked hard enough to achieve them—but mostly he came here for the privacy that his VIP booth gave him. Tonight, however, it was strictly business.

"Yes, here I am," Ellis said with an unusual hint of sarcasm. Kyle hadn't been with the company long enough to know that this was the table Ellis had reserved for nearly ten years. He sat with three others, including two of the investors who were present in Kyle's presentation.

"Thank you for inviting me, sir. Is Larry not here?" Kyle seemed a little disarmed without his mentor.

"No. I thought it would be good to meet you on your own." Ellis smiled as he sipped his single malt.

"I see." Kyle ran his fingers over his tie-knot.

"I was wondering, young Kyle, when exactly *did* you tell me about the meeting you were having today with my friends here?" He motioned his arm to the men at his table. "I've been reliably informed by these fine gentlemen it was implied that I was drinking in here instead. That the case?" Ellis asked rhetorically, his eyes drilling holes through Kyle's face.

"You know something? I must have forgotten to let you know about the meeting," Kyle floundered. "What with being new and all it must have slipped my mind. I'd assumed Larry would anyway." He loosened his tie away from his sweating neck.

"So, it was *Larry's* fault?" Ellis pressed.

"Well, he is the boss ... as well as you of course, sir."

One of the investors coughed as Kyle's confidence waned palpably.

"You know, the next smart thing to do would be to apologize for embarrassing me in front of my friends. I've always attended every meeting unless otherwise stated and on this occasion my wife was unwell," Ellis chided.

Kyle sipped his drink. "Of course, sir. It won't happen again."

Ellis smiled his reply.

"So how is everything going?"

Kyle took another sip.

"Everything's fine. At the meeting I said–"

"I know what was said, Kyle," Ellis interrupted, gesturing to his investors next to him. "What about the staff? Are they happy?"

"Of course, sir–"

"How are my two new recruits?"

"They're doing just fine, sir." Sweat beads began to form on Kyle's upper lip.

"Shona workin' on the trucks like I ordered?"

"I believe so," Kyle lied again.

"Good," Ellis nodded slowly, eyeballing him.

It seemed a natural moment for the conversation to pause and for people to sip their drinks. One of the investors got up to use the bathroom, and the other two walked over to the bar hollering as they recognized somebody.

"Sir, do you think it's good for morale to have a colored man and a woman working at the site? Daynes is booming at the moment and there are more deserving people who wanna work here. Some have even moved house to get a job in this town. You know what I'm talking about?" Kyle leaned forward.

"No," Ellis responded flatly.

"They're making the workers go crazy. I've seen it with my own eyes, sir!"

Ellis sipped his single malt. He paused, then looked Kyle dead in the eye.

"Tell me, have they ever stolen anything?"

"No," Kyle replied, leaning back in his seat.

"Have they ever shown up late?"

"Not yet! But I reckon–"

"Have they ever refused work?" Ellis interjected, still yet to blink.

"Not that I'm aware of."

"Then we're done on this subject." Ellis sat back.

Kyle sighed and finished his drink.

"Good evening, Mr. Ellis," he smiled and shook Ellis's hand, seething as he got up and left.

Chapter 21

Shona found Cuban sitting on the floor by the small fire he'd made just outside the back door of the tool room. She'd been finishing up for the evening that Wednesday, putting the tools away and wiping down the benches when she saw the door ajar. Cuban seemed distant, tapping a melody on the side of an old tire a few yards away from his makeshift bed.

"Hey," Shona said. He stopped humming. "No, don't stop on my account. That was beautiful."

"Thanks."

"You OK? Didn't get a chance to see you much today."

"They just playin' their games again tryin' to get me to take the bait but I ain't gonna bite. I need the money too much."

Shona shifted an old crate out of the way and sat on the floor next to him.

"There are some real jerks here. But it won't be long and we'll be out of it, right?" she said, trying to reassure him.

"Maybe." Cuban drummed his fingers on the tire again, slower this time.

"What's up?" Shona asked softly.

"Even if I do manage to set foot outside o'here, they're waiting. *The Klan*." He spat out the last word as if it were snake venom. "The safest place for me is here, in this goddamn place!"

"I'm sorry. Wish there was more I could do."

Shona pondered that thought. Maybe there was something she could do for him. He was nothing like what she'd been brought up to believe. Not a *thieving, raping, murdering bastard* like her father had ingrained in her mind. She had to try to help him. He couldn't stay here like this. He had nothing: a wooden bed, dirty satchel pillow and a tiny fire. It had to be small though, to avoid attracting attention to the fact he'd been staying there the last few nights.

"Hey, I got an idea. Why don't you come back to where I'm staying at the moment," she began, her words tumbling out before she had given herself the chance to register the magnitude of what she'd be asking of Tom and Ruby.

"You kiddin'? Ain't nobody gon' want a colored staying under their roof!" Cuban said.

"Well, technically, I'm not under *their* roof – I sleep in the barn outside. I'm sure we could make space? Come home with me tonight and we can at least ask. If they say no then you lost nothin', right?" Shona made a watertight case.

"OK, but we gotta wait until dark. I don't wan' be seen out there." Cuban pointed towards the field which backed onto the tool room.

"Deal. We'll stay here another hour or so. By my reckonin' it'll be just fine by then." Shona held her hands in front of Cuban's fire. They smiled at each other as they shared the peace and quiet of the evening.

As night fell, Cuban stared into the flames, transfixed.

"You alright?" Shona asked.

"I heard today that three coloreds gon' missin' from town.

The guys in the canteen were talking about it, calling it *population control*. One of them's my friend." Cuban choked back his emotions.

"My God!" Shona exhaled.

"He's a good man too. He does cleanin' at a school in town. Did a few shifts for him when he had to take one of his kids to some hospital appointments. One night, I 'member tellin' him I felt like I was being watched when I locked up, but he said nothin' would happen 'cause too many people were around. Think his wife took over my job when I left."

"She missin' too?"

"No, they only mentioned a *guy who works at the school*, so that'd be my friend. That's all I know. Somehow I don't think the sheriff will be looking for three coloreds on his watch, do you? I can promise ya, it won't end with good news."

"Jesus," Shona whispered.

"Yep, I really need *his* help right now."

They both sat quietly in front of the pathetic fire. It wasn't big enough to keep a dormouse warm at night, but it was arguably better than Cuban being caught sleeping there.

Chapter 22

"Mornin', young Shona." Elbie, on his hands and knees, looked up to greet her as she walked into his little workshop at the back of the tool room, early for work as usual that bright Thursday morning. It was Elbie's little haven – a place he could be alone with his thoughts and keep his private things. His best tools were lovingly stored on purpose-built shelves. He seemed to have everything in this cupboard, from tacks to billhooks, all neatly labeled – his meticulous organization a testament to how long he had worked there.

"Good morning, Elbie. What you up to?" Shona asked.

"Sssshh ... this is where I keep my secret stash," he replied.

Shona smiled and got down on her hands and knees too. "Where you keep what?"

"My stash! Liquor, some cash ... and my diary. Those up in the offices would turn this place upside down if they had any idea!"

Elbie traced his fingers along one of the floorboards near the wall, finding the one that was loose. He wiggled it upwards with his penknife until its lip was exposed enough to lift.

Underneath was a box and sure enough there was his brown, leather-bound diary, a hip flask and a few crumpled dollar bills.

"This is my *escape box*. That's what I call it in my head."

Elbie pulled out his diary and began flicking through it. Shona watched him with sadness in her eyes. He was an outsider here too. The fact that the only place he felt he could keep his things completely secret was in a little box underneath some floorboards spoke volumes.

"How often d'you write in it?"

"Most days. Just a line or two. Trust me, there's always something to write about with what goes on around here. Writing in this thing makes me feel close to my wife, like she can hear my thoughts. And if I listen close enough, I can hear her talking back to me," Elbie drifted off, gazing into space as he spoke.

"Yeah? What does she say?"

"To *get the goddamn hell out of here as soon as I can*." He pointed at Shona.

They both chuckled.

"I would say that's great advice!" said Shona.

"Here, this is a picture of her." Elbie took out a small black and white photograph from the inside cover of his diary and placed it in her hand.

"She's gorgeous, Elbie."

"She was a stunner. Too good for me."

"Elbie, don't you think it would be safer to keep this diary at home? People here'd go crazy if they found it!"

"It's my damn memory. I have to write things down straight away!" He spoke with the first tinge of bitterness Shona had witnessed since meeting the old man. "I can't remember a damn thing by the time I get home. It'd just be a blank page." Elbie choked back tears.

Shona put a reassuring hand on his shoulder, which he patted as he cleared his throat.

"Hey, if you ever need a drink, you know where it is now," Elbie said as he shook the hip flask, the liquor inside sloshing.

"Here you are," Cuban said, finding Elbie and Shona in the tool room just before their 10 o'clock break. He'd seemed brighter in the last few days since he'd been staying at Tom and Ruby's, bedding down in the opposite corner of the barn to where Shona slept. They were reluctant at first but Shona had convinced them that it was only short term. They agreed on the condition that nobody in town knew he was staying there, as the Birds didn't want any trouble brought to their door. He had to take a different route home from work every night to ensure he wasn't followed.

"Hey," Shona smiled.

"Boss man's givin' out the wages. We need to go." He cocked his head to the door for them to follow him.

The workers were gathered in the usual place underneath the balcony in the canteen. Each worker's name was called out for them to collect their envelopes from Deputy Paul.

"Elbie!" Deputy Paul hollered. Elbie took his envelope from him, emptying the contents into his hand.

"Jackson!" Shona collected her envelope.

"Nigger!" Head down, Cuban made his way over.

"There you go, everybody back to work," Deputy Paul ordered.

"I haven't been paid right, you?" Shona kept checking. She looked at Cuban who seemed equally dismayed.

"No, I've come up short too." He didn't sound surprised.

"Me too, those thievin' son'bitches," Elbie screwed his envelope up.

"I'll go see Deputy Paul. I'm not having this!" Shona

marched over to try and catch him before he headed back up the winding steps to the management offices.

"Excuse me? EXCUSE ME! Deputy Paul!"

"What?" he snapped his head back.

"We haven't been paid right. We're all coming up short!"

"That's what they're payin' you."

"But I got people relying on me to help them!" Shona's face radiated fury.

"Not my problem." Deputy Paul turned his back and continued up the steps.

"You *know* this ain't fair. We've done nothin' wrong. We work damn hard, goddammit!" Shona yelled in vain at the back of Deputy Paul's sweaty shirt.

"Well, go see the boss! I'll let Mr. Bruce know you'd like to complain ... or leave."

She stood glaring at him as he reached the top, hearing the clump of his footsteps walk around the balcony and into an office. She knew it was futile trying to reason with him. She made her way back to the tool room, punching one of the cleaning cupboard doors on her way past.

That afternoon, Shona was ordered to clean the kitchen until she could see her reflection in every pot and pan.

"Jackson! Get your ass over here."

Shona folded her cleaning cloth, put it on the side and made her way towards the booming voice. She found Deputy Paul at the bottom of the balcony steps, his cold eyes fixed on her. He led her up the steps, stopping right outside Larry Bruce's office. Turning to face her, he flashed a sly smile as he knocked on the door.

"Yeah," a voice bellowed from the other side.

The deputy entered and shut the door behind him. He was gone for about thirty seconds then reappeared.

"In you go," he smirked.

"Mr. Bruce, sir?" She spoke as confidently as she could muster as she entered his office.

"Get in here, Jackson!" Bruce was sitting down. On his desk there were photographs of him taken with the most influential people in town. He looked up from the papers strewn out in front of him and shot a look of disgust at her.

"You wanna work here, don't you?" He raised an eyebrow as he spoke.

"Yessir."

"Then why the *fuck* you talkin' back to your superior?"

"I just asked about our wages, sir. They're not the same as everyone else's." Shona lowered her eyes from his angry red face.

"That's because you're *not* the same. Do you hear me? All three of you rejects. You're lucky you all still *have* a job."

He rose out of his chair and stood directly in front of Shona, close enough for her to smell the liquor on his breath.

It was a familiar smell to her.

His mustached mouth curled as he circled her. Shona froze, feeling his breath on her neck as he lingered behind her.

"The thing that's been playin' on my mind since you had the audacity to walk into my company was *why*? Why would a pretty girl like you wanna work here? Now, I got my suspicions. She either wants to drive the men wild and get some *business* for herself in the evening or something ain't quite right with her!" He looked her up and down, wrinkling his nose as his eyes drifted over her shapeless, baggy overalls and heavy work boots. "Tell me, Jackson, why *did* you choose here?" Menace dripped from each word he uttered.

"I needed a job."

Shona stared at the wall behind Bruce's desk.

"Hmm," he whispered in her ear. "The guys tell me they think you're cute but they can't work you out." Shona felt her blood run cold. "Hell, maybe you could be some use to the men here after all. Work some *tension* out of 'em."

He began tracing his forefinger down Shona's back, her body flinching with repulsion as he did so.

"Now, get the fuck out of my office." Bruce growled.

Chapter 23

"You're too slow, old man!"

That sweltering Thursday morning, Elbie's first job was to move some heavy, steel tire rims out of the path of a tractor waiting to reverse into the fields. As he passed him, Kyle callously pushed Elbie into the pile he'd made. The old man squealed in pain as a sharp edge of steel ripped a hole in his work pants. A halo of dark red blood seeped through the ragged tear.

"You OK?" Cuban ran over and slid his strong arm underneath Elbie's shoulder. He smiled his gratitude and glanced at the half dozen men around him who could have stepped in to help him up.

"Come on, friend, let's get you patched up," Cuban said as he smiled back.

~

Cuban managed to get a bowl of lukewarm soup and some bread from the serving counter at lunch time, then made his way, through the usual taunts and insults, to the table at the back of the canteen where Shona was eating alone.

"Hey, how you doin'?" she asked.

"Fine. You?"

"I'm certainly finding out about that Mr. Chambers. Telling me how I belonged in the kitchen scrubbing floors. Yeah, me and him don't see eye-to-eye."

Shona slurped soup hungrily off her spoon. Just at that moment, Elbie also sat down with his equally sparsely laden tray.

"He seems like another damn idiot if you ask me. Corrupt as the rest of 'em. Although Miss Chloe's not," Elbie added.

"Keep your guard up with her, though. She still sits in the management office, remember?" Shona snapped back coldly.

"What's going on over there?" Cuban's attention was diverted to a couple of tables away. Randy, one of the mechanics, was surrounded by three hulking brutes who were throwing his hat around. Very quickly it became a circus of whoops and cheers, with Randy being the main attraction.

"Come on, big boy, come get it!" The tallest man tempted Randy, who huffed and puffed as he tried to force his huge bulk into a half-jump, his belly wobbling every time he rose and fell. His sweaty, red face was contorted into a pathetic scowl as he squealed his displeasure, which only served to egg his tormentors on more.

"Greg, it ain't funny no more!" Randy pleaded.

"I got his keys!" another member of the pack cheered.

"They're unbelievable," Shona said. "Even the damn bosses ain't doin' nothing!"

Elbie looked up to the balcony where Kyle and Deputy Paul were watching.

"So, d'you want the hat that *Mrs. Randy* got you or your keys that are kinda important for your job? Come on, fat boy, choose!" Greg reveled in his power. He tossed the hat and keys between his fellow tormentors. "Randy, just see it as me helping you lose a few pounds!"

By now, a three-person-deep circle had formed around Randy, waving their arms in the air and jeering.

"I've had enough of this." Shona jumped up.

"What's she doin'?" Cuban exclaimed.

Barging her way into the center of the crowd, Shona grabbed Randy's hat out of one man's hand.

"Give him the keys, Greg! Or you gon' hit a woman?" She fronted up to him, a defiant look on her beautiful face.

The crowd hushed, their eyes fixed on Shona.

"I'm gon' hold out my hand and you gon' place the keys down! Y'all had your fun now," Shona said. The tension in the room was palpable.

"Who are you, his mother?" Greg laughed in her face.

"No. Keys." Shona held out her palm.

All eyes were now on Greg.

Hearing the commotion downstairs, Chloe emerged out of her office and looked over the balcony. "What's goin' on?"

"Nothing, just the guys lettin' off some steam," Kyle replied.

Back on the ground floor, Greg pressed his nose into Shona, his sweat dripping down onto her cheekbone.

"You need to be careful who you make a friend in here and who you choose to make an enemy, darlin'," he sneered in her ear.

"Keys." Shona stared at him, her blue eyes calm.

Shocked, he looked up to the balcony for advice. Following his eyeline, Shona spotted Chloe standing next to Kyle who nodded his decision.

Greg huffed and slapped the keys down hard into Shona's palm.

"Come on, everybody, show's over," Deputy Paul barked, his eyes fixed on Shona as she handed a grateful Randy back his possessions, then returned to the table to finish her lunch.

Chapter 24

The following morning, Randy called out to Shona as he made his way over to her outside the mechanics' yard.

"Yeah?" Shona stood up straight, holding her broom.

"I just wanted to say thanks for standing up to those guys in the canteen yesterday. You didn't have to."

Shona felt sorry for him. He was short and round with thinning messy hair, eroded away from constantly wearing his tatty cap. He always seemed to have on the same dirty overalls day after day, the same shoulder strap always hanging loose.

"No problem. That happen a lot?" Shona squinted in the sunlight.

"Yeah, but who do you complain to, right?" he shrugged.

"How long's it been going on for?"

"Since Mr. Bruce took over. But he told me that nobody else in Daynes would give me a job and that I was lucky that Mr. Ellis did so I should be grateful."

The 10 o'clock buzzer sounded.

"You coming in?" she asked him.

"Nah. M'wife made me sandwiches. I like the quiet out here in the fields anyway. Best twenny minutes of the day for me!" Randy half-smiled.

"OK, well, I'll see you in a while."

Shona made her way to the canteen, got her food and sat down in her usual seat, scoffing down her breakfast. Ten minutes before the return-to-work buzzer was due to sound, an exhausted-looking Cuban walked into the canteen and headed up to collect his food. He held out his plate and braced himself for the typically inaccurate aim Chef Lou had when serving him. This time, Lou went one better, holding his ladle to the far left of Cuban's plate and slopping his portion onto the canteen floor.

"That's y'lot, move along."

"Could I just have some bread?" Cuban asked calmly.

"When you gon' realize you ain't welcome 'round here?"

"Can I just have some bread. Please," Cuban repeated. He was starving.

"When you've cleared up that mess." Lou looked over his counter at the brown greasy sludge on the floor.

Picking up some paper towels, Cuban got down on his hands and knees.

"Where he belongs. Go on, scrub!" Lou mocked. Workers in the canteen started to join in.

Bits of bread flew over at him, hitting Cuban as he tried to duck. When he was finished cleaning, he stood up and faced Lou.

"Can I have my bread now, *please, Chef*?" Cuban fixed his blazing eyes on the wall behind Lou, trying to contain his fury.

"Of course." Picking up a small bread roll, Lou took a huge bite, leaving remnants of his saliva on it, then gave it to Cuban. "Now, what do you say?"

"Thank you," Cuban replied through gritted teeth.

"Good boy."

Cuban joined Elbie and Shona at the table. Seeing that all he had was a tiny half-eaten bread roll, Elbie pushed his plate towards him, offering him the last of his eggs and refusing to take no for an answer.

"I'm gon' put all this in my diary, y'hear? They'll pay for it one day, I goddamn swear it!" Elbie was furious.

"Diary? With all due respect, sir, what's that gon' do?" Cuban was raging inside. He knew it was wrong to take it out on Elbie but he couldn't control his feelings of humiliation.

"When I get out of here, I'm gon' give it to somebody and maybe they can help when they see what's really going on here. I won't have anything to lose then," Elbie said as he tried to calm his friend down.

Cuban ate the few spoonfuls of food that Elbie had offered him. They sat there in silence for the remaining few minutes of break.

Chapter 25

That Friday afternoon, Shona approached Elbie who was sweeping up outside the mechanics' garage. She bent down to pick up a dustpan and held it on the ground for him.

"Elbie, I got a question." She looked up at him as the last of the debris was collected safely in the pan.

"What's that?"

"Why is Mr. Ellis so OK with colored folk?"

"Because he owes 'em," he replied simply.

"Owes 'em?"

"You see, Ellis's father ran a successful transport company about an hour from here. It was in the middle of nowhere. He built it up from what his father had started and little Jeffrey used to play around the yard most days after school getting into mischief. Ellis senior used to employ coloreds and pay 'em next to nothing to do all the dirty jobs other workers refused to do. He couldn't stand 'em."

"Go on–" Shona prompted.

The old man paused, leaning on his broom.

"One day, little Jeffrey, only about nine or ten years old, goes off into the fields behind his father's plantation and slips down a ten foot hole. It was blazing hot and he twisted his ankle on the way down so he couldn't climb out. He would've been cooked alive right there under that sun if he'd have stayed out much longer."

"Then what happened?"

"He called for help but his father couldn't hear him." Shona's eyes widened. "A little while later, two heads appeared looking down at him. It was the black fellas who worked for Ellis senior. They were on their way home and heard his cries for help. Now, these men were being underpaid, beaten, starved and humiliated by Jeffrey's father–"

"So what did they do?"

"They could've got the ultimate revenge on Ellis senior. Jeffrey was his heir, his world. They could've left him in that hole, walked away and nobody would've known."

"And? Come on Elbie, what happened?" Shona said impatiently.

"They did exactly that. They walked away," Elbie said matter-of-factly.

Shona was dumbstruck. That was not the line she'd expected him to say.

"Wait, what? They walked *away*?"

"They walked away. But they came back a few minutes later with two of their buddies and a rope from the yard, hollering to Ellis senior to follow them. When he arrived, he saw those 'evil' black men pull his scared, dehydrated son to safety!" Elbie smiled.

"My God."

"Yep, from that day on, Ellis senior never treated 'em bad again, even gave 'em more money. Jeffrey hung out with their children and everything. He owes his life to those black fellas."

"Wow. How come y'know all this, Elbie?" Shona smiled.

"I worked for Ellis senior many years ago and I never forgot seeing little Jeffrey being brought back that day, cuts all down his legs from the fall. That's why he's got that limp. When Ellis senior passed on, Jeffrey always promised me a job no matter what. I seen him grow from boy to man and I'm proud of him," Elbie concluded.

"You got a lot of stories goin' on in there, ain't ya!" Shona pointed at Elbie's head – he smiled and nodded.

"Come on, I'll show you a picture of Ellis senior and all of us at the old site. The black fellas who saved Jeffrey are in it too."

They wandered back over to the tool room, deep in conversation, and leaned their brooms up against the wall as they went inside.

"What the–"

Elbie's horrified face froze. His eyes slowly panned across the scene, the wrinkles on his face more pronounced as he frowned in bewilderment. The place had been completely trashed, broken stools and benches lying all around the once immaculate room. Tools had been snapped, then thrown around indiscriminately.

Shona sighed and set about picking up the remnants of broken tools and papers off the floor. Nuts and bolts were littered everywhere.

A terrifying thought pierced Elbie's mind, causing the color to drain from the old man's face as he ran towards his little workshop. Shona followed closely behind, hearing a strangled cry of relief as he realized the plank in the wooden floorboard had not been disturbed.

"GODDAMN this place!" Elbie clenched his fists.

Shona shut the door leading out to the corridor to give them their privacy and began sweeping up the broken glass on the floor inside. Looking up, it was now Shona's turn to be surprised.

"Elbie, look!"

"What the hell–"

They stared open mouthed at the two words gouged into the wooden door. *NIGGER LOVER*

Meanwhile, Kyle stalked around his office like a caged lion, running a frustrated hand over his neatly combed hair and loosening his tie. His desk was clutter free with just the bare minimum of office supplies any self-respecting executive should have – including the obligatory bottle of whiskey and glass in the desk drawer. The quiet calm of his surroundings belied his mood, however, as he paced around the desk on the phone to his mother in Pittsburgh.

"What are you talkin' 'bout?" He stopped dead.

"They came back, this time demanding money. What the hell you got yourself into down there, Kyle?" his mother shrilled over the phone.

"It's nothin'. I'll deal with it." He pinched the bridge of his nose.

"Nothing? Your father paid them off ... this time. Said you owe money to other people too, that right?"

"'Course not. They're just foolin' around tryin' to frighten you."

"Well, it *worked!* We don't want this anymore, Kyle. Time and time again we bail you out when you owe no-good thugs money for God knows what! Your father is livid."

"Yeah? It's not like you can't afford it, Mother," Kyle snapped back. There was a long pause. "Look, Mom, I'm sorry. I didn't mean that, I–"

"Son ... I've always, always defended you, even though it's caused nothing but upset between me and your father. You've had the best upbringing, the nicest house and you went to the best school. But this has gone too far."

"Uh huh. So, you're happy to let your only child get beat up? What kinda mother's that?"

"The kind of mother who paid those other thugs off last year in secret so your father wouldn't find out," she fired back.

"Yeah, I bet you have a lot of secrets from each other, huh?"

"Why you saying this?" Kyle's mother sounded tearful.

"You should be helping your son. Why's that gotta be a secret?"

"Because you've got yourself involved with the wrong people, Kyle. Drugs, gambling? You're thirty-four years old, for God's sake. You've had more than enough money out of us."

Kyle sat down and took a swig of whiskey straight from the near-empty bottle.

"Didn't realize there was a limit to my mother's affections." He rolled the whiskey over the front of his teeth, sucking the air through them.

"That's not fair, Kyle."

"The truth ain't, is it, Mother?"

"That him?" Kyle heard a deep voice in the background.

"Kyle?" His father barked.

"Father."

"I'm gon' give it to you straight now; I've paid 'em. But they said you owe more. You're on your own. Don't you dare speak to your mother like that and, in case you're wondering, you ain't getting a goddamn PENNY of inheritance after the money you've blown. You're a disgrace, the dirty deals you've done to some good folk back here! You're no son o'mine."

The line went dead.

Kyle was left with the dull burr of the dial tone as he drained the last dregs of his bottle and swept his arm along the smartly organized desk, sending his letter tray and notepad flying.

90

Chapter 26

"What the hell is it this time? We have more goddamn meetings than Eisenhower!" Elbie scoffed under his breath to Shona and Cuban.

Everybody made their way to the usual place in the canteen late that Friday afternoon, pleasantly surprised to see Jeffrey Ellis emerge up top, giving everybody a warm smile.

"Wish he was around here more," Shona leaned in to whisper to Cuban.

"Good mornin', everybody. I know y'all busy so I don't want to take up too much of your time," Ellis began, leaning over the balcony.

"Take as much time as you want, m'friend!" Elbie said in a low voice.

"I want to take this opportunity to introduce to you one of the new managers here at Ellis and Bruce."

Shona looked to the right of Ellis as Larry Bruce and Kyle walked out and stood together, not looking happy.

"I've been impressed with his professionalism, integrity and hard work. Please join me in congratulatin' Mr. Ron Black." Ellis swept his right arm outwards.

A tall, balding man emerged onto the balcony. He looked to

be in his late thirties and was as smartly dressed as Ellis in his three-piece suit. Ron Black was an island at the company, a safe pair of hands who never caused a fuss and never joined in with the harsh treatment. He just did his job.

Ellis concluded his introduction and instigated a round of hearty applause. Bruce and Kyle slow clapped, the outpouring of affection for Ron grating on them.

During the applause, Ellis leaned in towards Ron, knowing his voice would be drowned out. "Ron, I want you to be my eyes and ears here. Tell me *everything* that goes on."

Ron nodded and smiled back at the cheering crowd.

∾

The meeting was called to a close and the workers began mingling below the balcony, none of them in any rush to get back to work. Elbie pointed across the crowded room.

"There she is, sweet little thing."

Chloe Bruce had made her way down the steps from the management balcony to wander amongst the workers when Cuban and Shona both glanced over.

"She spoke to me when I was out in the field the other day. She seemed to really listen," Cuban added.

Spotting the three of them across the distance, Chloe began making her way over.

"I'm goin' back to work," Shona said quietly as she passed behind Elbie and headed towards the door leading outside.

"Shona, wait!" Cuban darted away just as Chloe neared Elbie, her face breaking out into the purest, most natural smile he'd seen in a long time.

Elbie had always been fond of the young Miss Bruce and, in the short time she'd been home, noticed that she'd matured into the total opposite of her brutish father. She was honest, kind and very considerate of the workers she'd soon inherit.

She always made time to check they were happy and helped where she could with their problems, even if it was just to listen. Elbie was protective of her when the less well-mannered workers dared to make any unsavory comments about her perfectly proportioned body. He always made sure those pigs were reminded just who was going to be paying their wages in a few years' time. That usually did the trick. Elbie relied on his wits rather than his less-than-intimidating physical strength to get his points across. He greeted her as she approached him, her eyes dimming slightly as she looked over his shoulder.

Cuban raced after Shona, who moved as if she was trying to outrun a lion.

"Wait, you OK?"

"I'll see y'later," she replied bluntly.

Cuban stared down the corridor at Shona's back as she turned the corner. Shaking his head, he headed back to his changing space to gear up for his next rancid job of the day, wondering what was eating away at his friend.

Nearing the door, a noise coming from inside stopped him in his tracks. He was shocked when he looked in to see Kyle decimating what little private space he had. Splinters of wood from his shelf and cupboard were everywhere, his metal locker completely caved in and its lockless door hanging by its broken hinges. What little clothing Cuban had was ripped to shreds, axle grease smeared all over his satchel.

Kyle approached with a smirk, knowing Cuban was powerless.

"Locker check."

"Anybody else been checked?" He forced the words through his clenched mouth, knowing the answer.

Kyle whistled to Deputy Paul who sauntered over.

"Don't like our rules?"

Cuban swallowed.

"You know what you can do? Fucking leave!" Kyle

pummelled the last two words verbally into Cuban's face, droplets of spit landing in his eyes.

"I suggest he comes with me, what d'you say, boss?" Deputy Paul's face was emotionless as he stared straight at Cuban, tapping his short wooden staff into the palm of his opposite hand.

"Excellent idea, Paul!" Kyle smirked as Cuban was strong-armed out of the changing space and down the corridor.

Chapter 27

Chloe Bruce had felt the dull ache of her restless spirit constantly since the day she'd returned to Daynes. Her studies in the city had finished and, with her older brother gone, she was needed at home to do as all good Southern daughters should. Her only escape from the monotony of her new corporate role was to saddle up that Saturday morning and put on a baggy cotton shirt, comfy slacks and riding boots. It was the only time her cluttered, swirling mind felt still and when she felt the soft breeze through her untied hair, her inner wildness was released.

Resisting the urge yet again to jump the fence of the paddocks that surrounded the family estate, she returned to the house to find her father in the living room slouched on the sofa, slugging whiskey and watching the same old game show he'd watched for years. He was still just as bad as ever at guessing the answers, his frustration growing with every glass of liquor that he sloshed down his throat.

"GODDAMN it. I *knew* it was that! I swear this damn show's rigged!" He drained his glass and immediately poured himself another.

"I'm going down to my den to do some painting," Chloe said

with a sigh, deciding not to linger while her father berated the contestants as he gulped his shot down and jangled the ice cubes in his glass at the television in condemnation of their incorrect answers.

"OK, Princess, but I wish you wouldn't waste your time doing that stuff. There's no money to be made there. The business is where you will make your money, sweetheart," he replied, his eyes not diverting from the screen.

"I enjoy it, Daddy. I think I'm pretty good at it."

She didn't get a reply.

"Yes! I *knew* that one," he screeched at the television, only being snapped back to reality by the shrill of the telephone.

"Yeah?" He listened for a moment, then looked at Chloe. "Honey, it's a private call."

"Sure." She sidled out of the room.

Bruce waited until he was certain Chloe was out of earshot.

"Yeah...Right...OK, I'll just tell Ellis one of the machines packed up and I took the money from the safe to fix it. You leave it with me. I'm on my way. Get the cards ready." He slammed the phone down.

Eleanor Bruce knew exactly what she was looking for that same Saturday afternoon. There was only one shop in town that was chic enough for her expensive tastes. As Larry's wife she wanted for nothing, the townsfolk revering her like a celebrity. She was the Bette Davis of Daynes, in her late forties and always immaculately dressed and coiffed. Her brown hair, with not even the merest hint of gray in it, was pinned up high in a bun on her head, combed and smoothed meticulously. Her stylish pale blue two-piece suit was this season's latest design, to go with her Chanel handbag and pumps. Mrs. Bruce was responsible for making or breaking local fashion establishments—a nod or recommendation from her would virtually guarantee a rush on a particular garment. Her business was a sought-after prize. As she made her way down the main sidewalk through town, window blinds twitched and shop assistants crossed their fingers that within minutes their door bells would tinkle.

Stella's Boutique was Eleanor's destination. Nowhere else would suffice today.

"Well, *hello* there, Mrs. Bruce. How are you on this fine day?" Stella greeted her with the usual over-the-top grace while subtly trying to organize her staff with a flurry of hand gestures behind a browsing Eleanor Bruce's back.

"Hi sweetie," Eleanor chirped over her shoulder.

"Now, what can I do for you, ma'am? What fancy dinner you goin' to this time?" Stella asked. Charlie, her assistant, looked over as he straightened out some clothes hanging on the rails with precise attention to detail.

"It's not for me, actually; it's for my daughter, Chloe."

"Well now, I heard she was back in town. Home where she belongs with you and Mr. Bruce, ain't that right, Charlie?" Stella shot a look towards her assistant who looked around sharply, broken out of his concentration. He nodded his agreement even though he hadn't heard the question.

"So, what's the occasion?" Stella continued, unashamedly prying.

"She has a date with Kyle Chambers." Eleanor announced the name of Chloe's date deliberately loudly, knowing the impact that statement was going to make with the town gossip. "Stella-the-teller" couldn't keep her mouth shut. It would be all around Daynes by the end of the day, and Alabama by the end of the week, no doubt.

But that was the idea.

"*Kyle Chambers*? Now, she is one lucky woman! But hey now, so is he. She's the catch of Daynes, hell, of all Alabama. They're a match made in heaven," Stella gushed. "And I'm sure if you can't find anythin' off the rack, then Charlie here could work his magic and make somethin' real special – he's got some lovely silk and velvet in the back!" Stella stared at Charlie, who nodded again, fiddling with the tape measure draped around his neck.

"It has to be something gorgeous. I want him to be completely hypnotized by her!" Eleanor clasped her hands together.

"Oh, he will be. How long has Miss Chloe been courting him?"

"Well, it's kinda like a blind date, you know?" Eleanor screwed up her face into a snorting laugh.

"So, Miss Chloe doesn't know 'bout it?" Stella asked, raising an eyebrow.

"She will, and when she does she'll be over the moon, just like we will be when they are the next power couple of Alabama. Who knows? A wedding may soon follow."

"You got this all figured out, ain't 'cha?" Stella wagged a finger.

"I'm not gon' let this one get away. I'll make Chloe see what a smart move it'll be to date him. Now, Stella darlin', show me those stunning dresses."

Chapter 28

As the blood-red sun dipped below the horizon, the Bruces sat in their opulent dining room on Sunday evening, ready to dig into the delicious-looking food their housekeeper was laying on the table. Antonia had worked for the Bruces as long as Chloe could remember. Now in her fifties, she was more like a friend to her–and made the best pot roast she'd ever tasted. This evening, though, Antonia noticed her absentmindedly pushing a piece of beef around her plate. As she refilled Chloe's glass with water, she put a gentle hand on her shoulder, her kindly features soft and warm as usual but with a tinge of concern for the girl she had loved all these years as if she were her own.

"Larry, your dinner's goin' cold. Put that newspaper down!" Eleanor chided for the third time.

"You seen this bullshit? Segregation in schools being banned. What's this damn world coming to?"

Bruce slammed the newspaper down and sat back in his dining chair in a huff, snatching his reading glasses from his face and pinching the bridge of his nose.

"El, I'm glad we paid for our princess to go to the best

schools without bein' around those kind. My God, if she had to share a class with a damn colored..."

Chloe picked at her food.

"You're right, dear. Now eat!" Eleanor instructed.

She put on her napkin and started her meal as Bruce picked up his knife and fork.

"D'you realize how good you had it, Chloe?"

Bruce wiped his mouth on his napkin as he felt his mustache moisten with spit and gravy. Chloe took a large intake of breath, releasing it quietly.

"You just don't know what diseases they carry. I mean, I heard you could die by just being next to them," Eleanor added, shivering.

"I met quite a few colored people when I went traveling on my time off from college and I'm still alive," Chloe said, her eyes not leave her plate.

Bruce stopped chewing. He and Eleanor stared at their daughter, the ticking from the antique gold carriage clock on the marble stone mantelpiece the only sound audible in the room for the next five seconds. Finally, Bruce swallowed the food he'd held in his mouth.

"I don't want you makin' friends with 'em. D'you hear me? They rape, they steal and they lie. They'll try and suck you in to liking them, then boom. Before y'know it, the whole town will be crawling with them like locusts. No, that ain't happenin', not while I still have air in my lungs," Bruce raged, flecks of food flying through his mustache and landing on the tablecloth.

"Have you actually spoken to Cuban?" Chloe put her knife and fork down gently onto her china plate.

Antonia bit her bottom lip to stifle a smile at Chloe's bravery. She really had grown up—and it was a breath of fresh air in this house of hostility. Antonia had never truly understood why two people as rich and successful as Larry and Eleanor Bruce could still be so bitter with the world around them.

Bruce looked up from his plate in surprise. "I don't care what he has to say, other than *Mr. Bruce, I'm leavin'*."

Chloe raised her eyebrows, meeting Antonia's equally tired-looking expression.

"Now, honey, he's probably crawlin' with God knows what. You stay away. I don't want you bringing anything into this beautiful house. Don't you go getting attached and feelin' sorry for 'em–that's how they trick you," Eleanor warned. "Anyway, sweetheart, on another more important subject, what d'you think of Kyle?" She changed the subject of the conversation effortlessly.

"Kyle?" Chloe looked at her mother in surprise.

"Yes," Eleanor said with a nod.

"Well, he's alright. I don't really talk to him much. He seems up his own backside most of the time. He's not very nice to some of the workers. Why?"

"We were just wonderin'. He's made quite an impression on the ladies who are eager to become *Mrs. Chambers*." A smile was creeping across Eleanor's normally icy exterior.

"Well, I would say..." Chloe paused to sip her water. "They're welcome to him!"

It wasn't the answer her parents were hoping for.

"Give the guy a chance," Bruce said.

Chloe remained silent. She made her peace with the uneaten food on her plate and rose out of her chair, itching to get to the sanctuary of her bedroom. When she was out of earshot, Bruce looked across to his wife.

"What we gon' do? You're gon' have to work harder on her, El."

"Don't worry. You leave it to me."

Chapter 29

The Copperpot Inn was the unlikely destination of the Ellis and Bruce workforce that following Friday evening. Jeffrey Ellis had hired the bar out in celebration of Ron Black's promotion and all of his employees, most of whom had never seen the inside of this normally exclusive venue, had been invited. After witnessing the abuse Cuban had suffered and the hostilities she'd experienced so far, Shona hadn't particularly been looking forward to the event.

"Hey Shona, you want another drink?"

Randy waddled over and sat at a small table next to her.

"No thanks," Shona replied, staring at the door every time it opened.

"Your buddy couldn't make it tonight. He got...busy." Deputy Paul swaggered over to the table, flashing Shona a grisly gray-toothed grin.

"Who? Cuban?" Ellis overheard Deputy Paul. "That man deserves to be here like everybody else!"

Larry Bruce rolled his eyes as he walked up behind Deputy Paul.

"Next time, Mr. Ellis," Deputy Paul replied, then glared at Shona as he and Bruce headed to the free bar.

"I'm just gon' get another beer, Shona, you sure you don't want one?" Randy lifted his large bulk from behind the round bar table.

"No thanks."

Shona hated the stench of smoke which contributed to the stale, thick air in the Copperpot. She was uncomfortable but figured she would stay long enough to be respectful towards Ron, Ellis and a few of the other guys she got on alright with. As the evening wore on, it became clear to her that there was an obvious divide in the workforce. It was playing out right in front of her tonight, the two corners of the bar gradually filling up with men choosing their side.

Randy returned to Shona's table and put his beer down, not registering that Deputy Paul had followed stealthily behind him.

"I wanted to say somethin', Shona–" Randy began. As he did so, Deputy Paul kicked the chair from underneath him just as he went to sit down, sending Randy crashing to the ground with the table landing on top of him. Riotous laughter broke out as they cheered the commotion and chanted for the *fat man* to get to his feet.

Shona sprang into action and struggled to help the prone Randy up.

"You alright?" she asked, brushing fragments of the broken bottle from his beer-soaked shirt.

"I'm fine," he replied, trying to pull himself together amid the chanting workers.

Bruce and Kyle could hardly contain themselves as they congratulated Deputy Paul on the evening's entertainment.

Just then, a cheer erupted from the corner nearest the door.

"Now there's a sight for my sore eyes," Shona heard somebody in the bar say as a pretty young woman glided in.

She was wearing a cornflower blue cocktail dress, the fine sequins shimmering in the bright lights of the bar. Her silky brown hair was parted on one side and held in place with a diamond-encrusted butterfly clip. Sighs of admiration rippled across the workers, with one small corner trying to stifle their wolf whistles.

Chloe Bruce had arrived.

~

"Here's my princess." Opening his arms wide, Larry Bruce embraced his daughter, giving Kyle a wink behind her back.

"You alright?" Shona whispered to Randy, who was sitting quietly and looking over at the crowd of men now fawning over Chloe Bruce.

"Yeah. It's just boys being boys. It's fine," he said, looking at the ground.

A few minutes of awkward silence passed between them until Shona decided to cut her losses and make a move. Cuban hadn't arrived anyway and no one else really wanted to talk to her. She walked around the table to say goodbye to Ron and to congratulate him again, shaking Ellis's hand as she passed him.

"What do you think of her, Ron?" Ellis asked, just as Shona was out of earshot.

"She's great. Works harder than most of the guys. Gets a tough time, though. I mean, I can't be everywhere."

"Hmm–" Ellis replied as he watched his star recruit stride towards the exit.

Across the room, another group had also clocked Shona's movements.

"There she goes," Kyle said to the little crowd that had gravitated over to him and Bruce. Chloe's head snapped around towards the exit, just as the door swung shut behind Shona. The others sniggered.

Chloe, meanwhile, was curious to meet this *Shona*—the girl who had got all the men talking, the managers' opinion divided and who she had only, to date, seen the blurry outline of as she was hastily leaving a room.

∼

It was gone midnight, long after Shona had returned home from the Copperpot, when she heard a creak of the barn door and the fresh air of the night sweep over her blankets. A dark figure moved tentatively in the shard of dust-speckled light between the doorway and the corner of the barn. It was Cuban finally returning home, his whimpers replacing the silence. He sat on his little pallet bed and took off his boots with a strangled cry.

"Hey. What happened?" Shona asked.

Hearing him shivering, she crept towards his hunched figure. Edging closer, she looked down to where his boots had landed, a pool of dirty ditchwater staining the wooden barn floor. Something else was mixed in, making the water rusty in color. She reached her hand down and put two fingers in it.

Blood. Lots of it.

"Cuban...what the hell happened to you?"

"I'm fine. I fell," he replied limply.

"You're bleeding, for God's sake!"

He rocked backward and forward on his bed, his arms wrapped around his stomach.

Shona went back across to her bunk, pulled her boots on in the half-light and headed to the little cupboard Tom kept a first aid box in. Pulling out a wad of bandages and a little bottle of iodine, she switched the light on to see how badly hurt Cuban was, but couldn't have prepared herself for the horror that greeted her when she saw him.

Dripping with blood, Cuban's leg looked as if he had caught it in a bear-trap. Cuts and scratches covered his shin bone, his right eye was swollen and he had a wide gash spanning the bridge of his nose. He looked broken.

"Christ. How exactly did you *fall* to make your face and leg look like that?"

"I don't know...I don't know!" he replied, rocking back and forth on his bunk.

"You're lyin', Cuban!" She sniffed and wiped her hand across her face.

"Someone chased me. I tried to take a different route home like Tom and Ruby asked me to do, but they musta followed me. They threw some kinda blanket over my head and knocked me down. I fell, then a damn dog got hold of m'leg. I don't wan' talk 'bout it no more. Please. I just wan' go sleep, OK?"

Shona silently patched him up, then switched off the light. She went back over to her bed, feeling tormented by the thought of the ordeal her friend had been through that evening.

Chapter 30

Despite the fact that she was one of his only friends, Cuban still hadn't told Shona the full story of what happened that night. The following Monday night after work, they were sitting chatting in the barn, sorting out the pieces of wood that Elbie had thought perfect for Shona to make her benches out of.

"You done much readin', Shona?"

"Nah, not really. You?" She picked up two pieces of wood and held them together, sizing them up as armrests.

"Well, I couldn't read until a nice white guy I worked for a few years back taught me, then I couldn't stop. I liked *Marjorie Morningstar* by Herman somebody. You heard o'it?"

"Nope!" She laughed, not expecting to talk literature while hammering two-by-fours together.

"It's about this woman who wants to change her life. Wish I could do that, just click m'fingers and be in that bar in New York playin' that smooth jazz. I can almost hear it now."

A smile crept across Cuban's face as he drummed a beat on a piece of wood with his fingers.

"Yeah? That sounds like a good place."

"You know, Miss Chloe was behind me in the queue today–"

"And?" Shona concentrated on her wood pile.

"I went to let her go in front of me and–"

She stopped what she was doing and faced Cuban. "What?"

His face dropped, unsure at why his light-hearted story had created storm clouds on Shona's pretty face. Her eyes, which had glistened with softness for him a moment ago when he talked about his dream, were now cold and hollow.

"And she let me go ahead of *her*, insisted on it."

"Really."

"You shoulda seen the look on Lou's face! She ain't so bad, Shona. I don't think she's like the others."

"Don't trust her. She didn't stop what happened to you, did she?" Shona's voice was harsh. Picking up three small pieces of wood, she analyzed them for flaws, then threw away the one piece that didn't make the grade. The other two pieces, one in each hand, were further scrutinized by their holder.

"Shona, she don't know! If she did, I think she'd try and stop it."

"Do you? You really think she'd come to your rescue?" She slammed the wood down on the stone floor, sending echoes rippling through the barn.

"Shona, what is your problem with Miss Chloe?"

"She's one of *them*. She won't ever help the likes of us. I'm goin' to bed."

"Christ! What happened here?"

Shona scanned Cuban's possessions as they littered the floor early Tuesday morning.

"Locker check. Not that anybody else ever has one."

"Look, sorry about last night. I'm just not as hopeful as you are that things around here can change! Ain't nobody gon' come save us." Her tone was blunt. "I think we gotta just get on with it and get out of here as soon as possible!"

Cuban tidied the last of his possessions up with Shona's help and rehung his spare pair of pants and an undershirt before attempting to bend the metal locker door back flat so it would close.

"Thanks for your help, Shona." He shook his head and put his hands on his waist. "Jeez man, that Chambers! You'd think going on a date with the boss's daughter would put him in a better mood!"

"What you talkin' bout?" Shona stopped what she was doing.

"He's got a date with Miss Chloe. Don't know what she sees in him."

"She likes him?"

"God only knows why and if she does, well...there's no hope."

Her face hardened. "She *is* like them," she whispered to herself.

Shona's strange mood swings were still playing on Cuban's mind. Tasked with clearing up some smashed glass in the kitchen, he gripped the bag with the shards in it too tightly, recoiling in agony as a white-hot sting ripped through his hand.

"Argh!" He stamped his foot in pain.

"You OK?" Ron Black heard the shriek.

"Yessir. It's nothin'." Cuban tried to hide the blood dripping through his fist and pooling onto the kitchen floor.

"I'll get something for that," Ron replied, inspecting Cuban's wound as he stared in disbelief that his boss would want to help him.

Ron Black burst into the meeting room trying to minimize his flustered appearance by smiling broadly and straightening his tie. *Not a good start to my first management meeting,* he thought as his eyes scanned the room, searching for his seat around the table. The only warm eyes were those of Jeffrey Ellis, who understood that the first meetings were always the worst.

"I'm sorry, sir! Cuban cut his hand real bad so I had to get a bandage and then I got caught up with guys who wanted to see me about some shifts and, well, you know–"

Ellis waved a hand to reassure him and invited him to sit down in the seat next to him.

"Should have let the son'bitch bleed to death," Deputy Paul said under his breath to Larry Bruce, who smiled in agreement.

"Right, me up first, isn't it? Is Chloe joining us?" Ron rustled his papers as he sorted them into neat piles and took a deep breath.

"She's in town on business," Bruce replied.

"It's OK, Ron, take your time," Ellis encouraged.

"Thank you, sir. Phew...Um...Well, I've had some ideas about the future of the company."

Ellis flashed a warm smile at his newly promoted manager.

Returning to his office after the meeting, Ron felt elated. It'd gone better than he'd imagined it would, especially considering how late he'd arrived.

Insisting the workers go home half an hour early, as they had worked so hard that week, was a decision that had irritated Kyle, who was still struggling to play second fiddle to Ellis's new star player.

"So..." Kyle leaned against the doorframe, his arms folded. "You're the do-gooder?"

"Pardon me?" Ron looked up from his desk.

"You know, *Mr. Popular*." Kyle sauntered into the office.

"Don't know what you're talkin' 'bout."

"Wanting to win over the guys?"

"Not especially."

"Wanting to impress the boss?"

"This all a problem to you, Chambers?" Ron sat up straight, broadening his shoulders.

Kyle smiled. "Me? No."

He picked up a small die-cast model of a Spitfire off the neatly arranged desk. Holding the plane by its wings, Kyle began to spin it, prompting Ron to lick his lips in the hope that he wasn't thinking of breaking it.

The little model plane had been a gift on his twenty-first birthday from his father, just before he and ten other brave American pilots left to fly with the RAF Fighter Command in July 1940, rejecting the neutrality laws and risking imprisonment for doing so. Ron hadn't seen his father again after that. He'd been lost somewhere over the Atlantic Ocean, but Ron had always kept a little piece of him on his desk to remind him of the bravest man he'd ever known and the importance of having honor in the workplace. He'd also received his father's Battle of Britain clasp attached to the Campaign Star that was awarded posthumously, but the sentimental value of that little Spitfire plane was far more important. It was the last thing his father had given him. He motioned with his eyes to put his prized possession down. Kyle did so, then leaned across his desk.

"Thing is, I'm just headin' home to get ready for a date with the boss's daughter. You know, *your* boss? I'm making a good impression here and my future relies on that fact. I just cannot allow anything, or anyone, to get in the way of that."

He stood up straight and backed out the door with his familiar swagger, leaving Ron to try and work out what the hell had just happened.

It *felt* like Kyle had just threatened him.

Chapter 31

"What are these bags doing here?" Chloe returned home on Tuesday evening and nearly tripped over three large sacks of books that had been left in the hallway. Antonia looked up from the windows she was cleaning and scuttled over.

"Your father asked me to pack 'em up. He's making way for new furniture in the lounge," she explained, removing one of Chloe's kitten heels from a bag handle loop.

"Oh, so they're going be thrown in the trash?" she asked, reaching down into one of the bags and sifting through the books.

"That's what he said."

Antonia walked into the kitchen as Chloe picked up a few of the books, then took them to her den down the basement steps. As she returned to her bedroom up the main stairs, her mother stood waiting by the door, a broad smile draped across her face.

"You need to get ready, Chloe darling. I bought this for you." Eleanor Bruce directed her daughter's attention to the midnight blue, off-the-shoulder evening dress she was holding.

"That's stunning, Mother. Are we going out to dinner?"

"You have a date," Eleanor smiled.

"A date? Who with?" Chloe was a little perplexed that, even though she was twenty-five years old, she was still having dates arranged for her by her mother.

"It's a surprise. The ladies in town are so jealous of you." Eleanor stroked the soft velvet of the evening gown.

"So everybody knows, apart from me?" Chloe put her hand on her hip.

"Quick. Go get ready." Eleanor scooted Chloe to the bathroom.

Chloe found it impossible to feel excited while getting ready, especially as she had plans for a simple night in her den finishing a sketch she'd started. She hated these types of occasions, where her parents would invite some boring executive over for the chateaubriand, champagne and show of wealth.

"You look beautiful, Princess." It was just before 7 o'clock when Larry Bruce, pouring his usual pre-dinner glass of whiskey, caught a glimpse of his daughter as she sidled into the living room.

"Thank you, Daddy. Who is the date?"

"You'll find out. He'll be here soon!" Bruce tapped her on the nose.

Ten minutes later, Chloe was still poking at her tightly-pinned hair in front of the mirror in her bedroom when she heard the doorbell ring.

"Chloe, come down, honey," Eleanor called up to her daughter from the bottom of the stairs.

"Here goes," she muttered to herself.

Gripping the banister for support as she swept down the

stairs, Chloe saw her mother beaming, her hands clasped against her chest. Her father raised his topped-up glass to her and nodded his head towards their guest–and Chloe's date for the evening. A tall, dark-haired man stood with his back to her, offered his jacket to Antonia. As she went to hang it up in the closet, she passed Chloe and squeezed her forearm lightly like she always did when she sensed her young mistress was nervous. Chloe's eyes followed Antonia, then drifted back towards her parents as their guest for the evening turned around.

Kyle Chambers.

Chloe's smile faded. It didn't go unnoticed.

"Honey, say hello." Eleanor raised her eyebrows.

"Hello," Chloe said evenly.

"You look stunning." He flashed his Hollywood smile as he kissed her hand. Chloe faked a smile as a reply, drawing her hand away. They walked over to the dinner table where Kyle held out her seat.

"Thank you," she said coolly.

"So, Kyle, how's things?" Bruce poured him a large glass of Cabernet Sauvignon.

"Well, Larry, things are going great." He took a slug of his red wine and smacked his lips. "You know, with your leadership n'all, I really feel I know where we're heading. I'm gon' ask for more investment and hire some real men if you catch my drift, sir. Not the *Jeffrey Ellis* kind, with all due respect. I mean, Ellis is great but his choice in personnel, well–"

Kyle and Bruce both chuckled, the latter wiping his mustache on a napkin.

Antonia served them their food, smiling at Chloe to check she was alright. She managed a pained smile back, listening to Kyle and her father talk with such disrespect about the workforce who were making them so much money every day.

"So your parents Kyle, tell me about them," Eleanor chipped in.

"Well, I'm very close to my parents, ma'am. My father did well for himself and built up a nice fortune in the steel business back home in Pittsburgh; he's one of the most influential people there," Kyle bragged, chomping on a piece of beef fillet. Bruce's ears pricked up as he rambled on about his father's fortune.

"You've hardly touched your food, sweetheart," Eleanor said, noticing Chloe's near-full plate.

Antonia observed but said nothing as she busied herself fetching drinks.

"I'm not hungry, Mother. It's not the food, it's delicious," Chloe added quickly, hoping she had caught her words before they had offended Antonia, but she smiled to reassure her it was OK.

"I did a sketch today," Chloe said, changing the subject. The table fell silent. Eleanor Bruce's potato-loaded fork hovered in front of her half-open mouth.

"Um...OK?" Kyle nodded, confused as to the relevance of her statement.

"It was of the little church in town," Chloe smiled, her face softening towards him for the first time that evening.

"Chloe does little sketches," Bruce announced through chewed food.

"Father, it's my passion." She stared indignantly at him.

"Honey, listen, I just don't think you should waste your time. There's no money in that field, ain't that right, Kyle?"

Kyle nodded as he mopped up his Bearnaise sauce with a hunk of bread.

"No, money is made in business. Being smart, using your head. Not drawing. You agree with me, don't you, Kyle?" Bruce stared intently at him.

"Absolutely, sir!"

Chloe felt like she was imploding. Her only contribution to the table all evening had been shot down.

"I need some air," she huffed, dropping her knife and fork.

"Sweetheart, you can't go out like this." Eleanor sprang up out of her seat to chase after her daughter but the front door had already slammed shut.

Chapter 32

Chloe's flame-red Chevrolet Deluxe roared to life as she turned the key in the ignition and sped off down the long driveway to the main road. Normally she would cruise along the Alabama roads enjoying the scenery, but right now her blood was fizzing through her veins. Reaching the open road, she stamped her foot down on the gas pedal, the hard, gray asphalt giving way to the open yellowy-green plains of surrounding farmland. The evening sun hugged the horizon as if inviting Chloe to keep driving forward. She turned onto a road parallel to the Weaver, the water twinkling as it caught the orange haze of the fading sun.

A flicker of movement in the distance to her left immediately caught her attention. It was somebody riding a horse on a road parallel to the one she was racing along. They must have been going fast as Chloe floored the gas pedal, struggling to keep up with their pace. The galloping horse kicked up plumes of dust in its wake, looking as if it was doing everything in its mighty power to fling its rider off at any moment. The accomplished-looking rider hung on, though, equally determined–they both seemed in perfect sync with each other.

Keeping one eye on the road, glancing across to the left

every few seconds, Chloe squinted to see who was riding so fast, then accelerated so she was level with the horse as if they were both racing for an imaginary finish line. Up ahead, the roads were due to merge so Chloe, adrenaline-fueled intrigue pumping through her, sped up to get there first. As expected, the rider also made a gradual turn but didn't appear to make any attempt to slow down.

With the distance between the racing horse and speeding car shortening rapidly, Chloe realized what was about to happen and came crashing to her senses. She thumped her right foot down and, with an ear-piercing screech of brakes, skidded the car along the ground. The next few seconds were a blur as she clamped her eyes shut, waiting for the impending thud of the horse crushing her shiny red hood.

But there was no impact.

The quick-witted rider pulled up just in time. Through closed eyes, she heard the sickening sound of the horse shrieking, the clump of hooves and the crash of the rider being bucked off and dropped like a sack of potatoes.

Opening her eyes, she waited a few excruciating seconds for the dust to settle, then slowly got out of her car. The rider was sitting awkwardly on the ground, shaking away a concussion. She clasped a hand to her mouth in horror when she realized the identity of the rider she had almost killed.

It was Shona.

Chloe squinted in the dust, bowing her head slightly as she approached her. "You're Shona, aren't you? We haven't been properly introduced yet. I'm—"

"I know who you are. But that don' give you no right to drive like a maniac into people."

Wincing, Shona stood up stiffly. Stretching out her back, she set about making sure she could still move all of her joints, then brushed herself off.

"I'm so sorry. I didn't mean to–" Chloe edged forward.

"You were drivin' pretty fast. You spooked m'horse." Shona turned away, concentrating solely on calming Storm.

"I know. I'm sorry, I was just curious to know who the maniac on the horse was!" Chloe attempted a joke to break the ice, but her humor had no effect on Shona whatsoever. "I'm glad it was you, though. I've been trying to catch up with you since I started working back here. I heard good things about you," she continued, edging closer still.

"I'm just busy. I work hard." Shona rested her thumping head against her horse's muzzle.

"Your horse?" Chloe asked softly.

"Kinda," she replied, straightening up her saddle. "Her name's Storm. She's owned by the people I live with. You ride?"

"Sometimes. But not much these days. I miss it." Chloe looked to the horizon.

It was then that Shona raised her eyes and looked at her properly.

Chloe Bruce was stunningly beautiful. She was an inch shorter than Shona, her low heels adding hardly anything to her height of five foot six. Her soft, light brown hair shone in the dying light, the evening dress she was wearing caressing every curve of her hourglass figure. Shona was hypnotically drawn to her eyes, but there was such a look of sadness in them. *What was going on in her seemingly perfect life to make her so sad?* Shona wondered.

Chloe looked back at Shona, their eyes locking together properly for the first time.

First to break away, Shona returned to petting Storm who had nudged her arm as if to remind her she was present.

"How come you're dressed up all fancy?" She couldn't help noticing the incongruity of Chloe's dark blue velvet evening gown against the dull yellow dirt, especially in the dusky hue of the setting sun.

"It was a bit of a disastrous dinner...date, whatever you wanna call it."

"Sorry 'bout that."

"That's OK."

"Got a real nice car here, designed to go fast. Ain't no wonder you don't ride no more, not when you can go faster in this beast!" She ran an admiring hand lightly across the fender, picking some dirt off with her strong fingers. "You should have that roof down, though. Feel the wind through your hair."

Chloe responded with an embarrassed smile. "You're right. My father said I shouldn't, though. Says it gives off the wrong impression of me and that I'm somehow *making myself available.*"

Chloe tapped her fingers lightly on the side of the car as if apologizing to it. Shona shook her head, knowing she had to be mindful of what she said about Larry Bruce.

"Well, if I had this car, you can bet your boots I'd be driving around with that roof down and letting the wind blast *my* hair." She hooked an arm over the car roof, whistling as she looked through the window at the stylish chrome finish on the instruments. Shona really did appreciate a fine-looking car.

Chloe grinned. "That sounds good." She stroked her fingers across the car roof.

"Anyway," Shona said as she ran her hand through her tousled blonde hair and motioned to Storm, "I need to get this one back."

"OK. But it was nice to finally get to talk to you, Shona."

"Likewise." She hooked her leg over Storm and rode off into the distance. Chloe smiled for a moment as she watched her leave before returning to her vehicle.

Half a mile across the fields where she had said her goodbyes to Chloe, a violent lurch erupted in Shona's stomach. She reared the horse to a stop, almost crashing to the ground for the second time that day. Hunched over, she staggered to a small sprouting of bushes and began to retch behind them. Struggling to breathe, she sank to her knees, the tears streaming from her eyes.

Not again! She thought.

Chapter 33

"I didn't hear you leave this mornin'."
 Cuban found Shona out the back of the tool room on Wednesday morning, sweeping the floor like she was trying to strip the concrete from it.

"Couldn't sleep. Thought I'd get in early. Might as well be doing somethin' useful."

"Some bruise you got there!" Cuban pointed at Shona's face.

"What? Oh, it's nothin'. I fell off Storm is all."

"You OK?"

"Yes, Cuban, I'm fine! Stop gettin' my goat, will ya!"

Cuban held his hands up in defense and backed away. He stood a few feet away from her, kicking at the ground with his heel. After a minute or so, she leaned on her broom exhausted, wiped her brow and smiled apologetically.

"I'm sorry. I didn't mean to snap, it's just, well, last night–" Shona began. "You see, I was on Storm...when–"

A cheery voice sliced through Shona's soft tones.

"Morning, Cuban." Chloe strolled over to them, her red and white halter-neck dress blowing in the cool early morning breeze. She smiled broadly, her left hand holding down her summer hat as she approached.

"Morning, Miss Chloe." Cuban tipped his cap.

Shona turned and bent down to scoop up her sweepings.

"Good morning, Shona." Chloe's brown eyes twinkled in the morning sunshine as she removed her cat eye sunglasses.

"Ma'am." Shona glanced up briefly.

"Jeez, that's some black eye you got there. I hope it doesn't hurt too much!" Chloe's voice softened with concern.

"Some crazy driver spooked my horse and I fell off." Shona threw the sweepings into a small metal trash can, slamming the lid down with a clang.

Cuban looked confused.

"Well, I hope you got a description of the car?" she continued, trying to breathe life into the conversation.

"Could have been anyone," Shona said flatly.

There was a long pause as Chloe stood silently watching Shona pick bits of straw and wood out of her brush head.

"OK, then...I won't disturb you any longer. Have a good day, both of you."

Chloe turned on her heels and headed back around the outside of the tool room and across to the main building. Shona slung the trash can over her shoulder, straining under its weight.

"Did I miss something?" Cuban asked, scratching his head.

"What?" Shona's tone was razor sharp. She stood toe to toe with him, pulling herself up to her full five foot seven height, her eyes blazing with raw emotion.

"I just don't get you–" Cuban's frustration had boiled over now. "D'you know how many people here would kill for Miss Chloe to make time for them? Every guy in here dreams every night of that happening and she came over to us!"

"You think it's a good idea for you to be seen talkin' to her? When every guy in here wants to beat you up for any reason they goddamn like! We gotta stay away from her and keep our goddamn necks off the block!" Tears welled up in Shona's furious eyes. There was a strangled pain in them that wrenched at Cuban's heart. He wanted to hug her but before he could move she stomped away towards the back door of the tool room and threw the trash can and broom against the wall.

Cuban and Shona hardly spoke to each other for the rest of the day, apart from a cursory nod as they passed each other in the canteen. The atmosphere between them felt thick and heavy, their fledgling friendship fractured. Cuban, lost in his thoughts, was sitting on the floor in the garage when a familiar gravelly voice snapped him back to reality. He put down the oily rag he was cleaning engine parts with and looked up to see Kyle's leering face bearing down on him.

"My car needs cleanin'. I gotta impress the ladies and I don't see why I should pay when I got a slave to do it for me for free, right? So when everybody goes home tonight, you come find me!" Kyle shrank down to his haunches. "Now, I'm sure I don't have to draw a picture of what happens if it's not all up to my very high standard, right?"

"Yessir." Cuban looked down.

"Good dog!" Kyle rose to his feet and strode away, the heels of his expensive black leather Oxfords scraping along the concrete.

Cuban sighed, knowing it meant another night of having to walk back to the Birds' barn alone through the darkness. He would have to trudge through the fields instead of along the main road to make it harder for the truck that seemed to follow him home each time.

They always seemed to know when he was leaving.

It was just after 6 o'clock when Shona packed up her satchel to head home at the end of a long day. As she did every night, she went to find Cuban, who was cleaning out one of the trucks that was due to go out on an overnight delivery. He looked like he had the weight of the world on his broad shoulders. Shona inched closer to him, worried that her outburst that morning had led to Cuban's misery. She felt bad; she hadn't meant to take her mood out on her friend.

"Hey, you ready to go?" she asked tenderly.

"I gotta stay."

"Stay? How come?"

"Just a job for Mr. Chambers."

"I'll stay to help." She rested her satchel on the ground.

"Go home. The simpler I keep things, the better."

"He threatenin' you again?" Shona's face hardened.

"Just leave it, Shona, for my sake. Please?"

She gritted her teeth and nodded. Grabbing her satchel, she rested her hand on his shoulder, then turned to walk home.

Half an hour later, after he had cleaned up his work area, Cuban headed up to Kyle's office and knocked on the door.

"Yeah?"

Cuban opened the door to find Kyle sitting behind his desk, a half-empty bottle in his hand. He was pouring another drink for himself and Deputy Paul who sat in the chair opposite him.

"I heard you're cleaning Mr. Chambers's car, right?" His rancid breath prickled the inside of Cuban's nose. He nodded, turning away to avoid the stench. "Well, after that, you gon' do my car too. And you will polish it until you see your dirty black face in it or you do it again. Understand?" Deputy Paul grinned.

"Here." Kyle threw his car keys at Cuban, who missed his catch. "You'd better get started. You don't wanna be here all night now!" he sniggered as he and Deputy Paul swigged their drinks, watching Cuban bend to his knees to retrieve the keys from the floor.

∽

Cuban had spent over an hour polishing the inside of Kyle's 1956 Continental Mark II when he noticed the driver's side door crammed full of old Lucky Strike packets, receipts and other junk.

"Jeez, you'd think a man lucky enough to own a car like this would have the goddamn decency to look after it!" Cuban shook his head.

Unsurprisingly, he found women's telephone numbers scribbled on scraps of paper. He discarded the trash but put the pieces of paper with the phone numbers in the glove box. As he did so, a scrunched-up letter fell out onto his lap. Unfolding it, he squinted his eyes to read the letterhead in the dim light of the garage. Realizing what he was reading, Cuban recoiled in surprise.

In the top corner, he saw the company logo: one word printed in black slanted font against a yellow background.

He read further down the letter to see Kyle's car registration details and two simple words written in dark red capital letters below.

FINAL DEMAND.

Chapter 34

"Cuban!"

"Miss Chloe," he replied, a little out of breath from lugging heavy trash bags to the trash cans the following morning.

"I remember you saying that you'd like to read more? I've read these anyway and I thought you might like them?"

Cuban's eyes were drawn downwards to the books Chloe held in her hands. A copy of *The Catcher in the Rye* stood out to him, its blunt edges showing the affection it had been held in over the years.

"Miss Chloe. I can't accept these, I mean...I want to, but it's too much, too much." He waved his hands in protest, taken aback by Chloe's generosity.

"Now hush your mouth. Take it as an order from your boss, then. I'm instructing you to have these books," she smiled.

"Well, alright, how can I say no to that?" Cuban's face lit up.

"Good! Let's see, here's one on Roosevelt," Chloe handed him a solid-looking hardback book. "Oh, and I though you might like Ellison's *Invisible Man*...and this is my latest favorite, *On the Road* by Kerouac. It's really good, only just come out, but I read it in a day!" she beamed.

"My goodness, I can really have all these?" he said, feeling the weight of the books.

"Of course, it would be my pleasure, Cuban."

"Thank you so much, Miss Chloe." He held the books as if they were made of glass.

"You're welcome. Anyway, I'd better go. I have a meeting in town with the delightful Mr. Johnson. Wish me luck!"

"Good luck, but you won't need it, ma'am." Cuban tipped his cap as Chloe mouthed "Thank you" and left.

As Cuban was reading the back of the books he had been given, Kyle was lurking just out of sight, fuming at the attention Chloe had given him.

"*Somebody's* teacher's pet!" Shona strolled up to Cuban.

"Can you believe it? How thoughtful is that lady!" he said, staring in Chloe's direction.

"I guess."

"Huh? That's one of the kindest damn things anyone has ever done for me. Well, apart from getting me a home and a job, that is."

"I'm glad you remember that!" Shona playfully punched him on the arm.

Cuban's smile faded as he spotted Kyle across the yard standing next to Chloe's car. He frowned as Kyle opened the driver's side door for her, then subtly cocked his head to the side seeing her skirt ride up slightly as she climbed in.

"Look at him. She's way too good for that nasty piece of trash. I hope she finds out what a goddamn dirty fraud he is."

"What d'you mean?" Elbie wandered over.

"I cleaned the son'bitch's car last night and found out he don't even own it! He's up to his eyeballs in debt with it; it's a rental!"

"What?" Shona screwed her face up.

"Yep, there he was telling the boys he paid cash for it. Damn liar! She's so kind, I hope she don't get stuck with him. He'll be after her goddamn money for sure."

Over on the other side of the yard, Kyle was conducting his latest charm offensive on a disinterested Chloe.

"Can you wait a minute?"

"I can't, Kyle. I have to shoot into town to speak with Johnson right now. I'm already late." Chloe put her hand on the car door and tried to close it, but he held on tightly.

"Alright, but I was just thinking we could start over and do that dinner again. Just the two of us this time?" He flashed a smile.

"Kyle, I don't get mixed up with guys at work. I hope you can understand that."

She finally managed to yank the door closed, then fired the car up and roared off into the distance, leaving Kyle choking in her dust.

"The dreams you have at night sound awful," Cuban broached the subject as he stood polishing the headlights on a truck an hour later. Shona was in the cab cleaning it with the door open. She put down her cloth and looked at him.

"I'm sorry, I keep waking you up, don't I?"

"No, I didn't mean that. You just don't talk about 'em, that's all...or about nothin', for that matter."

"I just like to keep myself to myself is all." She picked up her cloth and rubbed it vigorously over the dashboard.

"Understood. But if you ever need to talk, I'm here. I mean, you've done more for me than you'll ever know."

Cuban paused, dropped his sponge and looked straight at Shona. She jumped out the truck, picked it up and threw it square at him.

"Hey!" Cuban spluttered as it hit his chin.

Shona grinned at him.

The buzzer sounded.

"Another break?" Cuban said, wiping the water off his face and squinting as some of the soapy droplets ran in his eyes.

"Yeah, right, an ass-kicking's more likely!"

Making their way into the canteen, they saw Elbie standing near the back of the already gathered crowd, mumbling their confusion as to why they'd been called away yet again from their tight deadlines. They looked up towards the management offices for an explanation, but nobody appeared from there.

"Do we have a thief among us?" a loud voice roared.

Everybody's head shot from looking upwards to looking over towards the lockers. Larry Bruce was standing there stony faced with Kyle directly behind him.

"What's going on? What's he talkin' 'bout?" replied the muffled voices in the crowd.

"We're conducting a locker search and we really hope we don't find anything that belongs to somebody else in there." Kyle was enjoying every minute of holding court.

Bruce strolled towards the gathering. "Now, does anyone want to confess to anythin'?" He scanned the faces in the room. Cuban's blood ran cold as Bruce's traveling gaze landed squarely on him.

"They're not searching *everybody's* lockers," Cuban whispered to Shona, who felt him freeze like a petrified statue.

"We found these, sir." One of Deputy Paul's cronies handed a small package to Bruce.

"Still don't wanna confess anythin'?" Bruce glared at Cuban. "These are *my* books from *my* home, you thievin' bastard," he blazed, spit flying through his mustache.

"No, sir. Miss Chloe...she...she gave them to me," Cuban pleaded as he felt a whack to his left cheek.

"Thieving bastard!" somebody repeated.

"Lynch him!"

Shona and Elbie were horrified. The crowd turned on Cuban like a pack of wild animals on a frightened stag.

"No, wait, this is wrong! Damn it, STOP! I saw Chloe give them to him!" Shona cried out. She tried to hold back the barrage of punches raining down on the prone Cuban, flinching as she caught a few nasty blows too. Elbie waded through the baying mob to help Shona, who by now was on the floor with her arms over her head to protect it from the onslaught. Cuban was at the point of collapse, almost relieved when Deputy Paul fought his way through the chaos to break it up. Reaching down, he grabbed Cuban by his overall straps and half-dragged him up the steps to Bruce's office.

"No, this ain't right!" Shona screamed as she was held back and forced to watch as her friend's battered body bounced up every cold metal step.

"Back to work, everyone. We'll see justice get done," Deputy Paul called from the balcony.

"What we gon' do?" Panicking, Shona stared at Elbie

"It all lies with Miss Chloe," Elbie replied, panting. The melee had taken the wind out of the old man's sails. He leaned down, resting his palms on his knees.

"She's in town at the Johnsons' place. I have to find her. Can I borrow your truck?" Shona's eyes shot hot darts into Elbie.

"You be careful." Elbie squinted as he handed her the keys, the sweat dripping into his eyes and blurring his vision.

Shona raced out to where Elbie's truck was parked and floored the gas pedal. Her left hand trembled with adrenaline as she wiped the blood from her cut eyebrow across her temple, turning a few strands of yellow hair red.

"Come on...come on." Shona shook her dazed head, searching for the right road until finally she saw the sign for Johnson's Truck Parts. She handbrake-turned the truck as soon as she spotted the familiar flame-red car in the parking lot, then, abandoning Elbie's truck in the first available space, sprinted towards the entrance.

"Excuse me, do you know where Chloe Bruce is, please?"

Shona's heavy breaths stunted any sense that she was hoping to make from the words tumbling out of her mouth. The woman at the front desk wore a mixed look of sympathy and disbelief at the distraught young blonde leaning over her desk.

"I'm sorry, who are you?" she replied.

"My name's Shona...can you tell me where Mr. Johnson's meeting is? I need to speak to Chloe...it's urgent...*please*?" Shona swept her long bangs out of her sweating face.

"Wait here a moment, please." The assistant rolled her chair backward and stood up. She opened her office door and made her way down a short corridor to a little group of offices about twenty feet away. Seeing her opportunity, Shona lifted the hatch on the counter and followed her, almost barging her out of the way as she opened the door to Johnson's office, where his meeting with Chloe was taking place.

"What do you think you're doing?" the assistant shrieked as Shona appeared behind her like lightning. She tried to grab her but Shona wriggled free.

Around a large solid-looking wooden table, several business-suited men stared open-mouthed at the out-of-breath, overall-wearing young woman who had charged into their sedate meeting. One blew out a large puff of cigar smoke and looked at the front desk assistant for an explanation. As the cloud dissipated, Shona saw an equally surprised-looking Chloe sitting directly in front of her.

"Shona?"

"You know this girl?" Johnson asked, putting his cigar down.

"Yeah, she works for me," Chloe replied, waiting for an explanation.

"I'm so sorry for interrupting you–" Shona tried to catch her breath, her emotions overwhelming her. "I need your help. It's Cuban. Please, will you come back with me? It's serious!"

"Would somebody mind telling me what the hell is going on?" Johnson demanded as he rose out of his brown leather chair and looked around the table.

"Of course I'll come with you." Chloe looked directly at Shona as if nobody else was in the room, despite it being one of the most important business meetings she'd secured.

"Thank you," Shona whispered, lowering her head in relief.

"What on earth's happened?" Chloe asked as they ran through the parking lot.

"It's Cuban. He's had his locker searched by your father... and Kyle. They're sayin' he stole them books and he's been beaten badly. He tried telling 'em that you gave 'em to him, but they didn't believe him."

"Oh God! I should've known better. This is my fault." Chloe was fumbling in her Chanel handbag for her car keys.

"I'll meet you back there—" Shona turned to head over to Elbie's truck.

"Get in mine. It's quicker!" Chloe ordered.

Shona opened the car door, moaning as she felt the dull ache of the bruising to her ribs where she had tried to protect Cuban. As they reached the end of the road, it suddenly dawned on Chloe that Shona was also hurt.

"You're bleeding," Chloe said, leaning across to touch the matted hair around Shona's bloody temple.

"I'm OK...It's Cuban I'm worried about." She dipped her head away from Chloe's hand and looked dead ahead, praying they would make it back in time.

Chapter 35

Larry Bruce rose from behind his desk and paced in front of the battered and broken black man kneeling in front of him. Cuban's face was now dripping with scarlet blood, both eyes swollen almost shut. Bruce swigged his whiskey and feigned outrage as Kyle began his interrogation of Cuban, who was shaking with pain, shock and fear.

"You know somethin'?" Kyle began. "You losin' your job ain't even the worst part of your day, y'know why? When I let you outta here it will be like feeding you to a bunch'a hungry wild animals who'll enjoy rippin' you apart! They've been waitin' for this!" Kyle was enjoying every intimidating second of this torture.

"Please...may I speak?"

"Shut the fuck up!" Kyle interrupted, digging Cuban in the back.

"No, let him speak! I'm just dyin' to know how he's gon' explain away havin' MY property in his locker!" Bruce put his glass down and moved in front of Cuban, whose arms were being pinned back by Deputy Paul.

"Miss Chloe, sir...she spoke to me a little while ago and asked me 'bout myself and I told her I liked to read. She came and found me today and offered me some books. I said to her it was too much, but she insisted." Cuban's words were tumbling out in heavy sobs, blood and spit bubbling from his quivering lips.

"Now, you listen here, boy. Don't you *dare* even *breathe* near my daughter, you hear? I know what men like you wan' do to her–"

Bruce punched Cuban in the stomach. He doubled over, struggling to breathe.

"This is from me—you stay away from Chloe." Kyle punched Cuban's face hard, his blood spraying over the floor. He landed face down, unconscious.

The door burst open just as Cuban dragged his heavy body off the cold floor and sat back against the whitewashed wall. Holding his battered face in his bloodied hands, he tried to shake himself into full consciousness, looking up through blurred vision at the two women standing breathless in the doorway.

"Father! What in the hell are you doing?" Chloe tried to register the carnage she had walked into, her eyes locking onto the puddle of dark red blood on the gray floor. Cuban whimpered with relief and closed his eyes. His prayers had been answered.

"This doesn't concern you." Bruce put his arms out to shepherd her back out of the door but she pushed him aside and crouched next to Cuban, wiping the blood from his mouth with her lace-trimmed handkerchief.

"If this man is here because of those damn books, it's *everything* to do with me. I took them. You were throwing them out. Some of them were mine anyway!" She glared at her father.

"Why in the world would you be standin' up for a colored?" he snapped.

"Because it's the truth. You should be ashamed of yourselves, all of you. You've wronged this man."

Kyle patted his palm with his stick, struggling not to roll his eyes at Deputy Paul, who was standing guard over Cuban.

"Are you OK?" Chloe wiped the remaining blood away from Cuban's lips.

"Yessum, I'll be fine. Thank you."

"Can you stand?"

Cuban groaned with pain as he tried.

"Now, I want you all to apologize to this man. This misunderstanding was *my* fault, not his!"

Chloe stared with hatred at Deputy Paul, who gritted his teeth.

"Sorry," he said reluctantly.

"Sorry," Kyle mumbled.

"I won't *ever* apologize to a damn colored! You've gone too far, Chloe." Bruce stormed out, slamming the door behind him.

Chapter 36

Early next morning, Cuban woke up with a groan. Chloe had insisted he take a few days off to recover from the beating he'd had, but he couldn't seem to get comfortable. Every movement was a dull agony for him as he lay on his bed, aching to the bone.

"Here–" Ruby Bird held the mug to Cuban's split lips as he took a sip.

"Thank you, ma'am."

"Why can't they just leave you alone?" Ruby sighed as she sat with him. Even though she and Tom had agreed to have little to do with Cuban while he stayed outside in their barn, her nursing instinct was too strong for her to forsake an injured man, regardless of his color.

"Because they're frightened. They think that if they give me a chance they might all realize I'm no better an' no worse than they are!" Cuban looked straight ahead.

∼

Shona sat alone in the canteen that morning on her 10 o'clock break. Food untouched, her fingers tapped on the table as she mulled over what she had witnessed the day before and the tenderness Chloe had shown Cuban.

"There you are. You OK?" Elbie came over with his tray, adjusting his cap as he sat down.

"I'm fine."

"How's Cuban doing?"

"He's OK. He don't want no fuss, you know what he's like."

"What about you? You got caught up in it too," Elbie said, pointing his fork at the scab on her eyebrow.

"I can't wait 'til we all get out of this damn place. Go where we don't have to look over our shoulders. We can just be...us."

Shona's voice trailed off as her thoughts drifted with it. She traced imaginary shapes on the table, then took a deep breath. "Anyway...I gotta go."

"Where?"

"To see Miss Chloe," Shona replied, pushing her chair in slowly.

"Now that's quite a surprise. Didn't think you could stand to be around her?" Elbie smiled, glad that she was starting to see the good in Chloe, just as he had.

"Well, she stuck up for Cuban. 'Round here that's rare, especially with her last name."

Shona said goodbye to Elbie and headed up the balcony steps. She felt nervous but she had played out the scene in her head several times that morning. *Keep it simple, then get the hell out of there,* she had coached herself. Taking a deep breath, she knocked on Chloe Bruce's office door.

"Come in," Chloe called out sharply from inside.

Shona poked her head in to see her boss frowning as she sifted through her overflowing in-tray while drinking her morning coffee.

"Sorry to bother you, ma'am, but do you have a moment?"

"Hi, Shona, how are you today?" Chloe's voice softened as she put down her handful of unopened letters.

"I can see you're busy...I'll come back later." Shona backed out of the office.

"No, it's fine. I'd welcome the distraction from these!" She gestured down to her letter-littered desk top. "Come in! Please, sit." Chloe hurried out from behind her desk and pulled out the guest chair.

"I can't stay. I just wanted to come and say thank you for what you did for Cuban. It was really brave of you to speak up for him like that," Shona said gently. It was the first time Chloe could recall hearing the softer side to her voice.

"You're welcome, and how are you feeling today?" Chloe asked, perching on the edge of her desk, her concerned eyes catching sight of the angry red cut on Shona's eyebrow.

"Excuse me?"

"Are you OK?" she repeated. "It can't be easy for you around here." Chloe looked intently at her.

"I'm fine. I can take care of myself." Shona tried to sound tough, but inside she felt confused by Chloe's sudden interest in her well-being.

"Good...well, you be sure to come up and see me if there's anything more I can do for you." Chloe returned to her seat. "Anytime, OK?" she added as she sat down and lifted her coffee cup up to her shiny red lips.

"Thank you," Shona smiled. She turned and left Chloe, who stared deep in thought for a moment at the closing door, then turned her attention back to opening her letters.

Chapter 37

The walk home from work seemed a little bit brighter for Shona that evening. The spring days were getting longer now, the nights lighter. Walking along the bank of the Weaver, she took in the way the lowering sun bounced off the shimmering cool water. A jumble of emotions ran through her mind: what was happening with Cuban, Elbie's diary, and how they were all just biding their time to get enough money together so they could go off and live their dreams.

And then there was the small matter of Chloe Bruce.

Shona hated to admit it but when Chloe was around they felt more protected at work, like somehow it felt less hostile there. Her presence was a blessing to them in more ways than one. She sat in her favorite spot by the river skipping stones across the surface, lying back among the sweet-smelling flowers with a maelstrom of thoughts whirling through her brain.

As the sun began to set, Shona picked herself up off the bank and headed home.

After dinner, Shona thanked Ruby for another delicious meal and said goodnight to her and Tom, kissing them both on the cheek. Walking into the barn, she turned to Cuban's side to check in on him.

"Hey," Shona whispered, not sure if he was awake.

"Hey." A deep voice resonated through the darkness.

"How's the patient?"

"Bored. Tom and Ruby won't let me help them with anything."

"Good, you need to rest."

"I can't. Every time I close my damn eyes, I see them."

"Who?" Shona frowned, straightening his blanket and tucking him in.

"The Klan! It'll haunt me 'til I die. I keep seeing my house burning with my wife and kids trapped inside! You know somethin'? When they beat me at work, I didn't want 'em to stop. I wanted them to finish me off and send me to my family. I prayed for the lights to go out. Every minute that goes by, it's more a punishment that I'm still breathing. I can't see a day when I won't have to look over my shoulder."

"Well, getting to New York and meeting with your friends, that's something to hold onto, right?"

"Let's be honest with each other here. It'll be a miracle if I make it out of this town alive, let alone all the way to New York."

Chapter 38

Larry Bruce slammed the newspaper down onto the meeting table that Monday morning. The tense atmosphere was broken after a few moments when he jabbed his finger at the front page and leveled his gaze at Kyle and Deputy Paul. Chloe sat quietly looking on.

"Look, the damn fair is in town! That's the reason Clint ain't at work this mornin'. I saw his father on the way in, said to me he'd met some young broad, got drunk and went back to hers until her parents came home, then he jumped out the goddamn window running away from her father pointing a shotgun at him. Twisted his damn leg and now he can't walk on it." Deputy Paul and Kyle didn't try to hide their sniggers. "I'm a man down, and he's an idiot." Bruce continued his tirade while pouring himself a large drink.

"I hope she put out, otherwise what a waste of time," Deputy Paul muttered.

Chloe looked straight ahead at the closed office door, not a flicker of emotion crossing her face. She'd had enough of the childish remarks. Coolly, she sat upright in her chair and directed her icy stare at her father.

"Would you be saying that if it was Cuban? Or would you be

straight on the phone to Jeffrey the very next minute to get rid of him?"

Deputy Paul and Kyle stopped smirking like schoolboys and stared open-mouthed at her in stunned silence. Bruce responded by pouring another drink, lost at what he was going to do with his belligerent daughter.

"I need some air," Chloe packed her things up and left the three men to watch her storm out of the room.

∽

"Elbie...how are you?"

"Why hello, Miss Chloe. I'm alright. How 'bout yourself?" Elbie tipped his cap.

"I'm fine. You being treated OK?"

"This place has changed a lot, Miss Chloe. I'm just glad I retire soon, that's what I *will* say."

"Well, Elbie, this company will be the poorer for losing you!" She tapped him fondly on the arm. "Listen, Elbie, you don't happen to know where Shona is, do you?"

"Yeah, of course, she's over by the tires, probably cleaning something nasty up."

She turned and headed off in the direction Elbie was pointing. He smiled, glad that his two favorite girls were finally getting on.

"Mornin', Miss Chloe. You lost someone?" Randy asked as he watched Chloe turn her head from side to side, scanning the area for the person she had come to look for.

"Randy, hi. You seen Shona? I was told she was over here."

"Just cleaning up an oil spillage over there." Randy pointed to near where a truck had been parked.

"Thanks, Randy."

Randy began to sweep the ground, surreptitiously inching closer to where Chloe had found Shona, and cocked his ear to listen in to their conversation. *What could the boss's daughter possibly want with Shona?*

"Hi," Chloe's bright voice pierced through the motor noise and the clangs of the mechanics hammering away.

"Hello, ma'am. You OK?" Shona stood up, her hands and arms mottled with splotches of dark, sticky oil.

"You know, it's so nice to hear that. Normally all I get is demands, moans and groans! I tell you, for people to actually ask *me* if I'm OK is quite rare," Chloe drifted off as she spoke. "Sorry, you didn't need to hear all that; that's me moaning now!" She smiled and refocused her gaze on Shona's calming blue eyes. "Anyway, how's Cuban doing?"

"He's doing alright. He's not a good patient, though."

"And how are you doing? You being treated OK?"

"I can't lie, being blasted up in one of those damn rocket ships they've started launchin' into space sounds just fine right about now. I'd happily volunteer for that just to get the hell outta here! If I didn't need the money then–" she stopped, seeing Chloe's face drop. Realizing how ungrateful she was sounding, Shona quickly backtracked. "But, I mean, well...I can think of better ways to spend a day, but it's a job, and that's what I need to get me where I need to, uh...get." Shona's words were becoming awkward now.

Chloe smiled, finding her honesty refreshing.

"Well, I feel that I owe you an apology too, so–"

"An apology? What for?" Shona interrupted.

"The book incident. You got caught up in it too," Chloe pointed to the cut at the corner of her eyebrow. "So, I was wondering if you would care to accompany me to the fair tonight. Unless you have a prior engagement?"

Shona picked at the oil stains on her hands, looking down at the ground. She shifted her weight from one foot to the other.

"Listen, you don't need to invite me out to apologize, so I'll decline."

"So, will you come because I'm tired of being around sweaty men all day?" Chloe joked, noticing a hint of a smile that Shona was trying hard to suppress.

"You must have a hundred friends. I'm sure you could find someone better to spend your time with." Shona bit the inside of her cheek.

"I don't really have anyone I can talk to anymore. I used to go to sock hops when I was younger, but all the girls I knew before I left for college are all married and at home with their babies. I don't fit in with them now. All they talk about is dirty diapers and whether Daz or Omo is better for their whites!"

"You don't want that?"

"What, sitting around all day in a housedress, chained to a washboard and waiting for a man to come home from work to find his dinner on the table ready? There's got to be more to life, right?"

Shona smiled at her, knowing Chloe was preaching to the choir there.

"Well, alright then, when you put it like that," Shona responded as nonchalantly as she could muster, putting her oily hands in her pockets.

"I'll meet you at the entrance at, say, 7:30? Or I could pick you up? Where do you live?" Chloe asked.

"About two miles farther down that road where we first met. It's just off to the right, near the Weaver. You can't miss it. But it's OK; I'll meet you at the entrance." Shona looked away quickly, feeling her cheeks redden.

"Alright, I'll see you later, then." Chloe waved and went on her way, the breeze blowing around the bottom of her summer dress, riding it up slightly.

Shona watched her leave. All of a sudden, with horrid predictability, the lurching in her stomach took hold of her yet again. She doubled over in pain as the sting of bile rushed up inside her throat. Covering her mouth, she ran behind the mechanics' shed before the noise of her retching could be heard by the departing Chloe.

Randy, however, standing less than ten feet away, had heard everything.

∽

"Jackson!"

Shona looked up from wiping the tables down in the canteen to see Kyle approaching, looking incredibly pleased with himself as usual.

"A delivery's coming later tonight and I want you to stay and wait for it. It's important, so you need to make sure you don't miss it."

"Um...OK, but–"

"But what? Not willing to work?"

"No, it's not that. I just made plans, that's all."

"*Unmake* them."

"But I was..." Shona stopped, realizing who she was talking to. She breathed out as calmly as she could. "Is Chloe around?"

"No, she's over at the Johnsons' place, trying to clean up the mess that was left, remember? And in the future, if you want to speak to her, you go through me first. You got that?"

"Could you let her know that I have to work tonight?"

"Of course. Consider it done." He smiled and left Shona to finish her cleaning. She kicked the table leg in frustration and sat on the ground with her head in her hands. *Maybe it's best I don't meet Chloe tonight*, she thought as she rubbed her still-sore, churning stomach.

∽

Meanwhile, Larry Bruce picked up the phone and dialed a number he knew by heart.

"It's me...Yeah, I'm good. Listen, I need you to do something for me. I need you to stir something up outside the gates and it needs to be convincing. Get some guys from the bar too." Bruce ended his conversation and hung up. He then made his second planned call of that Monday afternoon to the editor of the local newspaper.

"Lewis? Yeah...Look, there's gon' be somethin' big happening here tomorrow. I want it front page! I'm sure you got someone there who's chompin' at the bit for a big story, but we need him on *our* side, you understand? OK, Sam, I'll leave it with you!"

Chapter 39

"Those are mighty fine drawings in your den, Miss," Antonia praised, her warm eyes dancing.

Chloe looked up from sorting her handbag and smiled at her.

"Thank you. I wish I had the time to do more but work seems to be taking over. It's so busy there."

"Well, honey, you should *make* the time. You sure got the talent. I noticed you have a new muse lately. Well, I shouldn't ask, I know...but who *is* that in all them sketches? You sure have a real eye for the details...Those cheekbones–"

Antonia knew that she could speak freely; she had known her young mistress practically all her life and Chloe had always insisted on no airs or graces between them. Antonia's opinion was the only one that really counted for anything and was the one Chloe could always depend on being the truth. But the mention of her latest sketches made her blush.

"Have you seen my red blouse, the one with the rolled sleeves?" Chloe looked away as she opened her closet and rifled through the clothes hanging there.

"You mean your *favorite* blouse? The one you always wear whenever you goin' somewhere special?" Antonia winked and pointed to the inside of the closet. "It's there on the right-hand side, next to the blue halter-neck dress."

"What would I do without you?" Chloe smiled and shook her head. She scooped up the blouse by its hanger and twirled to show it off to Antonia, who laughed as an excited Chloe went to the bathroom to get ready for her night at the fair.

∽

Arriving just before seven thirty, Chloe parked her freshly cleaned car near the entrance, gaining a few admiring glances as she turned off the ignition. Reapplying her bright red lipstick in the rearview mirror, she fixed her hair again even though not one single strand had moved. One day, though, she'd like to take her friend's advice and drop the roof to feel the rush of the wind through her hair. Just once.

Not normally out on nights that weren't about business, Chloe was nervous and unsure in this unfamiliar territory, but something about Shona had intrigued her. Taking a deep breath to calm her nerves, she looked out of the car window to see if Shona had got there just as early. All she could see were couples and families amid bright colors and happiness. The latest hit music was playing in the background as teenagers mingled with each other wearing their best poodle skirts and saddle shoes. The smell of candy apples and melted butter on popping corn lingered in the carefree air.

Chloe waited.

And waited.

∽

Thirty minutes dragged by and the Monday evening sun started to set. Families with small children started leaving, making way for the teenagers to crank up the jukebox.

Shona was never late for work and Chloe strongly doubted that she would be now when meeting the boss's daughter. Something was wrong. Heads turned as she meandered through the crowd looking for her, hoping that she'd misunderstood where they had agreed to meet.

A mixture of emotions flurried within her but by 8:15, she decided enough was enough. Shona wasn't coming. Chloe exhaled deeply as she climbed back into her car.

On the other side of the entrance, half-hidden by thick bushes, a tall, stocky man dropped his cigarette butt on the floor and crunched it under his heavy boot.

Earl, the eldest of the three Bullen brothers, climbed into the passenger side of the green truck that was parked out of sight.

"Mission accomplished! That poor lil' girl left waitin' like that? I almost felt sorry for her...ha-ha, *almost*. Head down!"

Ernest, his younger brother, shrank behind the steering wheel as Chloe sped past their stationary truck, her blinding headlights beaming straight through their windscreen.

"That Kyle Chambers is one mean bastard!" Ernest cackled as they drove off in the opposite direction.

Chapter 40

A few days had passed since Cuban's beating. He returned to work on Tuesday morning, feeling sore but a little more optimistic that now Chloe was keeping an eye on him.

"Good to see you, Cuban. How you feeling?" Elbie greeted him.

"I'm OK," Cuban replied, a faint smile creeping over his fragile lips.

"He can do my jobs today, see'n as though he's had the most rest outta all us," Shona joked as she walked in. Within seconds, Chloe charged into the tool room behind her, glaring and cocking her head, instructing Shona to follow her back outside.

"Everything OK?" she asked as they stepped into an empty room nearby.

"Everything *OK*?" Chloe snapped back. "You think everything would be OK when you make plans with somebody, then they just don't bother to turn up? I'd feel bad if something terrible had happened to you on the way there, but I watched you stroll in here just now lookin' like you didn't have a care in the world and everything looked fine to me!" Chloe's arms flailed outwards.

"What are you talking about?" Shona shook her head in

confusion, taken aback by the sheer rawness of hurt present in Chloe's normally soft brown eyes.

"Last night...the *fair*?" she raised her eyebrows, trying to get a flicker of recognition from Shona.

"Oh, yeah, I had to stay late here and wait for a stupid delivery that never came. I did ask Kyle to tell you–"

Shona's attempt to explain fell on deaf ears. Chloe huffed and marched back up to her office.

~

"You're looking a little stressed, Chloe," Kyle remarked as she walked into the meeting room half an hour later, her files clasped tightly against her chest.

"I'm fine," she lied.

"Right, let's get started." Larry Bruce called the meeting to order. He shuffled his papers and instructed his secretary to pour the three investors who were in attendance a large whiskey each. Windows creaked as they were opened and notepads rustled.

Halfway through the meeting, one of the drivers burst in, red-faced and panting from rushing up the stairs.

"Sorry to interrupt, but we have a problem! There's a heap o'people outside having some sort of protest; it looks like it's gettin' out of hand."

"We'll handle it," Bruce replied as he flung himself out of his seat to the window.

"My God. What's going on, Father?" Chloe stared at the congregated mob below.

"Maybe Ellis will listen now–" Bruce said coolly.

The angry crowd was waving banners and placards reading *No more niggers* and *Coloreds don't belong here.*

"I think it's quite clear how we deal with this." Kyle got up and joined Chloe at the window, invading her personal space.

"We get rid o'Cuban, for everybody's safety, or the company will lose business." His coal-black eyes bore holes through Chloe's puzzled face.

Staring at Kyle, then back out the window, Chloe walked calmly over to the phone.

"Linda. Can you call the sheriff to arrest these people outside, please? They're trespassing–"

"NO!" Bruce grabbed the phone, shaking his head to quiet Chloe. "Listen, I'll deal with it. Do *not* call the sheriff!"

"What's going on? These people could hurt our workers. They could come in here and cause damage! Why are you not doing anything?"

"Because they have a point," Bruce replied evenly as he replaced the receiver.

Chloe looked around the room for support, but there wasn't a flicker. Looking back out of the window, she noticed the local press had turned up and were taking pictures as the chanting became louder.

"How did *they* get here so fast?"

"People talk," Bruce's voice was eerily calm as he reached for the whiskey bottle.

"Alight, well, if you're not going to deal with it, *I* will!" Chloe headed towards the office door.

"You stay out of this one, Chloe. That's an order–as your boss, understand?"

Bruce sat back in his seat, taking a swig of his drink.

"Now, where were we?" He gestured to the assembled group to continue the meeting.

Chloe looked thunderstruck by the sharpness of her father's direct order. She sat back down in silence.

"There he is," Shona clenched her fists as she stomped across the yard outside the tool room.

"Hold your horses, girl. Be careful," Elbie frowned as he called after her.

"Where's she goin'?" Cuban asked.

"To have a little word with Chambers. He screwed her over, apparently. Serves that nasty piece o'shit right if she punches his lights out!" Elbie stifled a chuckle.

"Excuse me, Mr. Chambers?" Shona called but received no answer from the man she was chasing after. "KYLE!"

Kyle spun around. When he registered who it was, a smug grin started to weave its path across his handsome face.

"Yes, Miss Jackson, and what can I do for you on this fine day?"

Shona wanted to knock that grin off his face. Her fingernails dug into her palms as she fought to steady her emotions.

"Did you pass on the message to Miss Chloe that I was workin' last night?"

"What?" He leaned forward with his hands in his trouser pockets, shrugging away her very simple question.

"Chloe. Did you tell her that I had to work last night?"

"You didn't give me any such message. You must be mistaken." His eyes glinted.

"I asked you to let her know. You said you would!" It was taking every ounce of composure not to lash out at him.

"Shona, you need to change your tone. Mr. Ellis wouldn't be pleased to hear you talkin' to your superiors like that, don't you think?" Kyle smirked. "Now, say you're sorry to your boss!"

Shona stared furiously at him for a few moments, realizing that arguing with him was futile.

"I'm sorry."

Kyle grinned at his victory and swaggered away from her.

"One day...one day soon...you'll get what you deserve, you piece of shit," she cursed under her breath.

Chapter 41

The young reporter raced from the copy room with the front page of Wednesday's paper in his excited hands, hot off the press. Forgetting to knock, he rushed through his editor's door, making Big Sam Lewis shoot his head up and glare at the charging bull that had rudely entered his domain.

"Sssssorry, sir...but I got the first edition here to show you!"

Lewis's angry face broke out into a satisfied grin.

"Come here, Joe. Show me what you got!"

He chomped on his cigar as he scanned the headline and opening paragraph.

"Perfect."

That Wednesday morning, the day after the protest, it was all the town was talking about.

"Jeffrey, it's me. You seen the front page?" Larry Bruce lit a cigar and took a seat at his desk, phone in hand.

"Yes, Larry, I've seen it. Anybody hurt? Any damage?" Ellis replied.

"No harm done, but this could put pressure on our

investors, Jeffrey. I mean, you know Tony Simms? He's lookin' to put money into us; he could pull the plug if we don't listen to the people of this town—"

"He stays, Larry. Cuban stays," Ellis interrupted.

"Well, it's you who's losing out, Jeffrey. We've been warned by the town about how they feel."

Bruce slammed the phone down. He took a few deep breaths and picked it up again, dialing that same familiar number.

"Earl, it's me…Even the goddamn protests didn't work! No, your guys were good…convincing, but Ellis isn't biting. He won't let this guy go. We'll have to think of another way."

Kyle's expensive Oxfords clumped on the floor down the long stone corridor. Bruce had told him five minutes earlier about his call to Earl Bullen and Kyle had come up with the perfect plan, but he couldn't execute it on his own–he needed help. He headed from his office to find Deputy Paul.

"I've got a job for you."

Chloe smiled at each worker she passed on her way up to her office after her morning meetings, receiving the usual array of "You look lovely today, Miss Bruce" compliments. Looking in through Kyle's office window, she stopped dead, seeing him hand Deputy Paul a bulging, brown paper bag. He slid the paper bag inside his jacket, nodded to Kyle and headed to the doorway. Chloe ducked behind the door as it opened and bent her body around the corner of the corridor, still keeping her suspicious eyes on Deputy Paul. He closed Kyle's door behind him and walked down the balcony steps.

Breathing quietly, she reached down to her feet and removed her heels, then tiptoed down the metal steps to follow him as he turned left, right and then entered the tiny broom cupboard Cuban used as his changing space.

After a few moments rummaging through Cuban's belongings, Deputy Paul pulled open his bent locker door and slipped the brown paper bag inside. Closing the door, he cackled in satisfaction that his mission had been accomplished.

"Finished?"

Deputy Paul spun around as if he had been electrocuted.

"Chloe. I mean...ma'am."

"What the hell do you think you're doing?"

Chloe made her way closer to Deputy Paul. He wiped sweat from his forehead.

"I got orders."

"Well, now I'm going to give you an order."

At lunchtime, Cuban, Elbie and Shona all took their usual positions in the canteen. They were used to sitting at the back now where nobody bothered them.

"You OK, Elbie?" Shona asked, taking a bite of her bread.

"Yeah." The old man sipped his water.

"You don't look it."

"I'm thinkin' o'retirin' early. I can't stay here, not with the way it's goin'. I hate to think of what it will be like in a month or two months–" His eyes were bereft of their usual twinkle.

"You can't leave us." Shona stopped chewing.

"I'd want you two to come too. I hate the way you both get treated. It's nothin' short o'barbaric."

"Well, I won't be far behind you, Elbie," Cuban added. "I've been speaking to a couple of guys from that little bar I go to sometimes. They're on their way up to New York next week.

They're gon' just settle in first, find their way, then get me a job there!"

It had been a long time since Shona had heard Cuban talk this positively about anything.

"That's great, Cuban," said Elbie. "You know, when I'm outta here, you two don't have to worry. I'm gon' send my diary to somebody real powerful and expose that Larry Bruce for the bastard he is!"

"You serious?" Shona said.

"Yup, been my plan all along."

"Oh, Elbie." Shona put her arm around the old man's shoulder.

"Anyway, what about you, Shona? You got any family anywhere?"

"Um...Well, you see, my life is a little...complicated. My mother died when I was fifteen. I say she died, but I know in my heart she was killed." Shona looked down at the table.

"Killed?" Elbie spluttered, almost choking on his mouthful of soup.

"Yeah. By my father. He's a drunk. One night, they were arguing over me. I went out of my room to see what was goin' on but my momma told me to go back in and not come out no matter what I heard. I hid under my covers. But then I heard a scream. I didn't know what to do, so I went to my door to see if I could hear anything...but it was all quiet. I opened the door, but my father caught me and said if I came out he would hurt my momma real bad so I stayed in my room until the next mornin'. By then, though, it was too late. Doctors said my momma tripped and fell down the stairs. That she died from her head wounds. But my father and I know that's not what happened! Nobody believed me, though."

She picked at a loose flap of Formica at the edge of the table.

"Shona, I...I'm so sorry. I know how painful it is to lose your loved ones." Cuban reached for her hand.

"What in the hell were they arguin' 'bout that was so bad?" Elbie asked.

Shona recoiled as the tip of her finger sliced open, leaving behind a smudge of blood.

"Goddamn it!" She put her finger to her lips and sucked the blood away.

"Where is your father now, Shona?" Elbie asked.

"Back in Louisiana, probably sitting at a bar getting drunk as we speak."

She ran the same finger again over the same sharp shard of Formica.

Chapter 42

"Some piece of shit has stolen my wallet! I can't believe it, man! Ten years I worked here, TEN, and I never had a damn thing go missin', till now! I bet it's that no good, dirty bastard over there! Shit, I'm gon' go ask him."

An irate Jerry marched over to where he knew Cuban was working that afternoon.

"Hey! Yeah, you!" he bellowed.

Cuban grabbed his rake and set about his work in the vain hope that Jerry wouldn't interrupt him.

"You got my wallet, you thievin' dirty bastard? Lemme come check your locker and I swear if I find it, I will put you in your grave m'self...I knew you was bad news. I knew it." Jerry's face was blood-red, his mouth speckled with spittle.

Just as Jerry launched himself at Cuban, Ron Black emerged from the back door of the tool room and grabbed Jerry, holding his arms firmly behind his back.

"What's goin' on here?"

Jerry wriggled himself free from Ron's grasp and pulled his wrinkled-up shirt back down over his beer belly. He wiped his mouth with the back of his hand and spat on the floor.

"Five guys today. FIVE! All of 'em said to me they've had

their wallet taken from their locker. That ain't no coincidence! No one's seen this guy all day and now people's property goes missin'? Only one explanation for that in my book!"

Cuban stared back blankly. No one had seen him, this was true, but no one ever notices the black guy doing all the jobs they don't want to do.

"OK, I hear you, Jerry, but we have to deal with this in the right way. There's no reason for violence," Ron replied.

"Putting a bullet in the back of his head *is* the right way!" Jerry spat.

Cuban saw no point in arguing. The blood was already boiling inside Jerry and no amount of saying he didn't do it was going to cut any sway with him.

"See, he ain't denyin' it! Guilty as hell," Jerry raged.

Cuban remained tight-lipped, taking heart that it was Ron dealing with it rather than Kyle.

"Let's go," said Ron. "We need to straighten out this situation. Cuban, walk in with me." He placed his body between Cuban, Jerry and the five angry, wallet-less workers that followed. They headed into the canteen and up the balcony steps.

The men stood outside the offices muttering and pointing their fingers at Cuban as Ron disappeared into the meeting room. It seemed like hours before he came out, followed by someone who Cuban knew he wouldn't stand a chance of getting a fair trial with.

"Everybody, listen up!" Kyle Chambers leaned on the handrail of the balcony, looking at the gathering crowd below. "It appears we have a thief in our midst. Wallets have gone missing. There's only one way to deal with this. We'll conduct a search of each man's locker."

He smiled. *It was all going according to plan.*

The baying crowd parted as Chloe emerged through the channel of empty space between the bodies, her face motionless. When Kyle saw who was accompanying her, his smile evaporated. Deputy Paul looked up at him, a panicked look on his pudgy face.

"Deputy, would you do the honors, please? Get the keys and go search every man's locker!" Kyle called down. Deputy Paul looked back at him and ran his flat palm horizontally across his fat neck, fingers outstretched, pretending to scratch the back of his head as he finished the motion. Kyle's eyes twitched as he tried to read the signal Deputy Paul was trying to send.

Slowly, Chloe made her way up the balcony steps, running her hand delicately along the rail. Reaching the top, she stood with her arms folded, waiting for her moment.

"It goes without saying that whoever's locker we find them in will no longer continue to work here." Kyle stared at Cuban, who swallowed hard.

"They better not find my wallet in that colored's locker! I'll smash a rock in his head, I swear it," Jerry growled.

"Kyle, I need to have a word with you?" Chloe stared at the side of his face.

"Not now. I need to sort this out." Kyle dismissed her with a flick of his hand.

"I think you should make a few minutes to hear what I have to say."

She walked directly into Kyle's line of sight.

"I said, NOT NOW!" he seethed.

Chloe set her face to stone and walked calmly into his personal space. Almost nose-to-nose with him now, her stare drilled holes into his skull.

"Do you know where those wallets are?" Chloe's voice was barely above a whisper.

"Of course not," he snapped.

"Well, you know what? *I do!* Now, *Mr. Big Shot*, if you look over my shoulder at your friend Paul, you'll see he is very nervous. He's sweating like a pig on a spit down there. You wanna know why?" Her eyes blazed as she spoke. "Because he's carrying something very interesting in his pocket–a little brown paper bag containing six leather wallets!"

Chloe saw the color drain from Kyle's face as he looked over to see Deputy Paul open his jacket a fraction and reveal a crumpled, brown paper bag. The six accusers and Ron Black looked on in confusion, trying to overhear the hushed voices.

Chloe continued. "I've just had a very lovely chat with him and, after I reminded him who the *real* boss around here was, he told me the very interesting story you two had cooked up. Every...last...detail!"

Gritting his teeth, Kyle looked back at Chloe, who knew from his face that he was beaten. He glared at her for a moment, then looked back down to the assembled crowd.

"Everybody back to work!" Turning to the six men, he smiled.

"Guys, um, give me a few minutes. Paul, up here. NOW!"

Deputy Paul took a deep breath and walked the torturous twelve steps to the top of the balcony and into the meeting room as Kyle slammed the door violently behind them.

"Chloe, listen, please. I can explain—" Kyle began.

"Oh, I'm just itching to hear your excuse, Kyle! You do realize doing something like this could get Cuban killed? The men are looking for any excuse to hurt him!"

"I had to do somethin'. The men ain't happy him bein' here. Neither is this town! You saw the protests at the gates with your own eyes. I'm worried it'll seriously damage the business. The business *you* are inheriting!"

"Hold your damn horses, Kyle! Are you seriously suggesting you did it for *me*? I attend the meetings with the investors and last time I checked they were very happy with our progress.

Only the other day I managed to convince Johnson to invest in us over every other competitor in the area! You expect me to buy that crap that you did it for *me*?" She stared at him wide-eyed and open-mouthed.

"Sweetheart, I swear! I'm not proud of what I did, but sometimes in business you gotta do what you gotta do! I was concerned at how you may get treated for taking the side of a colored. I thought I could help."

"Kyle, you only care about *you*! I only care about what is right and what you did is just wrong. Now, what am I gon' tell my father about these wallets? It would serve you right if he fires you BOTH on the spot!" She looked back and forth between Kyle and Deputy Paul, tilting her head to the side as she chastised them both.

Kyle's demeanor changed at the mention of the man he was trying so desperately to impress.

"We're gon' say that someone handed those wallets in just now. A delivery guy stole 'em, had a crisis of conscience or somethin' and dropped them back, no questions asked. As long as the guys get their wallets back, ain't no more questions gon' get asked, OK? And after all, Larry ain't gon' want to believe your version of events and get rid of me for the sake of keeping a colored out of the firing line. This story is best for everyone, OK?"

Kyle perched in front of her on the edge of the desk. Chloe thought for a moment. It really was her word against his, unless she had an ace up her sleeve. Backing up to the edge of the door, she bent her neck and called out to her father's secretary.

"Linda? How many delivery guys were here this morning?"

"I'll just check the log, ma'am–" Linda chirped back.

Chloe didn't take her eyes off Kyle the whole time they waited. Trying to work out what she was doing, he could almost hear the blood rushing through the veins in his head.

After an excruciating minute or two, she piped up. "It looks like none yet, ma'am, nothing due in until 4 o'clock."

Chloe looked at Kyle, her face like stone.

"And that's definite, Linda? No delivery guys have been in here at all today?"

She needed to be sure.

"Yes, ma'am, I checked twice," Linda confirmed.

Chloe's attention switched back to Kyle, who was sweating now that he'd realized what she'd clarified.

"So, here's what I want in return for not telling my father, and Jeffrey Ellis, what a liar you are. You leave Cuban alone, OK? No one in this place goes near him from now on. He does his job like everyone else here. And while we're on the subject, you call your mob off Shona and Elbie too! Just let 'em do what they're paid to do here, you got that?"

Kyle squeezed his teeth together. He knew he had no choice.

"Fine." Kyle faked a smile.

Chloe's face lightened. "Excellent...Now, remind me, what are you going to tell those guys out there? And Kyle, in the future, *don't* call me sweetheart!"

Chapter 43

"I just can't choose! The blue gown with the bow near the shoulder or the green evening dress with the mink stole wrap. What do you think, Chloe?"

Eleanor Bruce was at the dinner table trying to decide what she was going to wear at the business function they were all going to attend in town that Wednesday evening. Chloe was picking at her dinner, lost in her thoughts and not remotely interested in what her mother had just said.

"Blue dress," Chloe replied, not looking up from her food.

"Oh, but I think the green one is so much more elegant!"

"Then why ask me?" Chloe dropped her fork onto her china plate with a clatter.

"What has got into you lately?" Eleanor frowned.

"I'm going out," Chloe exhaled, getting up to leave the dinner table just as her father entered.

"Where are you goin', young lady?" Bruce demanded, his head snapping around to follow Chloe's movements.

"Out."

"What about the function?" Eleanor called out.

"I'm sure people will make deals whether I'm there or not."

"That's looking pretty good." Cuban returned to the barn at the Birds' house that evening after helping Tom to fix one of the yard fences. He blew his cheeks out in admiration at the perfectly shaped armrests on the bench Shona was lovingly sanding down.

"Thanks." Shona swept her bangs out of her eyes and wiped sweat off her forehead. " I think I'm done here. I'm gon' go see what mood Storm is in." Shona dusted her hands off.

"Good luck with that. I heard her kicking against her damn door as I came in," Cuban replied.

"I'm sure I can handle her jus' fine, no need to worry 'bout that! Ain't no filly gettin' the better of *me* tonight!" Shona threw a cloth at Cuban, who caught it and laughed. She closed the barn door behind her so he wouldn't be disturbed by the last dying embers of sunlight streaming through as he rested his weary, aching body on his bunk.

The evening air was balmy, the sun starting to nestle down under the horizon. Shona loved this time of year when evenings became longer. It felt like work wasn't the sole focus of the day, like there were still a couple of hours of precious daylight to do something other than come home at night and go straight to sleep. She exhaled deeply, taking in the vast surroundings of the farm, its yellowy-green grasslands and peach trees, the black cows mooing softly and the white perimeter fence that kept all of it inside. It was this time of year that the wildflowers were at their most colorful, speckling the dull grass with flecks of bright oranges, reds and purples. For the first time in a long time, Shona felt a modicum of peace inside her.

As she stopped for a minute by the side of the barn to admire the view, a small red shape with dust clouds billowing up underneath it caught her eye in the distance.

Squinting, Shona put her hand up to shield her eyes from the glare of the sunset. As the car drove closer, she was able to better make out the shape.

"Who is that at this time?" Tom called out from the yard to Ruby, who made her way to the front door as the car pulled up outside the farmhouse.

"Hello?" Ruby called through the door.

"Hi, it's Chloe Bruce."

Ruby opened the door to Chloe, who was standing there, her red, polka-dot summer dress blowing in the evening breeze.

"Hi, please come in, Miss Bruce."

"Ruby, who is it?" Tom's heavy work boots clumped on the wooden floorboards as he entered the kitchen.

"It's Chloe Bruce, dear," she replied, surprised to have the town's most glamorous young lady in her house. She offered her a seat at the kitchen table, wiping down the chair with the cloth she was holding.

"It's OK. Sorry to just turn up out the blue like this but...is Shona around?" Chloe wrung her red leather driving gloves through her hands.

"She's out back," Tom replied. "You wan' come see?"

Chloe smiled and nodded her response.

As he led her into the stable, Chloe heard the stomping of hooves and Shona's soothing voice.

"Shona, you got a visitor. I'll leave you two to it," Tom said, shutting the door behind him.

Taking a deep breath, Chloe walked over to Shona. "Hi." She waved with a flick of the gloves in her hand.

"Everything alright?" Shona asked, raising an eyebrow as she stroked the grunting horse's head.

"I just wanted to come and say sorry. For thinking you had

better things to do than meet up with me the night of the fair?" Chloe stepped forward, spooking Storm slightly, who snorted to remind her she was there. Shona stared back blankly.

"You don't remember?" Chloe's face dropped.

"Of course I remember." Shona shook the surprise from her head. *Chloe came all the way out here just to apologize?* she thought.

"Well, as I said, I'm sorry for not giving you the chance to explain. When I heard you trying to blame work, I should have given you the benefit of the doubt!" Chloe looked down at her shiny round-toed Mary Janes, dragging one heel lightly through the dust.

"I did ask Kyle to give you a message, to tell you that I–"

"I believe you. Trust me, I *know* you gave him that message." She met Shona's piercing blue eyes with her own, causing the churning feeling once again to rear its ugly head in the pit of Shona's stomach. She fought, as usual, to suppress it, to control it, until the dull ache subsided. Storm, noticing the attention she'd been getting had stopped, petulantly broke the silence by kicking up a plume of dust, causing the two women to cough and laugh at the same time. Shona patted the mare affectionately and rubbed her nose.

"Anywaaaay..." Chloe beamed brightly.

"You got no plans tonight, ma'am?" Shona nuzzled her nose into Storm's cheek.

"I did have plans. But when you've been to one business dinner, you've been to them all. It's the same faces, the same conversations, who has the most money..."

Her words trailed off as she stared at Storm, her eyes glazing over as she witnessed the calmness Shona was effortlessly able to instill in the restless, wild horse by simply stroking her and whispering in her ear. The mare seemed at one with Shona, nodding at her indignantly when her petting hand moved away from her muzzle.

"Well ma'am, that won't happen here, I can assure you o'that. None of us has *any* money to brag about so that's one less conversation to have, right, Storm?" Shona nuzzled the horse with her nose again. Chloe beamed, quite taken by how much pure affection there was between her and the animal.

"So, this is Storm?"

"Yep, she was the one who threw me off when–"

"Oh yes, sorry again."

"That's alright. Here, you can pet her if you like." Shona tugged the reins, masterfully commanding Storm to behave.

Chloe tentatively approached and stroked her mane, her face lighting up as the mare responded as instructed.

"Well, look at that, she likes you! And she's tough to please, believe me," Shona smiled.

"I like her too. She's gorgeous. She may be a bit wild, but she just wants what we all want, doesn't she? To be understood..."

As she spoke, Chloe turned her head from the horse to look directly at Shona, whose heart began to beat faster as she noticed out of the corner of her eye.

"Well, she can also be a pain in the ass too!" she replied, trying to break the intense atmosphere between them. As if on cue, Storm broke wind loudly.

"Storm! Behave! *Goddamn!*" Shona was mortified as Chloe wafted the air in front of her face with her glove, making Shona hold her hands up in mock defense of her horse's little *indiscretion.*

"Is Miss Chloe stayin' for supper?" Ruby called out as she knocked on the stable door.

Shona looked at Chloe.

"I'd love to, thank you."

~

Shona sat at the Birds' kitchen table opposite their famous guest, who looked over at her constantly. The churning in her stomach reminded her it was there every time she caught Chloe's gaze. Luckily, Ruby and Tom were never shy of conversation. Within minutes, the room was filled with laughter, from the funny stories they all took turns telling to deep conversations about anything and everything.

Chloe had never felt so relaxed, so welcomed around a table. She told them all about her paintings and the sketches she'd done recently, with Ruby saying she'd like to see them one day. The house felt like a home, with no talk about business deals or who had the most money or who was getting fired. There was just pure happiness radiating around the room.

"Well now, Shona can take you out ridin' if you like! Don't worry. I'm sure she'll let you ride one of the *calmer* horses we have here."

Shona froze as Tom volunteered her to spend more time with Chloe.

"I'd like that, as long as it's OK with you?" Chloe looked at Tom, then Ruby...then Shona.

"Sure. Don't worry, I won't make you ride Storm," Shona replied, swallowing hard and taking another calming deep breath.

The stunning waitress, who had caught Kyle's roving eye, brought two more whiskeys over and placed them on the VIP table he was sharing with Larry Bruce at a bar in town that same Wednesday evening. As Bruce sat gazing into space, Kyle slipped a wad of dollar bills in the waitress's hand and winked at her. She tucked the money into her bra and sidled away. Kyle slouched back in the booth, elated that his poker game that evening had gone so well. For the moment at least, his money worries were gone, the three-hundred-dollar prize nestling snugly in his jacket pocket. Bruce refocused his eyes on Kyle and exhaled deeply.

"My daughter, Kyle! I don't know her anymore. It's like whatever I say to her, she doesn't listen. And worse still, she sympathises with coloreds. Do you know what that could do to my reputation? Tonight, I don't even know where she is. She just got up and left. I went to the function earlier but I couldn't concentrate on a damn thing."

"She got any friends she might have gone to visit?"

"Before she went away she had quite a few friends, but since she came back she spends most of her damn time in her den doin' those silly drawings."

"A secret boyfriend, maybe?" Kyle took a swig of his drink.

"Not that I know of, but you know how I feel about that. I want you to date my daughter! I trust you. I want you and her to take over the company when I'm gone."

"That's very kind of you, Larry. I'm honored."

"In the meantime, I want you to keep an eye on her. I'm worried she is getting mixed up with the wrong kind. Will you do that for me, son?"

"It would be my pleasure, sir."

Chapter 44

That Thursday morning, all the usual faces were convened in the boardroom, the investors making sure their money was being used productively and telling the same, lame jokes week in, week out. It was a whiskey-and-lewd-comments affair, with only the gentlemanly conduct of Jeffrey Ellis raising the tone around the table. He rose above the comments, checking them occasionally when they went too far and reminding them that there was a lady present, which Chloe appreciated. But she still counted the minutes until it was over.

As soon as the meeting had concluded, Chloe shot out of the room, Kyle following closely behind prompted by a nod from Larry Bruce.

"Shona?"

Shona sat chewing a mouthful of bread she'd just dunked in her soup as Chloe made a beeline over to her on her lunch break. She swallowed as quickly as she could, wiping her mouth on her sleeve.

"Hello, ma'am, how are you today?"

"Good, I'm good...boring two-hour meeting, but I don't tell them that!" She winked. "How are things goin' around here with you all?" A glimmer of a frown crossed her face as she looked down at the tiny bowl of soup Shona had been given by Chef Lou.

"Well, since you ask, it's actually been quite calm around here for us. It's kinda nice to only have to worry about the job for once and not have to watch your back all the time!"

Chloe smiled. "Listen, Shona. Thank you for last night. You have no idea how good it felt to be...normal. I really enjoyed myself. Tom and Ruby are adorable."

"That they are...and you're welcome. I mean, Tom and Ruby said you're welcome anytime." Shona coughed and swallowed hard.

"You wanna meet up sometime; go to the diner in town or something?" Chloe asked, casting her eyes again over Shona's meager rations.

"OK...Saturday?" Shona surprised herself by how quickly she answered.

"Perfect." Chloe's radiant smile illuminated her whole face.

"What's perfect?" Elbie sat down opposite Shona, tray in hand.

"The peach cobbler that you make, Elbie," Shona joked, changing the subject.

"I'll let you two get on with your food. Eat up, both of you. That's an order!" Chloe smiled at Elbie as she turned and left.

"Now that is one beautiful young lady. Any man who snaps her up is one lucky bastard," Elbie said, dipping bread in his soup.

Shona watched in silence as Chloe walked up the steps to her office, closing the door behind her. She exhaled and looked down at her bowl, feeling the ravenous appetite she'd had only minutes earlier evaporate.

Ed's was the most popular diner in Daynes. It was Chloe's childhood favorite and familiarity was what she needed right now as, for some reason, she felt nervous about meeting Shona.

Chloe took a seat in a booth by a window facing the door. She'd arrived earlier than the 8 o'clock time they had agreed on and every time the bell above the door tinkled, she looked up expectantly.

"Can I get you a drink, Miss?" the waitress asked, holding a steaming pot of coffee at the ready.

"No thanks, I'm just waiting for somebody."

Thirty minutes later, a few yards up the road outside, Shona jumped off the bus and made the short walk to the front of the diner. She took in a deep breath, straightened her clothes and ran her tanned hand through her hair, matting her long bangs to the side with her licked fingers using the window of the diner as a mirror.

Chloe looked through the glass and smiled with relief. She twirled a cardboard coaster on the table with one hand as Shona entered the diner, nearly taking out the waitress and her tray of drinks as she waved a goofy hand to Chloe when she spotted her in her booth.

"Sorry I'm late. I got the early bus but there was an incident. A white lady refused to travel on the bus with an old black guy on it, even though he was sitting in the correct seat at the back."

"What happened?" Chloe frowned.

"Driver kicked him off! The poor old guy could hardly walk!"

"That's awful."

"I know. It just makes me think of Cuban and what he must go through every day. The bruises I see him with all the time give away most of it." Shona shook her head in sympathy.

"I wish I could help him," Chloe said.

"You do. He speaks very highly of you," Shona replied, attracting the attention of the waitress to order a soda.

Chloe leaned back in her seat and smiled playfully. "So, why Daynes? What's your story, Miss Jackson?"

Shona had been dreading this question.

She breathed in deeply, her usually clear blue eyes clouding over as she tried to find a suitable place to start. A few more seconds of thinking time were bought when the waitress reappeared, placing Shona's drink in front of her.

"Well, I'm from a little town back in Louisiana. My momma died when I was not much past m'fifteenth birthday so my daddy was left to raise me. But he was a drunk, always coming home late from the bar. He used to blame me for stuff. It wasn't good, so I left as soon as I could."

Shona fiddled with her straw.

They talked for the next hour or so about the elements of Shona's history that she was prepared to share. Chloe was intrigued to hear her funny stories and how she'd battled to make it in men's jobs.

"*Wreckers*? That's a strange name!" Chloe said, nearly choked on her mouthful of coffee.

"Yep, that's its name! This place in Mississippi I settled in for a while after I'd moved around a lot since leaving Louisiana. It was a big workshop, mainly for trucks. I was there for just over two years. The guys treated me well an' I loved my job. I managed to save up a little bit of money too. They finished at midday on a Friday and we got time off if you needed it. The boss was all about looking after the staff and the food was amazing!"

"Then what?" Chloe leaned forward.

"I left."

"Why, if it was so good?"

Shona felt the heavy weight of Chloe's inquisitive stare.

"It don't matter. Let's talk about something else."

"OK...alright." Chloe sensed Shona's discomfort but chose not to push her.

A coin dropped into the jukebox and the happy tones of *Stupid Cupid* filled the awkward space between them. Shona and Chloe broke out in giggles at the very appropriate timing of Connie Francis's sweet, uplifting voice.

"As it is *this* song that's playin', let's play a game," Chloe challenged.

"Okaaaay?"

"I call it 'Make out, marry or kick to the curb'!" There was a glint in Chloe's eye as she bit her lip mischievously. "I'll pick three guys and you tell me if you'd make out with them, marry them or kick 'em to the curb."

"I tell you what, how 'bouts you go first," Shona replied, bending her straw over and over in her fingers.

"Alright then, you pick the guys."

"OK, lemme see. OK, I got three. Ron Black, Kevin the delivery guy and...*Kyle*."

Shona tried to read Chloe's reaction to the last name on the list.

"OK. Well, I would make out with Ron because he's kinda cute, but I know his lovely wife, so...um, I would probably marry Kevin as he's sweet and I like that in a person." She paused for a moment. "So I guess that means I'd kick Kyle to the curb—"

Chloe noticed the straw had split in Shona's hand.

"—but that can be our secret, right?" she added.

"Sure." Shona put the broken straw on the table and swiped it away.

"Now it's your turn," Chloe took a sip of her coffee and licked her red lips.

"Can you make swans? Out of napkins?" Shona blurted out.

"Excuse me?" Chloe shook her head, wrong-footed again by the swerve in conversation.

"Swans. Here–" Shona reached over to the napkin holder on the table.

"OK." Chloe blinked and stared as she watched Shona expertly fold the napkin into a perfectly shaped swan and hand it to her.

"Wow." Chloe held the swan up, genuinely impressed but frustrated by the sudden subject change.

"My momma taught me that," Shona said, looking down at the table.

"Can you teach me?" Chloe whispered, leaning forward again.

"I can try." Shona lifted her eyes.

The five attempts that followed, even though they gradually got better, couldn't hold a candle to Shona's original.

"You keep touching your necklace. It's beautiful," Chloe noticed.

"My momma made it for me. It's not worth a dime to anybody, but it's worth all the money in the world to me. We were walking along the river near our house one evening when I was ten and she picked up this small pebble, somehow put this hole in it, then pulled some string through. I've never taken it off since. My father was so annoyed, though. She never did *anything* like that for him. He's a jealous, bitter drunk and that's the *nicest* thing about him." She looked from side to side, keeping her eyes on who was in the diner.

"Why do you keep looking around? You seem nervous," Chloe said.

"No reason." Shona fidgeted in her seat, her hand resting on her stomach.

"Oh my, where are my manners," Chloe began, "I invite you to a diner and forget to order you some food! You must be starvin'! Here, what would you like?" Chloe slid a menu in front of Shona and raised her eyebrows apologetically at her.

"No, really, it's fine. I wouldn't expect you to buy me dinner.

I already ate anyway, but thank you, ma'am," Shona felt her cheeks redden. "It's gettin' late so..."

"You need me to drive you home?" Chloe offered, noticing Shona's sudden agitation.

"It's OK. I'll get the bus. But thank you. See you on Monday."

"Bye, Shona. Oh, and thank you for coming...and not standing me up this time." She grinned just as Shona was about to protest. Shona smiled back, realizing Chloe was fooling around.

"Thank you for inviting me." Shona waved as she pulled the door and stepped outside.

Chloe leaned back in the booth, a strange warmth fizzing in her stomach.

Shona tried to suppress a similar feeling, although to do that it meant she had to stop seeing Chloe Bruce.

And that was the last thing in the world she wanted.

Shona opened the barn door as quietly as she could, so as not to wake Cuban. As she got undressed, she could hear him whimpering on his bunk behind the divide.

"Cuban, you OK?"

"Shona, they're everywhere I go."

"Who?"

"The Klan!" He held his head in his hands. Just then, he realized the late hour of her return. "Where you been tonight?"

"Just out," she said softly.

"Out?" The whites of his eyes caught the thin shafts of moonlight peeking through the cracks in the wooden walls of the barn.

"Yeah, with Chloe. She invited me."

"That's nice...real nice, being able to go out, not have to look over your shoulder!"

If only he knew that it wasn't so easy for me either, she thought.

∼

Where the Copperpot welcomed a more sophisticated clientele, Red's was the perfect example of its antithesis. The seats were torn, the floor sticky and the less the waitresses wore the higher the tip tended to be, stuck sleazily under the strap of their sequined bras. The rooms upstairs were always available for the more *exclusive* of parties. Later that same evening, a well-dressed young executive was sitting up at the bar drinking alone.

"Can I get you anything else, sir?"

The sexy bartender, dressed in a red leather miniskirt and black crop top, was blatantly preying on her customer, the glint of his gold Rolex Oyster Perpetual catching in the bar's low lights as he raised his glass. Her eyelashes fluttered as she put his next drink down on a napkin and lazily draped herself in front of him.

"How much for you...for an hour?" Kyle drawled, unfolding a huge wad of dollar bills from his poker win a few nights ago.

"Well, I'm sure we can come to some arrangement," she replied, her eyes lighting up at the sight of the money.

Chapter 45

The following Friday afternoon, a massive sense of relief resonated around the site. A huge order for cotton bales had come in that week and the workers had just finished loading up the last of the delivery trucks. All that remained was for the order to be signed off and the workers could get to their celebrations.

After she had rinsed herself off under the faucet and picked up her satchel, ready to go home, Shona bumped into Ted, the foreman, who wearily thrust a clipboard into her hand.

"You got young legs, Jackson. Go sprint up to Miss Chloe, will ya? It just needs a signature. Then we can all go home, so hustle, will ya!"

Shona sighed, took the clipboard and headed up to the balcony.

"Excuse me, ma'am," Shona peeked around Chloe's open office door.

"Hi." Chloe's strained eyes softened at the sight of her.

"Oooh, tough week?" Shona screwed her face up at Chloe's paperwork-strewn desk.

"I feel like I'm constantly drowning in this stuff! You?" she replied.

"I'm just heading home. The foreman asked me to bring this up. He needs you to sign off the order, then they can go off to the bar." Shona walked over to Chloe's desk and handed her the clipboard.

"You going with them?" Chloe asked as she looked down to sign the document.

"Nah. I'll leave them to drink and gamble away their cash. I got better ideas for mine." She tapped her top pocket which held her week's wages snugly inside. "You?"

"No. I got too much to do here still. They won't want their boring heel of a boss around anyways."

"Oh, OK, I'll leave you to it, then. Bye."

"Oh...OK, bye Shona." Chloe twiddled her pen through her fingers.

Shona stopped after walking three steps and turned around.

"Say, you don't wan' go ridin', do you? By the Weaver? It's lovely this time of year. The flowers are all in full bloom and they smell amazing. I understand if you're too busy, though." She gestured towards Chloe's desk.

Chloe breathed out as if that was just what she needed.

"I'd really like that, Shona, very much. You free tomorrow?"

"What did your folks say about you comin' out to see me?"

Shona and Chloe were riding their horses at walking pace along the bank of the Weaver that balmy Saturday morning. There was just enough of a breeze to keep the sun from sweltering them, the flowers and trees smelling as sweetly as Shona had described.

"I didn't tell them. I got changed in the car. You know what my father's like," Chloe replied.

"Here." Shona halted Storm, climbed off, then grabbed the

reins of Chloe's horse to help her dismount. She took out a blanket and laid it on the ground next to the rippling river for them to sit and enjoy the picnic that Ruby had made for them. It was total isolation, hardly a sound in the air other than the lapping of the water, rustle of leaves on the bushes and the birds chirping in the trees.

Chloe sat down and stretched out, arching her back and groaning as if all her little aches and pains were starting to melt away in this little oasis of calm.

"Like it?" Shona knew it was a rhetorical question.

"Like it? I love it. I can totally understand why you come here."

"It's my secret place," Shona said, lobbing a pebble into the river.

Chloe turned to Shona, who stared into the distance.

"I'm sorry for the way you're being treated at work. I am trying to change things for the better for you all, believe me."

"I know you are. It can't be easy for you either. To be honest, though, it has got a little better recently. Cuban's had a bit less heat on him since those six wallets turned up out of the blue the other day. He ain't had another locker check since then, can you believe that? I reckon someone musta put in a good word for him!" Shona smiled sideways at her.

Chloe felt her cheeks redden.

"I liked what you said about the conditions at Wreckers. I'm gon' take those ideas and see if I can put them into practice. Would that make things better for you?" Chloe asked.

"Well, it'd help the guys, I'm sure," Shona replied, tossing another stone in the water.

"What about you?"

"Me? I probably won't be there much longer anyway."

Chloe felt her heart flip.

"Why? Where you goin'?"

"I'm headin' to the West Coast as soon as I can. Saving every cent I can spare," Shona said.

"When?" Chloe's face was still frozen from Shona's sudden revelation.

"Cuban and I will probably leave in a month or two. He'll head north to New York and me west to California."

"Can't say I blame you with how you've been treated, but I'm not gon' lie, it'll be a real shame." Chloe looked down.

"Look at this!" Shona drew Chloe's eyes to a stunning-looking pebble on the ground in front of them, its surface glistening with bright shades of rose quartz. She handed it to Chloe.

"That's beautiful."

"It matches your scarf," Shona observed, pointing towards the pastel pink chiffon draped around Chloe's neck. Shona took back the pebble and discreetly put it in her top pocket, hoping Chloe wouldn't insist on keeping it.

Talking for another two hours, they lost themselves in conversation about everything from politics to the weather. Chloe noticed she was the one doing most of the talking. Shona was an expert listener but when she did have something to say, Chloe hung on every word.

Slowly but surely, black clouds started to appear above them, hanging low in the darkening sky.

"We better get goin', there's gon' be a storm!" Shona sprang up from the riverbank to pack away the blanket and picnic basket, then quickly untied both horses just as the dull roar of thunder rumbled in the distance.

"What a shame. I was having a lovely time," Chloe huffed.

"We can do it again sometime...if you want?"

"I'd like that."

As Chloe spoke, an almighty bolt of lightning crashed directly over their heads. The heavens opened, with the rain taking moments to drench the parched earth around their feet.

"Damn it, we won't make it back in time," Shona cried, swinging her agile body over the back of her horse, with Chloe following suit just as nimbly. They both rocked their bodies to get their steeds to gallop quicker but the downpour had already made the ground too slippery for their hooves to grip.

"Well...we ain't gon' outrun it, so we may as well enjoy it!" Chloe shrieked, holding out a hand to catch the raindrops. Knowing they were still fifteen minutes' ride from the barn, they both climbed off their horses and walked them back to the farm.

"Easy, girl." Shona tied Storm to the post by the barn door, then helped Chloe do the same with her mare. They were both completely soaked through to the skin, their hair matted to their heads.

"Well. *That* was an adventure!" Chloe laughed, wiping the raindrops from her face.

"I'm sorry, I—" Shona began, noticing Chloe's smudged makeup.

"Don't apologize. It's the most fun I've had in...well, a long time. Thank you!"

"You're welcome."

As she ran a hand through her wet hair, Shona's smiling face darkened when she realized Chloe had begun to shiver in her thin cotton shirt.

"We need to find you something dry to put on, you'll catch your death..."

"It's OK, I got changed in the car, remember? I can just change back," Chloe replied.

After escorting her back to her car, Shona headed straight to the barn to get dry herself, almost bumping into Cuban who was standing just inside the doorway.

"You have a nice ride out with Miss Chloe?" he asked evenly.

"Yeah, why? Thought you were her biggest fan?" Shona replied, frowning.

"I am, you know that. The only thing I got against her is her father."

"You and me both...but–"

"I don't want you to go through anything like I do. It's dangerous for you to spend so much time with his daughter!" Cuban interrupted her.

"We hang out sometimes like friends are allowed to do. What's wrong with that?" Shona raised her arms in the air, not registering how short her tone had become.

He stepped back in surprise.

"What's going on, Shona? Really?" Cuban's voice penetrated the awkward silence that had fallen between the two friends.

"Can we just drop it, Cuban? *Please!*"

Shona pulled her arms across her stomach as the groaning ache pounded through her gut. Her cheeks twitched as she tried to gulp down the bile fizzing up in her throat.

"I'm sorry, I'll stop. I just want you to be on your guard, that's all. You're dealin' with dangerous people."

Shona knew how dangerous meeting up with Chloe Bruce was to her. But, like a refreshing drink on a scorching hot day, she was finding it impossible to resist.

Chapter 46

"Good mornin', ma'am! How are you today?" Rushing to get into work that morning, Chloe had forgotten to make lunch, so she popped in to the local convenience store in town to pick up a sandwich. As she browsed, her eyes lingered on a small postcard with a photograph of a rocket ship on it.

"I'm fine, thank you, Patty. How are you?"

"Well, it's Monday mornin' and my knight in shining armor hasn't arrived to whisk me off yet so, what can I say? But *you*, on the other hand, I bet you had a great weekend—you know?"

"No, I don't know." Chloe looked blankly at her.

"Kyle Chambers, of course. Now, I'm not one to gossip as you know, but I heard that you and he have a bit of a thing goin' on?" Patty wrinkled up her nose like a hamster.

"Did you now? From who?"

"Well, from your mother initially when she bought a dress for you over at Stella's and the news just kinda spread. Then Kyle came in a couple of days ago and I sort of...asked him." Patty sensed Chloe tensing up and shrank back behind her counter.

"And what did he say?" Chloe could feel her blood pressure rising.

"He said that things were slow but moving in the right...direction."

"Did he? Well, I'll tell you this and I hope you repeat it like you do everything else in this town. There is nothing, and I mean *nothing*, going on between Kyle Chambers and me."

Patty nodded her understanding, firmly put in her place by a fuming Chloe, who dropped a dollar bill onto the counter for the sandwich and postcard, then marched out of the store.

"10 o'clock! The best part of the morning!" Shona cheered as she took a seat in the canteen next to Cuban and opposite Elbie.

"You're damn right it is," Elbie agreed.

"Shona, do you have a moment?" Chloe passed their table and cocked her head for Shona to follow her.

"Yeah, sure." Shona rose from her seat and followed her into a side room.

"Here. I went to the store to get a sandwich and I saw this."

Chloe handed over the postcard. Seeing Shona's blank expression, Chloe began to explain.

"What you said the other day? You told me you wished you could be blasted up in one of those funny little rocket ship contraptions? Well, I can't make *that* happen, but I saw this and...thought of you." He eyes were fixed on Shona's reactions as she stood silently staring at the picture on the postcard. "I *do* draw the line at callin' you *Sputnik Shona* though, alright?"

Chloe grinned as she attempted the joke, biting her lip as she waited what felt like an eternity for Shona to say something.

"I love it. Thank you," Shona whispered finally as she held the postcard and lightly traced her finger across the embossed gold edging and textured picture. With tears pricking the corners of her eyes, she slid the precious postcard in the top pocket of her denim shirt, smiled and headed back into the canteen, with Chloe watching her all the way.

∼

Carefully fixing the postcard to the wall space beside her bed was the first thing Shona did when she got home that evening. She lay back and stared at it, wondering what it would feel like to be that free, to travel beyond the stars.

She couldn't stop thinking about Chloe.

What did it mean? The question rolled around her head repeatedly.

"Hey." Cuban knocked on the dividing wall between their bunk spaces.

"Hey."

"Nice picture. Where'd you get that?"

"Chloe gave it to me. I mentioned to her a while ago how I wanted to go up in one of those stupid rocket ships...just like when you told her about wanting to read more and she gave you those books," she added, looking Cuban in the eye, trying to deflect any other possible reason for Chloe's generosity that might have crossed his mind.

"Uh-huh," he nodded, holding back. "Well, what'say we go out tonight? C'mon, we ain't hung out together in a while. I know a safe route we can take and I won't take no for an answer, y'hear?"

"Yessir!" Shona mock-saluted as she got up off her bunk and grabbed her jacket.

Chapter 47

The Cell Block was *the* safe place for black people in Daynes to enjoy a night out, attracting the best musicians who played the sweetest-sounding jazz and blues for miles around. For safety, it moved between all the near-derelict, forgotten buildings in town, never in the same one twice in a row. The regulars were responsible for the transportation of the barrels of liquor and letting the black townsfolk know of the next location.

Monday evening's address was on the corner of a dimly lit, rarely visited street on the edge of town. The revelers inside prayed that the Klan wouldn't consider that the old, leaky storage house may have been converted for the night.

Cuban and Shona took a table to the left of the jazz band that was playing. Tapping her toe as the beat thumped through her, Shona smiled every time the trumpeter faced towards her, emphasizing every note he played with a tilt of his head. The conversation didn't flow as well as it usually did between the two friends. It was more Cuban making an effort and Shona giving one- or two-word answers.

Cuban's eye was drawn to a commotion by the main door. A middle-aged lady looked inconsolable, tears streaming down her face as she was guided by a crowd of anxious-looking friends to a table on the other side of the bar.

"Who's that?" Shona asked, leaning into Cuban.

"That's Maria. Her son Woody's been missing two days straight now and it ain't looking good. The poor son'bitch can't exactly run fast either with half his right foot missing from last time the Klan caught up with him."

"Jesus Christ," Shona exhaled.

"Yep, he's the only one who can help that poor bastard now. Can you see the sheriff being interested?" Cuban asked rhetorically.

Shona sipped her drink, unable to take her eyes off the devastated Maria.

"Hey, maybe you could ask Miss Chloe? I've seen how you two get along. You got an understanding. She seems like she wan' help all the time. Maybe she can talk to the sheriff?" Cuban looked at his friend hopefully.

Shona took another sip of her drink.

"I suppose I could try. I mean, if I see her I can ask." Shona shrugged.

Cuban smiled and nodded his thanks.

Early Tuesday morning, Shona sprinted up the balcony steps and knocked with a *rat-a-tat-tat* on Chloe's door.

"Come in!"

She opened the door and half-stepped inside. "Sorry, didn't mean to disturb–"

"Shona, hi!" Chloe's face brightened instantly. "That's OK, we're finished here." She raised her eyebrows to Kyle, who huffed as he collected his files and eyeballed Shona as he left, deliberately leaving the door ajar. Chloe rolled her eyes at his belligerence.

"Shut the door if you want," she said. "Sit down. Would you like some coffee? I got some nice cookies in here if you'd care to join me?" Walking over to her hot plate, she poured two cups, smiling as she did so.

"No, thank you, ma'am, I can't stay for long. I gotta get back to work."

Chloe bit the inside of her cheeks as she put her coffee jug down and snapped the lid back on her little red tin of Pepperidge Farm cookies she'd brought in specially that morning.

"Um, ma'am ... I'm not sure if I should even ask, but you're kinda the only hope for these people–" Shona picked at the nail on her left index finger.

Chloe turned around and sat in her office chair, nodding gently for Shona to continue.

"There's this boy, a black boy called Woody...He's been missing for a coupla days now, but the sheriff won't listen to Maria, his mother. She just wants to know what's happened to her only child, especially as she lost her husband to the Klan too!" Shona's eyes filled up with emotion as she spoke. "Will you talk to the sheriff? Please? He'll listen to you."

Chloe sat back in her chair. "Shona, I can't, and I won't, promise anything. I don't want anybody getting their hopes up, but I will go and speak to the sheriff if you think it will help."

Shona's face lit up. Chloe dropped her eyes to her desk as she caught herself mirroring Shona's infectious smile.

"Thank you. I'll leave you in peace now." Shona turned and headed to find Cuban to give him the good news.

∼

"Hartley! Get your fat ass in here, boy. When I say I like my coffee strong, I mean it! I ain't drinking this rat's piss." Sheriff

Landon spat out a mouthful of watery brown liquid on his paper-strewn desk and returned to chewing on his cigar butt.

"Sorry, sir, lemme sort that for you."

Deputy Hartley walked into his boss's commodious office and grabbed the steaming mug off the desk. His sweat-stained shirt clung to every part of his body as he rushed to refill his boss's mug.

"Um, sir? We have young lady outside asking for you."

"Who?"

"Chloe Bruce. She's asking for you directly."

"Well, don't just stand there, boy, send the lady through." Landon straightened his tie as his deputy went to fetch their esteemed guest.

"Miss Bruce, how can I be of service to you on this fine day?" the sheriff drooled as Chloe was shown into his office. She was used to people falling over themselves to pay her special attention due to her surname, but this time her status could actually serve to do some good.

"Hello, sheriff. I came for an update on a missing boy. A black boy named Woody?"

"You come here about a colored kid? Does your father know you're here, ma'am?"

"No, why would he?"

The sheriff waved his hand. "Carry on."

"His mother Maria has been in here before to ask for help, so I just wanted to know how your no doubt thorough investigation into this matter was progressing," Chloe said, her eyes leveled at him.

"I'm sure my boys have followed procedure, but um, to make you happy, Miss Bruce, I'll have them out looking for the boy and even visit Maria to let her know what's happening. How's that for service?" The sheriff took a puff on his cigar.

"I appreciate it sheriff. Thank you," Chloe replied, smiling as she turned to leave.

Chapter 48

Chloe spotted Shona sitting at her table in the canteen that Wednesday morning break time, halfway through writing a letter. Deep in thought and tapping her pen against her smiling lips, Shona contemplated her next sentence. Chloe approached the table and looked down momentarily over the beautifully clear handwriting, just as Shona saw her and quickly covered it.

"Chloe, hi." She folded the letter and slipped it into her top pocket.

"Sorry, am I disturbing you?"

"No, it's fine. You OK?"

Chloe eagerly sat down next to Shona to tell her the good news. Her excitement didn't go unnoticed by Randy, who was stalking nearby.

"I spoke to the sheriff. He said he'd look into it and send some officers around to talk to Maria."

"Oh, Chloe, that's fantastic. Thank you so much."

"You're welcome," she replied, her heart beating faster seeing Shona so happy.

They were so lost in the moment they didn't hear the footsteps of Cuban and Elbie, who arrived a minute later, trays in hand.

"Hi, Cuban, Elbie. I better go. Let me know if you hear of anything, Shona." Chloe rose and headed back up to her office.

"Good to see you two getting along so well," Elbie remarked, chomping on his sandwich.

"What? Oh...She's trying to help us find Woody."

"Woody?" Elbie asked.

"I'll explain later." Shona gulped her water and smiled at Cuban.

"That's quick work from Miss Chloe. Jesus, what did you say to her to make her act so fast?" Cuban let out a low whistle of admiration.

Shona blushed as she fought to contain her swirling emotions.

Just before the end of the working day, Shona strolled into the tool room to find Elbie hunched over his diary, writing furiously. He jumped when he heard footsteps but shrank back relieved when he saw it was only his friend.

"What are you writin' there, Elbie? Somethin' else happened today?"

"Dynamite, that's what's in here! I tell you. You heading home now?"

"Yeah, soon, I can't wait to get home and finish that bench. Listen, you got anything that'll put a hole in this thing?" She pulled out the small pink pebble she'd found by the Weaver.

"Sure, this should do it." Elbie handed her a small, thin drill bit.

"Thanks."

"What's it for?" Elbie asked.

"Oh, nothin' special...thanks, Elbie."

She put the bit into Elbie's Craftsman drill press on his bench and bored a perfectly clean hole in the pebble, then threaded some tough, black string through it. She held her creation up to the light, her eyes shining as she twirled it through her fingers.

~

Meanwhile, a Ford Sedan police car pulled up outside a run-down house on the outskirts of town just as the sun had begun to set.

"This it?"

"Yeah, come on."

Two officers from the sheriff's department knocked on the paint-chipped front door.

"Hello." The door opened a crack behind the screen door.

"Maria?"

"Yes?"

"We've had a report from Miss Chloe Bruce that your boy, Woody, is still missing. That correct?"

"That's right."

"Well, the sheriff would like to reassure you that we have men out there looking for your boy and we'll be in contact as soon as we find anything."

"Bless you. Thank you. I'll thank Miss Chloe too. Thank you, what lovely gentlemen you are." Maria wiped away a happy tear as she bid farewell to the policemen and closed her door.

Back in the car, the two police officers turned to each other and smiled.

"Yeah, I reckon she bought it!"

"I know...as if we're gon' waste valuable police time lookin' for a damn fuckin' nigger boy!"

Chapter 49

Shona couldn't get to work quick enough the following morning. Normally, the two-mile hike was a chore, but this bright and sunny Thursday dawn Shona practically ran the entire distance, the pink pebble necklace safely tucked away in her jacket pocket. Arriving at the main entrance just before 6:30, Shona saw Chloe's Deluxe already parked up outside and headed straight up to her office, knocking lightly on the door.

"Um...Miss Chloe?"

"Good morning, Shona. How are you?"

"I'm good, thank you, ma'am. I just wanted to say thank you. You know, for trying to help Maria."

"Well, they haven't found Woody yet. I called the sheriff again last night but nothing, so I don't know how much good I've been." Chloe sighed, fiddling with her pen.

Shona smiled and took a deep breath. "Listen, I wanted to give you this." She reached into her top pocket. "I made it from the pebble...from the riverbank, remember? Hopefully it'll remind you of a good day, if things here start to get you down, I mean. Like when you gave me that postcard..."

Shona's heart was thudding as she handed her the delicate necklace.

Chloe was silent for what felt like an age as she twirled it around her fingers. Shona started to panic, feeling she had overstepped the mark.

"It's OK, you don't have to wear it. You probably got like a ton of diamond necklaces...But...Um, oh, I don't know. I'll leave you to it." She turned to leave, her cheeks burning.

"Shona, it's beautiful!" Chloe gasped. "The way it catches the light, it sparkles like a diamond. It's *better* than a diamond."

"You like it?" Shona's ocean-blue eyes were shining.

"I LOVE it! I'll put it on now."

Chloe struggled to tie the string behind her neck. After a few moments, Shona edged forward to help but eventually it stayed put, looking stunning as it sat perfectly in the hollow of her neck.

"It looks great on you." Shona took a step back. "You wanna come to the Cell Block tonight? Cuban sometimes gets up to play."

"I'd love to."

Just as Chloe and Shona began planning their evening, the carefree atmosphere of the office was shattered.

"Good morning, ladies, how are we both this fine morning?" Kyle swaggered in, not even bothering to knock.

"Kyle." The light in Chloe's eyes faded.

"Hi, Shona, how are you? Things OK?" He flashed a bright smile.

"Fine. Have a good day, Miss Chloe."

Shona smiled at her and gave a cursory nod to Kyle as she left, wondering what kind of head injury he'd received overnight to make him act so nice to her.

As the door closed, Chloe turned to Kyle.

"That was nice to hear you speak to Shona like that, Kyle." She smiled warmly at him for the first time since they'd met.

"Well, I guess I feel a bit sorry for her. I spoke to the mechanics yesterday and apparently she ain't as good with those trucks as she seems to think she is. They let her have a tinker sometimes when I'm not looking, but they don't seem impressed. I ain't got the heart to tell her so we'll keep her on, but doin' what she's doin for now, OK? She can't damage anything cleaning, can she? Anyway, from what I hear, she won't be here much longer. Once she's got enough money to move on, I heard she's outta here."

Chloe's eyes clouded over again as she listened. But she was grateful to Kyle for deciding to go easy on Shona. She stood by the window looking out onto the yard as Shona bounced her way over to a group of mechanics, who seemed genuinely pleased to see her as they tossed her a wrench.

Strange, she thought, after what Kyle had said. She furrowed her brow as she gently ran her fingers over her precious necklace.

Chapter 50

Loud jazz played in the background and, as their evening wore on, Cuban and Shona were starting to get used to people coming up to their table and thanking Chloe for trying to help Maria. Some just wanted to catch a glimpse of the famous Miss Bruce in the flesh, not quite believing that somebody of her influence wanted to spend her valuable time with them.

"What do you think?" Shona said loudly, leaning in to Chloe.

"About what?" Chloe replied, tapping her foot to the beat.

"This place!"

"I love it! It's just a shame it all has to be a secret."

"Yep, for their own safety. They had to move again!" Shona added.

"I wish that one day people won't have to hide themselves away anymore," Chloe murmured.

"So, Cuban, you gon' play some sounds?" Shona asked, a sudden blast of trumpets swallowing up Chloe's last statement.

"Yeah, why not? They got some guitars all ready; I'll go check 'em out."

He jumped up out of his seat with more vigor than Shona

had ever seen in him. The musicians in the band were only too happy for Cuban to jam along. Chloe breathed out slowly, her expression distant.

"What's up?" Shona asked, hoping it wasn't because she was bored.

"You know something, Shona? I can be myself here. I ain't gotta impress anybody, be in charge of anybody or close any stupid deals." She paused. "I've never felt so free! It's like I'm discovering new things around me all the time!"

Chloe gazed around the room. The revellers looked as if they were moving in slow motion, all smiling and enjoying the happy atmosphere. She wiped away a lone tear as it trickled down her lightly powdered cheek.

"Well, you're *always* welcome here. Look, they adore you." Shona encouraged Chloe to look behind her to see the admiring glances being cast their way.

"Miss Chloe?" Maria made a beeline over to her.

"This is Maria, Woody's mother," Shona told her.

"Oh, hi! Listen, thank you for my flowers, they were gorgeous. I really hope the sheriff finds your son soon," Chloe said, resting both her hands tenderly on Maria's forearms.

Shona sat back and took in the moment. Never did she think that somebody with the Bruce family name could be so compassionate to a black person. After a few minutes of kind words exchanged, Maria left Chloe to get back to her drink–and her conversation with Shona.

"So, Shona-of-few-words. Was there a guy back in Louisiana...or Mississippi?" Chloe began casually.

"Uhhh–" She choked a little on her drink and fiddled with a beer mat. "Not really, no. What about you?" Shona deflected that question once again.

"Uh-uh." Chloe wagged her finger at her. "As your boss, I'm *ordering* you this time to tell me more."

Shona's head started to spin, her gut twisting as she wiped her forehead.

"That's a long, boring story," she replied finally, fidgeting in her seat.

"The reason you left?"

"Kinda." Shona looked everywhere except at Chloe.

"Well...we got time. There's no rush."

"But here isn't the place."

"Ooooh. I wanna know what's behind the cool, mysterious Miss Jackson that nobody knows about."

"Trust me. You don't! It's not a pretty story. Anyway, it looks like Cuban's about to perform." Shona angled her body away from Chloe's frustrated gaze and faced towards the stage.

Cuban strummed his guitar along with two other musicians, the audience nodding along to the thumping beat. Unable to take her eyes off Shona, Chloe bit her lip to hold her back from pressing her more. Just as her curiosity almost got the better of her, she felt a light tap on her elbow.

"Excuse me, ma'am?"

She turned to her left to see a young black boy, no more than fourteen years old. He was breathing fast and sweating, a small, fresh-looking cut sitting above his left eye.

"Yes?" Chloe replied, noticing Shona turn around also.

"I was told to give you this note from somebody outside." The boy handed Chloe a folded-up note. It read:

Get out now, for your own safety.

By the time she looked up, the boy had vanished. She looked over at Shona, who froze when she saw the expression on her face.

"We need to get Cuban!" Chloe breathed, her terrified eyes blazing.

Shona jumped out of her seat and raced over to interrupt

Cuban's performance, yanking him unceremoniously off the stage by his guitar strap.

"What the hell—"

"We gotta go, NOW! Some kid...There's no time to explain!" Shona dragged him back to their table and, with her other hand, grabbed Chloe, pulling them both through the dancing crowd and towards the exit. Instantly, the happy atmosphere of the Cell Block was fractured as the frantic screams of the boy messenger sliced through the smoky air.

"Get out, GET OUTTA HERE! RUN!" he yelled.

Chaos broke out as hordes of people stampeded towards the exit, almost crushing Chloe as she tried to pull open the door, her blood running cold when it opened to reveal several shadowy figures standing in a line in front of the building, each shrouded by a bright white cloak. Even though their pointed hoods masked their own identities, there was no doubting who they represented. This wasn't the first time the *white cloaks* had caught up with the constantly moving venue of the Cell Block.

Each figure held a burning wooden torch and stood chillingly still. After a moment of watching the mayhem unfold, one figure stepped forward ominously, his calmness a stark contrast to the screams and wails from the black men and women weaving in and out of each other like scalded ants. He walked over to one of the building's boarded-up windows, lay his burning torch down, then prized the wood off with a crowbar. With cold-blooded precision, he picked up the torch and dropped it inside, stepping back as the fire ignited the little pools of alcohol that had been spilled on the dry, wooden floorboards by tipsy dancers. Ferocious orange flames began licking up around all edges and corners, lighting the building up like a Christmas tree within seconds.

Screams and cries echoed in the air. Crowds frantically tried to run away from the Cell Block, only to be taunted by the masked members of the Klan cackling with glee as they obstructed their escape. Shona, Cuban and Chloe sprinted in the opposite direction to safety, the roaring flames completely engulfing the peaceful bar they had minutes earlier been sitting in.

"My God!" Chloe's eyes were wide with shock as the three of them hid behind a wall fifty yards away.

"Welcome to my world," Cuban gasped, trying to catch his breath.

"Whoever did that clearly didn't want *you* harmed, Chloe. Are they following you now? How did they know you were here?" Shona cried out, pointing back towards the fire that had illuminated the night sky.

"Your father? Do you think the warning note was sent by him?" Cuban raged, the flames reflecting in his smoke-filled, bloodshot eyes.

"I don't know. I didn't tell anyone where I was going tonight!" Chloe looked at both of them in confusion.

"Well, *someone's* following you!" Shona shouted back, coughing as the thick, black, acrid smoke choked the air around them. She hadn't meant to sound cruel but her harsh tone caused tears to well up in Chloe's stinging, red raw eyes.

Chapter 51

"You alright?"
Cuban spoke softly as he sat down next to Shona in the canteen that Friday morning on their 10 o'clock break.

"I guess so. You?" She poked at her eggs.

"It's nothin' I ain't used to. But Miss Chloe ain't safe in my world! I know it's not right what's happenin' out there, but people are gettin' hurt this way. We gotta protect her too, remember, her kind ain't gon' be happy if she's associating with coloreds! Can you imagine what that could cause in this town if she was seen doing that? There would be outright war!"

"Or her influence could make it so we can all finally live in peace together," Shona mused.

"That ain't never gon' happen, Shona, not in our lifetime. I haven't known peace anywhere I've ever been, even if we'd had a *hundred* whites on our side. For now, we just have to keep moving, keep hiding," Cuban said, the despair in his voice tangible.

"I know." Shona got up and trudged back to work without eating a bite.

∽

Outside, Shona clenched her fists as the injustice of the night before turned over and over in her confused mind. She stomped by, staring at the ground and almost crashing into Kevin the delivery guy, his cheery, *"Excuse me. Where's the fire, girl?"* comments infuriating her even more.

"You seen Miss Chloe?" Kevin was still smiling, despite receiving her most murderous glare.

"No, I ain't." She shoulder barged past him and carried on walking.

"Oh shoot! I need to give her this package."

"She's in there somewhere," Shona shouted back.

"Thanks. Oh, by the way, you live in the barn, don't you? By the Weaver? I heard the weather report on the radio on my way over here. Some bad weather comin' in tonight. Make sure you got a storm shelter near you, OK?" Kevin yelled after her, then shrugged as he watched her walk up to the trash cans by the back door to the tool room and kick one over. Heading back from his break, Cuban saw her fall to her knees behind the tire-mound and sob her heart out. He exhaled, wishing to God his friend would open up and talk to him.

Pulling the reins hard, Shona fought to slow her skittish mare from a canter to a trot, then finally a slow walk as she ended her ride that evening by the Weaver. Lost in her thoughts, she was jolted back down to earth by a deafening rumble of thunder.

"Damn it, not again!" she cursed as a spooked Storm began bucking. Torrential rain began pelting down, stinging the skin on her bare arms as she kicked her heels hard into Storm's flank.

"What the hell you doin' out in this? You'll catch your death!" Cuban came running out of the barn as soon as Shona returned, the rain taking seconds to saturate his white cotton shirt.

"How was I to know it was gon' be this bad?" she yelled back, her face dripping wet.

"You ain't thinkin' straight at all lately. You're not y'self, girl! Don't take a genius to see that. I'm worried about you; you're my friend!"

"I don't know what you're gettin' at, Cuban." She couldn't look him in the eye, her head steaming with pent-up emotion.

Not wanting to risk going back outside and return Storm to her stable, she tied her up in the far corner of the barn, then marched over to her bunk space. Finding some dry clothes, she began to undo her wet shirt, the adrenaline rushing through her fingers making it nearly impossible to grasp each slippery button.

"CHLOE!" He watched Shona's reaction closely as she pulled on a pair of dry pants, then wiped her face with her hands. Raw anguish seemed to consume her at the mere mention of that name.

She inhaled deeply, rubbing her temple with her twitching fingers.

"What about her?"

"I don't know what's goin' on, but I'm worried you're gon' get hurt."

"Cuban, I don't know what you think you know, but–"

"OK, here it is," he began.

Hailstones rattled the tin roof above their heads, the wind whipping up violently around the barn.

"I think you have some kind of tender feelin' towards Miss Chloe. There, I said it...Now, go on. You tell me I'm wrong."

∼

"What in the hell are you sayin'? How *dare* you think you know me! You of all people–" Shona yelled, the rain hammering down on the roof.

"Me of all people? You mean a *nigger*, right?" Cuban snapped back. "So, I start asking for some truth from my friend and you come back with that shit? My God, Shona, maybe I didn't know you at all! Maybe you are just like the rest of them!" His eyes brimmed with hot tears.

"ME? I found you, you ungrateful son of a bitch. Convinced Tom and Ruby they should let you stay. I get treated like trash at work along with Elbie for defending your sorry ass...But, yeah...*I'm* like the rest of them. How fucking DARE you compare me to all those animals out there who want nothing more than to string you up 'cause they *despise* you?" Shona collapsed backward onto her bunk, spent after her tirade.

Cuban stood motionless.

"Spoke from the heart there, Shona. Almost as if you know what it's like to be despised." Cuban nodded slowly. "That's why you've helped me so much, ain't it? You understand, right, 'cause you've gone through it too."

Tears obscured Shona's vision as she held her head in her hands trying to choke them back, her head spinning, her stomach ripping itself in two. She flew off her bunk and banged the palms of her hands against the wooden planks of the wall, retching as she crumbled inside.

Cuban rushed to restrain her, but her heightened emotional state gave her strength beyond his own considerable might. She shrugged his arms from around her shoulders and punched the wall so hard that the skin on her knuckles shredded, leaving bloody smudges behind on the splintered wood.

"Shona! Stop it...STOP IT!" Cuban pleaded.

"What in the goddamn HELL is going on in here?" Tom burst through the door, soaking wet and disheveled from the gales outside. Taking full advantage of the distraction, Cuban wrapped his arms around Shona again, who this time didn't struggle. She held on to him tightly, her tears cascading like waterfalls down her red-hot cheeks.

"Tom! TOM!" Ruby crashed through the barn door seconds later, looking terrified.

"What?" he shouted back to his wife, not sure who to look at in his confusion.

"IT'S COMING THIS WAY!"

Taking one look at his wife's panic-stricken face, Tom didn't hesitate for a second.

"We gotta go. NOW!"

"Come on, Shona. Come on, girl," Cuban whispered in her ear, scooping her fragile body up.

Moving as fast as they could through the driving rain, the four of them ran towards the storm shelter in the farmhouse basement.

"Come on! We're in its path," Ruby cried out, yanking open the door to the shelter.

"What?" Cuban shouted back, his deep voice drowned out by the howling wind as he struggled to balance Shona in his arms.

"There's a twister coming straight for us! Tom's got the horses into the stable and most of the cows have found the shed but we ain't got much time! Come on!" Ruby hollered back.

Tom ducked instinctively as a massive branch came crashing down only a few feet away from him. His eyes widened with the shock of his near-miss, meeting with Cuban's, who blinked several times to squeeze the grit out of them.

"Come on, Shona, do as you're told for once in your life!" Cuban pleaded, losing concentration on his surroundings momentarily and banging his head sharply on the doorframe. His right eye throbbed as hot dark blood began to seep out and blur his vision. Shaken out of her daze by Cuban's cry of pain, Shona put her feet on the ground and staggered down the steps, reaching back to ensure her friend made it safely too. Tom struggled to close the door behind them with the ferocious wind wrenching it out of his shaking hands every time he tried. Shona shook her head again to clear it, then stumbled back up the steps to help him, both of them grunting with relief as the bolt eventually clunked home with only seconds to spare. Descending the basement steps, they shuddered as they felt the eye of the twister pass overhead like a freight train echoing through a long, dark tunnel.

Looking around the basement, they each chose a corner to bed down in for the night. Realizing the room she was standing in, Shona glanced vacantly around what seemed to everyone else like relatively safe surroundings. But a palpable look of terror was etched on her face as she sank to her mattress on the ground, completely drained. Her strange reaction didn't go unnoticed by Cuban who, worried sick, decided he would watch over his friend that night.

Chapter 52

"Nooooo...Get off me! Please—"
"Grab her...hold her mouth!"

The first man, wearing his usual white overcoat, his glasses firmly planted on his bearded face, squeezed his hand around her throat as the second, much smaller man, held a tin mug to her lips. Forcing her to drink the foul-tasting liquid inside it, he pinched her nose to make sure it had all been swallowed. They both stood back waiting for the medicine to take its usual effect.

Within less than a minute, Shona felt her stomach lurch and twist, sending her crashing forward and rolling off the thin mattress she'd been forced to sleep on during her treatment. She writhed in agony as the liquid rushed like acid through her veins, her eyesight blurring as her breathing became labored.

Within moments, the desired effect was achieved. Shona rolled face first over a pile of magazines and photographs she'd been forced to look at during her incarceration periods in that dank, musty basement.

"Look at them...LOOK! What do you see?" the man in the white coat demanded.

Shona's left eye opened a crack. She looked down at the center-fold and saw the hazy outline of a beautiful, naked woman lying suggestively on a bed, her arm draped over her head, her plump red lips and large brown eyes staring seductively into the camera. The second Shona's eyes ran down over the naked woman's pert breasts and slender legs, her stomach growled as the bile rose and stung her raw throat.

"Don't you dare take your eyes off that...LOOK AT HER!" The second man grabbed Shona's messy blonde hair tightly in his fist and forced her eyes open with the fingers on his other hand. His grip slipped on her tears as he shook her until she submitted. She took one last forced look at the naked woman in the photograph before falling forward, the shaking of her spasming body too much for her to contain. Retching uncontrollably, her fingernails dug into the sheet that had once covered her, but now lay crumpled on the ground covered in the first flushes of Shona's vomit. Tears streaming from her eyes, she groaned and writhed as the medicine coursed through her like wildfire.

They weren't finished with her just yet though.

"Hold her down," the first man ordered the second one, who obeyed.

The man in the white coat opened the small, leather bag he brought down with him every time and took out two long leads; one red, one black. He handed one end to the second man who knew exactly what to do; it had been the same procedure almost every night for the last three months.

Shona felt the second man's strong hands pin her arms above her head and press her wrists into the ground. The man in the white coat then ripped her undershirt up and attached two soft pads to her bare breasts, pausing momentarily to find a patch of unblemished skin, which, after months of treatment, was becoming increasingly difficult. He finally found two clear patches of pale skin and stuck the pads down firmly. Shona, drained of any energy to fight him off, lay there prone, waiting for the pain.

"Flick the switch, Lenny!" the man in the white coat ordered, standing back.

Shona's body convulsed as the electricity pulsed through her, her mouth clenched in stunned agony. Three more shocks were triggered as the man in the white coat held the magazine in front of her face.

"It's disgusting, isn't it?! IT'S WRONG! SAY IT!" he screamed in her face, flecks of angry spit clinging to his neatly trimmed gray beard. Shona's head lolled around on the cold, concrete floor as she hovered on the brink of unconsciousness.

But the man in the white coat was determined.

He tore the pads off Shona's puckered red skin and ripped her loose pants down to her ankles, parting her legs roughly. He stuck the pads down, one on each of the insides of her thighs, as close to their meeting point as he could get and looked up at the second man, nodding his instructions.

The jolt of electricity caused Shona to let out a bloodcurdling scream. Once again, the man in the white coat held the centerfold in front of Shona's sweating face and forced her eyes open.

"LOOK! Say, 'It's wrong'. SAY IT!"

Shona turned her head weakly, a plume of vomit and spit erupting from her mouth, now blood-red from biting on her tongue.

"It's...w...w...w...w...wrong. It's wrong!" she gurgled helplessly.

The men looked at each other and smiled.

"Good girl...that's better. We'll give you more treatment tomorrow."

The man in the white coat bent down, put his leads away in his little leather bag and did up the buckles. He smiled at Lenny, who gestured to the door to see him out. Shona's eyes slowly closed as the darkness finally consumed her, her last vision being that of the thick wooden door shutting behind them.

Lying motionless on the cold floor, a lone tear dripped from the corner of her eye and onto her bare shoulder as she passed out, the magazine deliberately left open by her side.

"SHONA! Goddamn it, wake up! WAKE UP!"

Cuban leaned over his friend, alarmed by her spine-chilling screams. Her nightmares had woken him many times before, but this sounded like the worst one yet.

"Wh...what's goin' on...what happened?" Shona's bloodshot eyes opened and darted wildly until the friendly faces of Cuban and Tom came into focus and calmed her down. Ruby stood behind them, looking equally concerned.

Shona pulled her blanket up to her neck.

"I can't stop the dreams. I don't know how to." She broke down again into pitiful sobs. Cuban, Tom and Ruby all decided to take two-hour watches over her for the rest of what felt like the longest night.

Chapter 53

Tom opened the door to the basement on Saturday morning, unsure as to what horrific sight would greet him. He climbed up the steps and stood, hands on his hips, surveying the damage. The roof had been ripped off at one corner of the barn and several fences were down, but surprisingly it didn't look as if there was too much to fix. The cow shed and stable looked mostly in good shape, the sound of mooing and neighing reassuring Tom that all inside had survived.

They had all been very lucky.

Ruby followed him out, stroked his arm soothingly, then set off into the kitchen to start breakfast. As Cuban and Shona emerged from the basement, Tom instantly picked up on the tension still fizzing in the air between them. They both looked exhausted, their eyes red and sore.

"I need to go and check on Storm," Shona excused herself and stomped over to the barn where she had tied the horse up the night before.

"What's going on with you two? What did I walk into last night?" Tom asked.

"I don't know," Cuban lied. "I'll go get started on the fences, see what can be salvaged."

Tom watched both of them walk away in opposite directions, hardly able to say two words to each other. His thoughts were disturbed by Ruby's shout over to him, just as he looked up and noticed the same thing she'd seen out of the kitchen window. As the vehicle heading down their driveway pulled up, Tom recognized the bright red Deluxe. He walked around the farmhouse and headed for Chloe's car, opening the door for her.

"Miss Chloe."

"Tom, hi. How are you all after the storm?" she asked softly.

She was dressed immaculately as always, her red and black halter-neck dress perfectly matching her driving gloves and quilted Chanel handbag.

"Not too bad, we're just surveying the damage. Anybody in town hurt?" Tom replied.

"Unfortunately, yes. Three guys from work, but hopefully they'll be OK."

Chloe looked over his shoulder and saw the gaping, jagged hole in the roof of the barn. She bit her lip and looked back at Tom.

"Is Shona around?"

"Yeah, she's over in the barn checking on Storm. Between you and me, that girl ain't been herself lately. We can't for the life of us get to the bottom of it. Last night, down in the basement, she had the most awful nightmare. I've heard her have them before sometimes, but this one was...different. Worse." Tom ran his hand over the back of his neck. "Miss Chloe, I hope you don't mind me sayin', but I really think she could do with a friend right now. She seems so alone."

Chloe's stomach flipped as she fiddled with the tiny buckle on one of her gloves.

"Would it be OK if I went over?"

Tom smiled his gratitude and pointed to the barn.

Opening the door gently, Chloe saw Shona stroking Storm's head, whispering in her ear trying to sooth the skittish mare.

"Shona–"

"Ma'am," she replied, then turned to press her cheek softly into Storm's mane.

"I just came by to see how everyone was doing after last night." She tilted her head to try and get Shona to look at her.

"We're fine. Thanks," Shona replied flatly.

"OK. Well, if you're sure? I guess I'll leave you all to it. Let me know if I can help you with anything, OK?"

After a minute or two of awkward silence, and watching all of Shona's attention fixed on calming the wild horse, Chloe let out a defeated sigh and turned to head out of the barn and back to her car.

Blinking back her own tears, Shona picked at the fresh scabs on her knuckles and watched from the yard as Chloe's car roared back along the driveway and out of sight. Lurching forward, she doubled over in pain and collapsed to the floor, pulling at her hair and sobbing her heart out as she pounded her fist against her churning stomach.

Cuban looked over from the fence he was hammering back together, feeling completely helpless.

"What the hell is goin' on here? Miss Chloe made a special visit to come see us. She goes to speak to you, then two minutes later she leaves in tears?"

Cuban had left it for half an hour before wandering over to the barn to talk to Shona, who had returned to her tender stroking of Storm's head.

"Shhhh...I'm here, I'm here...shhh, it's OK," she whispered in the mare's ear.

"Shona? Did you hear me?" Cuban repeated as he came nearer.

"Yes, I heard you. She'll be like the rest of 'em, that's what you said? I should stay away from her, right? Well, I *am* doing that, OK? It's for the best."

"The rest of 'em? You mean Bruce, Kyle and Deputy Paul, right? I just said don't get *too* close! I din' mean make her cry!"

"Just leave it, Cuban!"

"No. This ends now, y'hear? I've lost enough people in my time, my whole goddamn family to the Klan! D'you think I wanna just sit back and lose you too? Not without an explanation. If you want me out of your life, that's fine, I'll walk away. But don't push me away if you don't mean it. What in hell's going on?" His voice cracked with emotion.

Shona stopped petting Storm. Still facing the mare, she began to cry, faintly at first, trying to disguise it. Cuban could see her shoulders shaking and when he realized she was breaking down, he raced over to catch her in his arms.

"Come here, s'alright."

After a calming minute in Cuban's arms, Shona broke away and staggered over to the other side of the barn where their bunks were, tears streaming down her cheeks. She turned to face him across the short distance, her eyes blazing with torment.

"It's not alright! Don't you see?"

"What are you talking 'bout?" His face creased with concern as he strode over to her.

"You ain't the only one on the run here. You ain't the only one who has to look over your shoulder all the time! You ain't the only one being hunted down, having to hide who you are every GODDAMN day!"

"Please...talk to me." He moved closer into her space.

"If I tell you, I'm scared I'm gon' lose you too–" Shona shook her head and slumped against the barn wall.

"You kiddin'? That would never happen! You ain't getting rid of me that easy. You're my friend for life, you understand? No matter what."

Shona wiped her tears on her sleeve. "I don't even know where to start–"

"Start at the beginning. I'm listening," he said, putting his arm around her and encouraging her to sit on his bunk.

She took a deep breath.

"Back in Louisiana when I was thirteen, I worked with my daddy on a farm for a few years. It was owned by a rich guy called Donald Chamberlain. He was a hard bastard, always shoutin' at people. My daddy was a drunk and often I'd have to cover for him when he fell asleep in the barn on his break. I did some of his work too–"

Cuban sat silently next to her.

"Donald...he had a daughter called Connie. She was seventeen. I found that I kept tryin' to think of something to ask her all the time, kept tryin' to see if she needed anythin'. Every minute in her company felt like precious seconds. My God, she was beautiful. Long wavy brown hair. She had a boyfriend, Nate, but she cried a lot over him so I used to go see her after work and we'd talk. She said that nobody listened to her like I did."

Shona breathed deeply, then continued.

"My father liked it. He felt I was makin' a good impression with a rich family, which might lead him to a better job, so he encouraged it. I sometimes think me bein' friends with the boss's daughter was the only time in my life he'd ever been proud o'me! But I couldn't help my heart beatin' faster when I was with her, especially when she talked one day about breakin' up with Nate."

She paused again. Cuban sensed she was getting to the crux.

"Anyway, one afternoon she seemed real upset, so I offered

to take her out ridin' to take her mind off whatever was eatin' her up. She asked me to wait in her room while she got changed in the bathroom. I couldn't help but look around. Then, I saw her mirror had lot of photographs tucked in all around the edge. There was this one picture I couldn't take my eyes off. She looked so damn gorgeous and I was totally in love with her at this point...but I couldn't tell a soul. My daddy told me many times about what happens to people who like their own *kind*! He said they...they *deserve to be punished*. I was holdin' the picture just as Connie came outta the bathroom and I didn't have a chance to put it back, I just kinda slipped it in my jacket pocket. I didn't mean to take it." Shona sniffed and wiped her nose with her fingers.

"Those few hours spent ridin' with Connie flew by way too fast. Every minute of them I was itchin' to tell her how I felt about her. She seemed to open up to me about how Nate had been foolin' around behind her back. It broke my heart to hear her so sad. We got back just as it was gettin' dark and sat on the porch for a while. But then I saw her shivering...so I took off my jacket and put it around her shoulders. She smiled at me in such a way that I really thought she was gon' tell me she felt the same as I did. But instead, she said her hands were cold...and when she put them in the pockets—"

His heart sank. He knew what was coming next.

"I'll never forget the look on her face. She was so angry I'd taken the picture from her room. I tried to explain, but I ended up tellin' her everythin'! I couldn't stop the words, I was only young...but the disgust on her face when she told me she never wanted to see me again. That she wasn't–never could be–one of my *dirty kind*."

Shona winced and held her side.

"She was yellin' so much at me that her father came out of the front door, wonderin' what was goin' on. He was so angry when Connie told him I'd stolen from his home and he wanted to know what else I'd been stealin' too! But when he found out from her why I'd taken the picture, he struck me so hard 'round the face I swear it lifted me off the damn ground!"

Shona exhaled.

"The worst bit was the names they were callin' me afterwards! The last time I saw Connie's face she looked at me like I'd killed somebody. That broke m'heart. Donald told m'father that he'd already been on his last warnin' and now, because of my *evil perversion*, he was fired. All I wanted to do was explain, but he beat me and told me that I'd brought disgrace on the family, not so much for the stealin' but because of what I was."

Shona paused to look at Cuban, trying to gauge his reaction. He remained silent and gestured for her to carry on.

"When we got home, I was sent straight to bed. Father told my momma and I heard them arguing over me. Later, she came into my room. I was so scared that she would hate me that I almost didn't want her to speak. But she held me tight and said she loved me, and that she was my momma no matter what. I just cried m'heart out in her arms. Then my father must have heard me cryin' and burst into the room. He saw my mother huggin' me and dragged her out of my room, slammin' the door behind him. He'd been drinkin' and was slurrin' his words as usual and crashin' around, sayin' how he didn't want to have a *damaged kid*, that I would be the talk of the town. My momma... the last words I heard from her were...'You don't deserve to have her as your daughter; I will love her no matter what.' Then...silence."

Cuban looked horrified.

"I was so scared. I didn't dare come out my room. I just lay there, covers up to my face, heart poundin' out my chest. Eventually, I crept out, careful not to make a sound on the floorboards. I opened the bedroom door to see out...and my father was right there. He said, 'If you come out, something bad will happen to your momma,' so I went back in. I didn't know what to do. He was drunk...He looked possessed! I didn't sleep much but early in the mornin' I heard voices downstairs. I opened my door and listened. It was the local doctor. I heard him ask what happened and my father said, 'She just fell down the stairs.' He was talkin' 'bout my momma! She'd fallen, but I knew he'd pushed her alright! That's what the noises were the night before. The bastard got away with it!"

Shona clenched her teeth, blinking the tears away.

"He spoke to that doctor about me. Made me admit to them both what I was and that I couldn't help being attracted to girls, then said I was crazy and needed puttin' right. Later that day I was taken away by a nurse, to live with her at the house she'd converted secretly into treatment rooms for *damaged people*. She made a livin' that way. I stayed there for six months, locked up. She told me I could only leave when I was cured of my *'disgusting proclivities'*."

"What happened at her house, Shona?" he asked patiently.

"She and a couple of doctors would, at different times of the day and night, come find me in the dark, damp basement they used as my treatment room. They kept me locked up, doin' horrible experiments on me. They would show me pictures of naked women then, when I looked at them, they would cut me, stick wires on me...make me drink the most god-awful things. They were designed to make me sick anytime I got those feelings again!"

She shuddered at the memory, the effects of which still haunted her deeply. Her violent stomach lurches were a constant reminder, especially since Chloe had appeared and opened up all her old wounds.

"My God, Shona. I'm so sorry. That's why you have those nightmares? Especially the one in the basement the other night. Memories, right?"

She nodded weakly.

"Then what happened?"

"One day I escaped. The nurse took a delivery and put it down in the basement. I pretended I was asleep, then made a run for it up the stairs and out the door. Afterwards, I moved around a lot. I'd learned about fixin' trucks and stuff on the Chamberlain farm so did that for a while, movin' from farm to farm. I kept hearin' my father was after me because I'd brought shame on his family and cost him a good job. He had nothin' to live for and nothing to lose. So, I just kept movin' on, spending three to four weeks in each little town I came across. Then, a couple of years ago, I settled in a small town in Mississippi. I broke my own rule and stayed longer than usual. I figured my father would've given up the chase by then. I found a great job at a place called Wreckers. The boss loved what I could do, said I knew more about fixin' trucks than any guy he knew!"

"What happened in Mississippi?"

"History repeatin' itself. A girl, around twenty-two years old, hung around the local bar every single night. It was right opposite Wreckers so she would often come in and talk to the guys. She looked a bit wild, excitin'...free. Her name was Lucy. Now, I wasn't exactly wise to the ways of the world, let's just put it that way. I didn't know at the time, but Lucy was a prostitute. That's why all the guys buzzed around her; they knew she was a sure thing. Later, I found out she was called *Loose Lucy* for obvious reasons. When I was at the bar, she would come up to me, even in front of the guys there when I was playin' pool. I couldn't understand why, the most beautiful woman in the room—coming up to *me*?"

Cuban shut his eyes.

"I started to like it, you know? I started to have *those* feelings again, the ones I dared not have for such a long, long time. I didn't so much as even look at a woman for years! Every time a pretty lady would talk to me, I made my excuses and left. I couldn't handle the sickness I got from the treatment I'd had. They probably all thought I was rude. But Lucy...she was different. She kept coming up to me whether I was in the bar, Wreckers or at the grocery store. I started to think about her more and more. I'd found a way to cope with the sickness, to suppress it by breathing deep and counting in m'head. Then one day, I asked her if she'd like to come for dinner and she accepted. I thought that meant I had found somebody, at last, somebody like me, who liked me the way I wanted to be liked, you know?"

She looked at Cuban, who nodded.

"The next evening, she came around. My God, she looked stunning. We had dinner and she then asked me to sit next to her on the couch, so I did. She put her hand on my knee. So, I put mine on hers. She leaned in to me...and just as we were about to kiss she pulled back and said, *'I knew it. I knew you were one of those screw-ups.'* Then, from nowhere, four of her friends jumped on me. Lucy hadn't locked the front door. It was all a setup. She'd got paid by some of the people at the bar to see if I was one of *them*! Then I got the biggest beatin' of my life. I couldn't see properly for a couple of days. I didn't go into work, couldn't say what the reason was, and left town."

"Oh, Shona."

"So, you see? You see why I'm terrified to get close to anybody, women that I find attractive, I mean. When Chloe was introduced to us all that day, all I heard was the guys around me say how cute she was, how they would like the chance to date her and all. But I had to stay quiet."

"Do you have strong feelings for Miss Chloe?"

"Yes, yes I do." Shona hung her head in shame.

"What do you think she feels?"

"No idea. There are times I just think she's being kind, like she just wants a friend, you know, someone to talk to? Then sometimes, I catch her lookin' at me and it's like I can read her mind...because I'm thinking the same. But Cuban, I'm petrified of gettin' found out or my past catchin' up with me. I just have to keep my head down, save some goddamn money and get out of here. I can't go through it all again!"

He leaned his head forward. "But you can't stop thinking 'bout her, right?"

"Every single minute of every goddamn day!" she replied.

Chapter 54

It was first thing on Monday morning and the workers had all been summoned to the canteen for a quick briefing.

"You OK?" Cuban said in a low voice to Shona, knowing Chloe was about to emerge onto the balcony.

"Yeah," she replied, looking everywhere else but up.

First onto the balcony was Ron Black, followed by Jeffrey Ellis, who laid a supportive hand on the younger man's shoulder. Seconds later, Kyle and Bruce appeared looking bored as they waited for Ellis and Black to address the crowd.

Then out came Chloe.

Her simple peach-colored blouse floated over her curves, her matching pencil skirt resting just below the knee and finished off by a thin white leather belt. Her hair was pinned back to the side by her glistening butterfly clip. Around Chloe's neck was her precious pink pebble necklace. She hadn't taken it off since Shona had given it to her. Her entrance drew admiring gasps from the men in the crowd, but Shona just took a deep breath and clamped her eyes shut.

Glancing down, Chloe deliberately looked to the back of the crowd, but the sight of Shona's strange expression caused her initial smile to evaporate.

"Good morning, everybody," Ellis began. "I know I don't come down here half as much as I should...apparently, according to some, I'm always at the Copperpot." He turned and glared at Kyle. "But I really felt for my town after such a devastating storm. Of course, we can prepare, but Mother Nature soon lets us know how insignificant we really are. But we have big hearts in this town! So, Ron came to me with an idea and I liked it. We're going to have a fete this coming Sunday to bring the community together—hold it here at the site! Tell your wives to make or do something to help bring in people to donate money to those who were most affected. Ron'll be around to give you more details, but if you have any ideas, come and see me anytime."

Bruce and Kyle looked at each other and rolled their eyes. For a split second, Shona opened her eyes and met with Chloe's anxious gaze, but looked away first. Cuban sighed to himself, noticing Chloe's downcast reaction.

"Shona, you and Cuban could build a couple of benches, couldn't you? Sell 'em real cheap at the fete to raise some money?" Elbie suggested.

"Yeah, OK," she replied

"Miss Jackson!" It was Kyle calling from behind.

"You go on ahead," Shona said to Cuban and Elbie, smiling to reassure them as they both reluctantly left her standing in Kyle's imposing shadow.

"Just to let you know, in case you've already put your mark on the money we raise, we won't be giving any to white nigger lovers like yourself," he whispered in her ear.

Shona stared emotionless at him, not in the least bit surprised that his consideration towards her in Chloe's office the other day had been a total sham.

That Sunday morning, the day of the fete, Shona felt like she'd actually been given a plum job for once, looking after the horses. She patted the placid mare Elbie had volunteered to bring along for the children to ride on.

"She's so pretty."

"That she is," Elbie replied, shooing Rosie into a horse box ready to take her to the fete, a makeshift stable waiting at the other end.

"I'll show her to Cuban later. I ain't ever seen him ride!" Shona grinned as she held her arm out of the truck window, the cool morning breeze running through her fingers as they pulled onto the long road that led to work.

"Momma...I can see the horse!" A little girl ran excitedly over to where Rosie was tucking into her bale of hay.

"Evelyn, come back here at once!" The mother gave chase, but the lure of the placid mare proved too much temptation for her daughter.

Cuban, who was tasked with cleaning out horse muck from inside the stable all day, found himself face to face with the little girl, who couldn't have been more than six years old. She had long blonde curls tied up in a bunch on either side of her head, a silky pink ribbon holding them firmly in place. Her little body was held in check by a very tight-fitting pink and white spotted crinoline dress, her lace-trimmed bobby socks the crispest shade of white Cuban had ever seen. The little girl stood there for a moment or two staring at the tall, black man with a puzzled look on her face.

"Uh, hey there–" Cuban said, backing away and putting as much distance between them as he could–for his own safety, not hers. She edged closer, though, intrigued at this dark-skinned man and his cute animal friend.

"Is that your horse, mister?" she asked, still looking curiously at him.

"She's ours today. You like horses, ma'am?" he asked, feeling the wooden planks of the stable wall press against his back. He looked side to side to see if anyone had seen her come in, sweat bubbling on his brow.

"Yes, I do. I'd like my own one day." The little girl continued to stare at Cuban, her inquisitive blue eyes picking up on something strange.

"Go ahead, ask. You wanna know why I'm black, right? If I ain't washed the dirt off my face for so long now that it won't ever come off?" Cuban spoke softly so as not to alarm the girl. He threw every crass explanation for his black face he'd ever heard at the little blonde girl, who continued to stare at him, her eyes unblinking.

"No," she said matter-of-factly. "I was just wondering how you hurt your face, sir. You got a big *ouchie* there...It looks sore!" She pointed her tiny finger up towards his right eye. The swelling, from the bang on the head he had received during the storm, had gone down, but the cut hadn't yet healed.

Cuban closed his eyes, thoroughly ashamed of himself.

"I'm OK, but thank you for your concern, ma'am." He took off his imaginary hat and bowed to her. She giggled and curtseyed in return.

All of a sudden, a middle-aged woman appeared around the doorway to the stable. She had dark swept-back bouffant hair curling forward around her ears, which held her expensive pearl earrings within them. Her eyebrows were shaped into arches and darkened with eye pencil, her cheeks rouged, and her lips bright red. Clutching her Gucci purse, she looked from side to side until she finally caught sight of the little girl and sighed with relief.

"Evelyn! Will you–" The mother stopped dead in her tracks, a look of pure horror and revulsion crossing her perfectly made-up face. She grabbed her daughter's milky white arm with her kid-gloved hand and put her body between her and Cuban.

"Momma, no! I was talking to the nice man about his horse," Evelyn cried.

"You stay away from my daughter!" The mother spat on the ground in front of Cuban.

"Momma, why d'you do that?" The little girl looked up at her mother, her eyes wide.

"Because he's dangerous. We don't talk to those with *black faces*, do you hear me?"

Evelyn's tiny, confused protests faded into the wind as she was dragged away, her shiny pink sandals churning up the dusty ground.

"And that's how it starts," Cuban whispered to himself.

Shona lifted her nose into the air and breathed in deeply, taking in the sweet aromas that were mingling in the warm summer breeze. She opened her eyes and caught sight of Elbie working his magic on the crowds and selling his crafts. She smiled, her fondness for the kindly old man growing by the day.

At that moment, the feminine outline of the most beautiful woman in Daynes emerged from a crowd of admiring towns-folk. Her hair shone in the bright light of the Alabama sun, her perfect cover-girl smile flashing at everyone who'd gathered around to offer her flowers and gifts for helping to organize the fundraiser for victims of the storm. She wore a pale yellow summer dress, complete with a pastel-lemon silk ribbon in her hair.

Shona fought the urge to look at her. Her heart fluttered, her head felt light and all she wanted to do was stride over to her and tell her exactly how she felt, but instead, she decided to wander back over to the riding section of the fete. As she got there, the sound of sobbing caught her attention. A small girl, no more than four years old, was crying hysterically just a few feet from where Rosie had been tethered. Her exasperated mother was in attendance, trying in vain to calm her.

"Hey." Shona crouched down to the little girl's level and smiled.

"She's just fallen over and scraped all up her legs!" her mother explained, upset at her child's obvious discomfort.

"You like horses?" Shona asked the young girl, who looked at Shona's open face and stopped crying.

"A little bit," she sniffed and wiped her nose on the back of her tiny hand.

"Well, how about you and your momma come with me to meet m'friend Rosie and if you'd like to, you can have a free ride on her, what d'you say?" Shona stood up, ready to lead the way. The little girl looked up at her mother, who nodded.

"Yes, please."

"Come on, then."

Shona led them around the adjoining wall between the riding arena and the stable where the mare was snuffling in her nose bag and drinking some water.

"Here's Rosie...wanna pet her?" Shona noticed the cuts on the little girl's knees. The little girl nodded, her tear-stained face brightening.

"How 'bout I lift you to sit on her and Mom...you, um–" Shona pointed to the cuts. It was the perfect distraction.

"She hadn't stopped cryin' until she saw you," the mother told her.

Shona got a clean, wet cloth and a Band-Aid, then lifted the little girl into Rosie's saddle. Her face beamed as Shona taught her about all the different parts of a horse – while her mother tended to the injuries, looking up every few seconds to check that her firm rubbing on her daughter's knees was not being noticed.

"Honey? Y'round here?" a deep male voice called out.

"We're in here, sweetie. It's my husband, Jack," the woman told Shona.

"There you are, honey. How're my girls doin'?"

Jack Edwards was in his early forties, had recently inherited his father's estate and was looking to invest his new money in the town. He tipped his hat to Shona, then walked straight over to his daughter.

"My God, she's stopped cryin'! How in God's name d'you manage that?" Edwards exclaimed.

"All down to this young lady!" Mrs. Edwards nodded to Shona. "Sorry, what's your name?"

"Shona." She held her hand out for Edwards to shake.

"Well, Shona, you're my new best friend," he said, shaking her hand vigorously.

∼

"The press are here, that's good." Ron Black stood near the refreshment stand drinking a glass of sweet tea next to Jeffrey Ellis, who preferred his usual tipple of scotch on the rocks.

"Yeah, it's goin' real well, don't you think?" Ellis replied.

"Some wanted today to fail." Ron nodded his head subtly in the direction of Kyle and Bruce who were standing in the distance chatting to Deputy Paul.

"But it didn't, so don't you worry about them!" Ellis reassured.

A deep booming voice sounded behind them.

"Ellis, my man! How in the goddamn hell are you?" Jack Edwards marched over to Ellis and Ron, extending his arm.

"Jack! You're looking well!" Ellis complimented, shaking his hand.

"Thank you, and how's your good lady wife?"

Ellis paused. "She's not been too good lately, Jack," he replied, his voice tinged with sadness. "Had the doctor 'round again last night but–" Ellis began explaining but was rudely cut off mid-sentence by the imposing figure of Larry Bruce.

"Edwards...Hi!" Bruce leaped in between Ellis and Ron and held out his broad right hand to Jack. Chloe stood a few paces behind her father, looking lost in her daydream as she scanned the crowds for the one face she wanted to see. As usual, Kyle stalked behind her like the shadow she just couldn't shake off.

"Larry...Kyle...Chloe, looking amazing as ever." Edwards shook all their hands one by one.

"Your wife here with you too?" Ellis asked, looking behind Edwards.

"There she is, over by the horse and that pretty young lady... Shona, I think her name was." Edwards turned around to see his giggling daughter trotting around the riding arena on Rosie, Shona gripping the tether as she led the horse. Chloe couldn't help her face breaking out into a huge smile, the affection she felt for Shona impossible to hide.

"She was fantastic with my daughter, Jeffrey! I tell you, this is a great event for the town."

They strolled to the riding arena, Kyle and Bruce trailing behind.

"Here she is! Did you have fun, sweetie?" Edwards scooped the little girl out of the mare's saddle. She had completely forgotten about her grazed knees.

"Can Shona and Rosie come visit us, please, Daddy?" Her parents both smiled.

"Of course they can," Edwards smiled at his daughter, then turned to Ellis. "I'd like to do some business with you real soon, and I mean a *lot* of business. I came over here to initially check it out up close. I'm lookin' to invest in real salt-of-the-earth family businesses. People like Shona and that old guy–Elbie, is it? They've made us real welcome today, and made my daughter feel real special!"

"That sounds good to us," Bruce said, reaching forward to shake his hand.

"Gentlemen...Oh, and ladies, could I take a picture?" Joe, the young reporter, stood in front of the group like an excited puppy, the huge flash on top of his camera making it wobble precariously in his shaking hands.

"Wait," Ellis interrupted, as people were shuffling together for the picture. "Shona...Hey SHONA! Come on, get in the picture...and bring Rosie!" Ellis grinned.

Shona jumped around when she heard her name hollered by Jeffrey Ellis. Joining the group, she stood on the very end of the line, with the mare on her left. The fear of being news for all of Alabama–and beyond, no doubt–to see, was temporarily forgotten, as the overriding emotion she felt that moment was the aching pain of having Chloe standing agonizingly close to her, less than six feet to her right.

Shona swallowed hard as a waft of Chloe's sweet perfume caught the breeze and nestled inside her nostrils. She breathed in impulsively, underestimating the effect it would have on her and, as soon as the picture was taken and Joe gave the all clear, she grabbed Rosie and made her excuses. Walking quickly back to the stable, she arrived seconds before feeling the gut-wrenching spasm ripple through her stomach, only subsiding on her tenth deep breath.

"Thanks a lot for what you did for this town today, Larry." Jack Edwards was getting ready to go home, patiently waiting for his little girl to have one last ride on her new best four-legged friend.

"It's our pleasure. Thanks for the donation to the cause."

"I can see Kyle has a thing for your daughter!" Edwards remarked, looking over Bruce's shoulder at Chloe, who was by the exit bidding farewell to some of the workers' wives.

"They'd make a fine couple, wouldn't they?" Bruce leaned in, grinning.

"Damn right. I mean, I don't know this Kyle, but you can tell he likes her! I want it to be that if I invest a lot of money, my clients will have the stability of using a company that will still be around after we kick the bucket!"

"Yeah?"

"And I think that company is going to be yours! With Kyle and Chloe at the wheel in the future, investors will be clambering over themselves to get a piece of it...They're the future, and that's what I want to invest in!"

Larry Bruce smiled, hardly able to contain the swell of ambition inside him.

Chapter 55

Jesters was the town's local barbecue joint, serving the best fried chicken and soul food for miles around. Their fried catfish with hush puppies and slaw was the talk of Daynes; nowhere in town did it better. Later that Sunday evening, the revelers from the fete all congregated there to fill up on fresh crawfish, skillet cornbread and Jesters' famous buttermilk biscuits with sausage gravy. The place was packed to the rafters, the sound of carefree conversations and laughter hanging in the air. Children were pressing their sticky fingers up against the glass chiller underneath the counter, drooling over bowls of banana pudding, peach cobblers and plates of pecan pie. Chloe and Kyle made their way straight over to the bar to get a drink.

"You looked ravishing today," Kyle drawled, wanting to stroke her hair. She tilted her head and brushed his hand off, not flattered in the slightest. In fact, she was annoyed. She'd spent all day the embodiment of perfection, as expected, but eight hours of being the *belle of the ball*–in four-inch heels that were killing her feet–had exhausted her tolerance to the breaking point. Her eyes searched the crowd once again.

"Can I get you a drink, Miss Chloe?" Deputy Paul appeared at her other side.

"Just a peach juice, please. Is everybody here tonight?"

"Pretty much," Kyle replied. His eyes fixed on the waitress as she bent over to retrieve a glass from the bottom shelf.

"Well...I'm going to go and say hi to all the workers; it's thanks to them that today was so successful."

Chloe slipped away, her perfume leaving behind a lasting memory of her. Kyle stared at her long, slender legs, frustrated that his seduction of her wasn't moving as slickly as he had been led to believe it would. It was looking as if he was going to have to try harder...or a different tactic altogether.

"Elbie, you go home, it's been a long day. We haven't got much else to do now, go on," Shona insisted, Cuban nodding in agreement. It was almost 10 o'clock, and the three of them had been made to stay at the site to clean up the mountains of debris left after the fete had ended.

"OK, if you're sure?" Elbie said, rubbing his tired eyes. He stood his broom up against the wall.

"Yes, we're sure. Get home safe, OK?" Cuban said, helping him into his truck.

As they watched him leave, a new set of headlights approaching stung their eyes. A feeling of dread engulfed the two of them, Cuban praying that the approaching vehicle wasn't a green Ford truck.

Shona held her breath, hoping the car wasn't red.

"Who the hell can that be at this time?" Cuban asked, trying to make out the shape of the vehicle.

"It's Chloe," Shona said coolly, recognizing the shape of the chassis across the closing distance.

"You gon' be OK?" he asked, noticing her stony face.

"Yeah."

Chloe's car crunched through the gravel, pulling up a few feet in front of them. An age seemed to pass before the door opened a crack and she slid out of her seat. As she did so, her yellow dress caught the breeze and rucked up slightly, revealing the merest glimpse of her bare inside leg. It was torture for Shona, who bit the insides of her cheeks, her fingernails digging into her clammy palms as she counted to ten in her head.

"Hi." Chloe smiled at Cuban, then lingered her gaze on Shona.

"Evenin', ma'am," he replied, politely tipping his cap.

"I've been looking for you both. I went to the Birds', but they said they hadn't seen you. How come you're not at Jesters, celebrating?"

"We weren't invited. We were told to stay here and clean up all the shit left behind." Shona's voice was flat and cold.

"By who?"

"Who do you think? Kyle! And that lil' sidekick of his, Paul!"

"He told me–"

"Told you what?" Shona fired back. "That we'd rather spend all night fillin' trash bags? That sound right to you?"

"Hey, watch your tone!" Cuban whispered.

"I'm sorry about that, I surely am. I wouldn't have allowed that to happen if I'd known, not after I'd arranged for you to be the one in charge of the horses today. I knew you'd like that, so..."

Chloe fiddled with the cuff of her white leather driving glove.

"Look, you both have a difficult time here, I know that," she continued, locking onto Shona's angry eyes. "If you can find it in your hearts to trust me, I want to work on putting a good team around me. That's why I suggested to Jeffrey that we make Ron Black a manager, but you need to understand it's difficult with my father ultimately being in charge too! Please understand where I'm coming from. I really am trying my best. I even had made a kind of an arrangement with Kyle that you both, and Elbie, would be left to do your jobs. Have things not been better for you all lately?"

Shona looked away, knowing Chloe hadn't quite succeeded at *that* one.

"I thank you for tryin', ma'am. That can't have been easy for you," Cuban said.

"Well, how 'bout I give you two a ride? Get you safely home." She tipped her imaginary chauffeur's hat, trying to lighten the mood.

"That would be most generous of you, wouldn't it, Shona?" Cuban nudged her.

"Thank you, that would be...nice," she replied quietly.

Cuban shrugged. It was the best he was going to get out of her right now.

"Great, hop in!"

Chloe opened the passenger side door for Cuban to climb into the back seat, Shona in the front. She ran around the front of the car, the headlight beam shining through her almost see-through dress. Shona looked away again and swallowed hard as Chloe jumped into the driver's seat and floored the gas pedal.

Back home at the Birds' house, Cuban took Chloe's handbag and gloves and put them by the front door, then went into the kitchen to put a fresh pot of coffee on. The atmosphere in the car had been fractious all the way home, with Chloe making small talk about the fete and how much money they had raised for the town. Shona smiled in all the right places but still looked distant, which pained Chloe more than she could put into words.

"Here." He handed Chloe a mug of coffee and pulled a chair out at the kitchen table for her to sit on. Shona leaned against the kitchen sink, out of her eyeline. Cuban shook his head at her and sat opposite.

"Tom and Ruby in bed?" Chloe asked.

"I guess so. They have to get up pretty early to feed the animals," he replied.

"How's Storm after the, um, *storm*?" Chloe giggled at the unintentional humor of her question.

"She's fine," Shona replied, missing the joke entirely.

"Do Tom and Ruby need anything? They OK?"

"They lost a cow." Shona stared at the floor, silently counting the tiles.

"Oh." Chloe clasped her mug to warm her hands.

A minute went by agonizingly slowly, the ticking of the clock seemingly louder with every stroke.

"I heard there's a new peach pie in Ed's Diner. Wanna come try it out with me sometime? You're both welcome?" Chloe looked at Shona, refusing to give up.

"With regret, as you can understand, I don't do many public places in this town, but Shona-" Cuban looked over towards the sink.

"My treat?" Chloe added with a hopeful raise of her eyebrow.

Shona's resolve finally cracked.

"If you throw in a strawberry shake, I'm in," she replied, the hardness in her demeanor lifting, her tone still cool.

It's a start, Chloe thought.

Chapter 56

"Chloe."
"Kyle."
"Nice evening?"

"Yes, thank you." She began opening her Monday morning mail.

Kyle watched her closely.

"I'm sorry, is there a problem?" Chloe snapped, feeling the weight of his intrusive stare.

"I asked your father this morning if you got home OK and he said you didn't return until real late. I was concerned. You shouldn't be out late by yourself." He tried his best to sound sincere, but to Chloe, it just sounded hollow.

"Kyle, I'm a big girl, and for your information, I wasn't by myself. I was with...friends. Oh, and in the future, don't go asking about business that doesn't concern you."

Chloe slammed the mail down on her desk.

~

"I'm glad you and Miss Chloe seemed to clear the air last night. It was nice to see." Cuban smiled at Shona, who was washing her hands after finishing a particularly grubby job.

"Well, I got this new thing I'm trying when I get those feelings. It seems to be working so far. Helps me to put those thoughts aside, for the sake of our friendship." Shona tried to sound convincing.

"Unless she feels the same way?"

Cuban's words hit her heart like a jackhammer.

～

Shona blew her cheeks out just before she knocked on Chloe's door that afternoon.

"Come in," came the cheery voice from within.

"Shona." Chloe beamed, her eyes sparkling as her door opened. It got to Shona every time, her heart thudding in her chest so hard she could scarcely believe no one could see it through her thin, white undershirt.

"Ma'am. I got a message you wanted to see me?"

"Have a seat, please."

Shona sat down in the guest chair that had been pulled out ready for her. She coughed, waiting to be spoken to. Chloe, meanwhile, tried to look professional, rifling through her wafer-thin pile of notes.

"Well, Miss Jackson, I've decided to speak to some of the staff to hear their ideas of how we can improve conditions here." Chloe fidgeted in her seat, trying to make the excuse for seeing her sound convincing.

Shona waited a few moments before answering, willing Chloe to read her mind so that the awkward, heart-piercing longing for her could just come out into the open.

"In what way?" she responded finally.

"What would make you happier here?" Chloe probed, her pen poised.

Shona paused as she considered the answer she really wanted to give.

"What have others said?" she ventured instead, backing out.

"I can't tell you that, of course. I'm interested in what *you* have to say. You normally have great ideas."

"OK, you asked for it! Let's start with the food," Shona began, folding her arms. "The food is *shit*. I wouldn't feed it to a dog! We need a better selection, some healthier stuff maybe? And more color! Well, just somethin' other than brown slop would be a start, for Christ's sake! And the uniform! This one itches the hell outta my ass! OK, while we're at it, we should only work a half day on a Friday. I bet you'll see morale jump right up. And a good damn pay raise! There!" She leaned back in her chair, smiling.

"Very honest, Shona. Some good suggestions there," Chloe said, writing them down, trying to stifle a blush at her *ass* remark.

"You're serious? You're gon' try to get some of those things introduced? All due respect an' all, ma'am, but your father and others will never in a month o'Sundays agree to them, especially if they knew they came from me."

"I'll make it happen." Chloe leveled her gaze at her.

"OK, well, I better get back to it."

Shona rose out of her chair and headed to the door, looking back as she left. She was certain she saw the tiniest glint in Chloe's eyes. Puzzled and excited, she walked out onto the balcony, feeling a glimmer of hope in her racing heart.

What she *didn't* feel, though, was even more confusing to her. The volcanic agony that usually erupted in her gut when she thought about or saw Chloe was incomprehensibly dormant.

Chapter 57

"**Y**ou hear the news?"
Elbie came and sat down at their table at break time the following Monday morning. Shona sat picking at her food. She hadn't slept much that weekend, mulling over the meeting she'd had with Chloe the week before and the strange energy that seemed to pass between them as they said goodbye.

"What news?" Cuban replied.

"Miss Chloe's outta town. Gone to Mississippi, so I heard." Elbie took a bite of his eggs.

Shona's head sprang up.

"Why Mississippi?"

"Not sure, something about visiting other businesses, to get ideas."

Shona's blood ran cold. *A research trip for information? Oh no,* she thought...*Please god, NO!*

∼

After three hours on the road to Mississippi in search of answers, Chloe pulled up in front of a bustling garage just off the main road and checked the name against the address she'd scribbled down.

Wreckers.

Several trucks were parked up in front, in various states of repair. Some had hoods and fenders missing, and some had mechanics lying underneath them on creepers as they changed oil filters. There was an atmosphere of calmness and order around the place; the workers looked happy and not in the least bit self-conscious about singing along to the radio as it played the latest Elvis Presley ballad. Chloe stepped out of her car, pausing to listen to the song, the words resonating with her. Just then, a cheery young pup raced over to her, forcing her to refocus her attention.

"Hello, ma'am, how can I help you on this fine day?" He smiled widely, his well-fitting denim overalls splattered indiscriminately with oil stains.

"I'd like to speak to the manager, please. Harry, is it?" Chloe removed her cat eye sunglasses.

The young mechanic looked crestfallen. "Is there a problem, ma'am—did we not fix your car right?"

"No, of course not," she added. "I'd just like to chat with your boss about some work ideas I'd like to share with my own lil' place and—" Chloe tailed off, realizing her cover had been blown as the boy's face illuminated with recognition—and panic—at who he was talking to.

"You're Miss Bruce, ain't ya! *Damn*, I seen you in all those magazines—I mean, I only read 'em for the articles, of course, not the pictures!" Reddening with embarrassment, he took his cap off and ran his oily hand through his short brown hair. Chloe smiled politely, willing him to stop digging a deeper hole for himself as he tried to explain.

"I'm sure you do. Is it possible to speak to Harry?" Chloe prompted.

"Oh yeah, of course, ma'am, allow me to escort you to his

office." He recovered himself and walked Chloe into the building, reminding her to be careful not to hit her head as they ducked underneath the truck-lift and sidestepped the work benches, air compressors and jack stands. Stepping past two men standing six feet below her in the mechanics' pit, it felt refreshing for Chloe to hear a polite, *"Good morning ma'am,"* rather than the usual wolf whistles she got most days.

"Miss Bruce! What an absolute pleasure to see you."

Harry came out of his office and greeted Chloe warmly. He was around fifty years old, his formerly dark hair going gray at the temples. Harry had the brown leather skin of a man who had worked his whole life outdoors, his calloused fingers showing the honest dent of where a wrench had sat snugly as he fixed thousands of trucks over the years. His clean blue denim overalls bore the Wreckers logo proudly.

"I won't keep you too long, sir. I just wanted to ask about how you run things here," Chloe began as she followed him back into his office.

"Come on, have a seat over here, somewhere comfortable. Marcie, could you fix us some drinks please, darlin'–" Harry called out to his wife, who stopped dead in her tracks when she laid eyes on Chloe, as if Grace Kelly herself had just walked in.

"Of course, dear–right away!" She buzzed out of the office as quickly as she had flown in.

"Thank you. Now, tell me about what keeps your staff so happy here?" Chloe began, taking out her notepad and pencil from her black Chanel handbag.

"Well, as simple as it sounds, I started with the grub! I found a food delivery service that is out of this world. Only the best for my guys! They work their asses off for me." Harry smiled proudly. "Oh, and overalls had to change. The ones we had before were too damn itchy," he added, making Chloe giggle as she remembered Shona's cheeky gripe regarding the Ellis and Bruce uniform. "I also decided that my guys should have Friday afternoons off, you know, to spend it with their families. It's made them ten times happier and upped productivity threefold. I can't even remember the last day I had a guy call in sick, so I guess my way works!" He leaned back in his chair, a smile of accomplishment on his weather-beaten face.

Chloe was impressed, but it wasn't the real reason she was there.

"You got what you needed, Miss Bruce?"

"Almost." She took a deep breath and asked the question she'd driven three hours to ask. "Do you remember a *Shona Jackson*?"

One of the clerks standing just outside the door by the in-trays looked up when he heard the familiar name. He listened in but kept his distance.

"Shona? Of course. She worked here for a period a while back. Why d'you ask?"

"Could you tell me about her? What was she like?"

Harry's eyes lit up. "Bless her heart, Shona was the best! Better than the best! Did more work around here than four of my guys, never had a day off sick, wasn't into drinking, and she was a real pleasure to have around. Everybody liked her. I mean, she kept to herself, but I respected that. But then–"

"What?" Chloe's back straightened in her chair.

"She vanished. Just like that. No word, nothing." Harry's voice lost its enthusiasm. "The old lady she rented a room from, Dorothy, rang up one morning to pass on a message that Shona had gone and to say sorry for letting me down. The poor old girl lives out there in the sticks all on her own again now, Shona used to take her shopping, and her rent money really helped the ol' gal out. Dorothy had this beat-up blue truck she kept out in the yard. It wouldn't drive so good, so Shona used to try and fix it up down here for her. I let her because, well, she was such an asset to this place I thought I'd cut her some slack. But then, when she disappeared without a word, I guess, well, you never really know people, do ya?"

"And you have no idea *why* she left?"

"Not really. I mean there was gossip, but unless I hear it from the horse's mouth I don't listen–"

Realising Harry had no more to tell her, Chloe rose to her feet and offered her thanks to him for his time.

A few yards away from reaching her car, she turned to see the admin clerk from Harry's office running towards her.

"Miss...*MISS*?" he yelled, almost out of breath.

"Did I forget something?"

"I'm Frank Smith. I'm sorry, but I heard some of your conversation and I may be able to help you."

Frank was in his late twenties, with slicked-back hair and a five o'clock shadow on his face.

"Really? With what?"

"With telling you the *real* reason Shona Jackson vanished."

"I got a real bad feeling about this," Shona whispered to Cuban when they briefly stopped for a drink while sweeping the yard.

"What d'you mean?" He wiped the drips from his chin.

"With Chloe gone, Ellis not here, there's an eerie calm around this joint, don't you feel it? God knows what she's findin' out about me right now. I jus' know she'll go to Wreckers, I know it–"

"And if she does?"

"Then she'll *finally* know the truth about me." Shona's face blanched at the thought.

"And you'll *finally* know how she feels about that," Cuban added sagely.

Chapter 58

After she left Wreckers, Chloe sped off in search of the little farmhouse with the blue truck in the yard. She pulled over several times to ask for directions, getting a little closer every time. Driving down the same road several times, she looked closer through the leafy trees and spotted the corner of a rusting blue fender. Poetically, the yard she had driven into was the very last house before the end of town. *Shona really did like her privacy.*

That sentiment resonated loudly in her mind. *What am I thinking? Why am I prying into Shona's past? What am I even going to say when I knock on Dorothy's door?*

She slammed the brakes on, finally coming to her senses. The crunch of her skidding on the gravel, however, drew attention from inside the house, the drapes in the front room gently twitching.

Chloe stepped out of her car and approached the house. Her mind was racing as she tried to think of a reason to give for being there. The house was made from simple whitewashed timber, the pale green paint peeling at the edges of each square window frame. It looked solid enough, a rocking chair on the veranda on one side of the front door and a porch swing on the other. Sturdy wooden beams held up each apex of the roof, and a plume of black smoke billowed out of the chimney stack in the corner.

Catching the scent of freshly baked cornbread in the air, Chloe made her way up the gray cobblestone path which was flanked on each side by the yellowy-green lawn. In the far corner of the yard, she saw a small partition fence with three black chickens pecking the ground inside. The battered, rusting blue truck sat in the front yard looking like a project that somebody had started but not finished, its hubcaps upturned on the grass.

She reached the front door and lifted her hand to knock.

"Can I help you, sweetheart? Are you lost?" A croaky old voice sounded from behind the door.

"Hi, are you Dorothy?"

"Yes, I am, dear. Who are you?"

"My name's Chloe. Chloe Bruce. Could I come in and talk to you, please?"

"Of course," Dorothy replied as she unbolted the wooden door.

Chloe was invited to sit in a small, high-backed armchair in the cramped front room. The air smelled damp, not helped by the small puddles of condensation on the windowsills, the putty on the insides black with mold. There was no sign of anyone else living here, only Dorothy. She watched silently as the old lady hobbled around the tiny ramshackle kitchen, leaning heavily on her walking stick. Putting the kettle on the little coal-fired stove, she waited patiently for the water to boil. She looked to be in her early seventies, with her white hair wrapped up in a bun on her head. She wore a long, pale blue pleated skirt, cotton shirt and a ratty old, light green knitted cardigan with a little hole near her left elbow. Her kindly features were wrinkled now, but her keen blue eyes still retained their sparkle. Even though her body looked ravaged by age–a small hump noticeable at the top of her back–her wits still seemed to be sharp.

After a few minutes of silence, Chloe heard the kettle whistle. Dorothy appeared soon after with two cups, handing one to her unexpected young visitor.

"I'm sorry just to come out and ask, but did you know a Shona? Shona Jackson?" Chloe asked, blowing the steam off her cup and then taking a sip.

"Why d'ya ask, dear?" Dorothy picked up the sugar bowl and offered it to her guest, who shook her head.

"I heard a rumor about why she had to leave town, but I wanted to know the truth. About the real Shona." Her voice trembled.

"Why?" Dorothy plopped two cubes of sugar into her cup and stirred slowly.

"Because...because she's my friend and I–" Chloe looked down at her cup. "She works for me and it's very difficult for her there. But we used to talk and spend time together. We went out riding once. It was such a lovely day, she really listens to me, you know?"

The old lady nodded.

"What a pretty necklace y'got there," she said, noticing that her guest hadn't been able to stop caressing the shiny pink pebble all the time she'd been speaking.

"It's beautiful, isn't it?" she smiled, her eyes shimmering. "Can you tell me about Shona? She did live here, right?"

"Yes, she did."

"What was she like? I keep hearing about her being this monster because of what happened with that woman, but, well, ma'am, I just don't see it. I've never felt it. Have you?" Chloe said, constantly twirling the pebble over in her trembling fingers.

Dorothy's eyes welled up. She gazed at the necklace as she took a long deep breath.

"Shona is...the kindest, gentlest, most thoughtful and funny woman you'll ever have the pleasure o'knowin'. There ain't a question in my mind 'bout that. I spent a great deal o'time with her. We talked and talked. She said I was the only person who knew about her life, her father and what happened to her when those people trapped her in that basement!"

Chloe's ears pricked up at her last comment. *What people? Trapped?* Not wanting to interrupt Dorothy's flow, she made a mental note to ask her about it later.

"She worked damn hard at Wreckers, often pullin' double shifts to support me. My husband died over in Normandy in '44 and by the time Shona turned up all the money'd run out. That's his truck out in the yard, but I just can't bring m'self to get rid of it. He often used to tinker with it and it makes me feel like he's just outside, you know? It keeps me goin' when I get lonely." Dorothy paused and turned her head to the side to look at the truck through the living room window. She smiled, a faraway look glazing over her aged face. "I've left Shona's room pretty much as she left it. Can't bear to have anybody else stay; the house just wouldn't be the same. She took care o'me, paid me rent, got my groceries on her lunch break. She was the daughter I couldn't have. My husband and I weren't blessed in that way, but y'know, life happens. Shona would help me up the stairs 'cause I busted my damn leg years ago and can hardly walk, so I just sit here and reminisce."

"If you don't mind me asking, how do you support yourself now? Financially?" Chloe asked, looking around Dorothy's modest front room.

The old lady winked. "My angel still sends me money."

"What? You're *still* in contact with her?" Chloe's eyes widened.

"I've never been *outta* contact! I'm the only one she can speak to, though I hear nothin' but good things about Tom and Ruby who've taken her and her friend Cuban in. She sends me letters all the time!"

"She tells you about her life now?"

"Of course! And her plans to leave. I told her to get the hell out o'that minefield as soon as possible. Oh, no offense, dear!" she added, seeing Chloe's face drop.

"Did she say when?" she asked, leaning forward.

"Soon. But I do know one thing. I know that she'll miss *you*!"

Chloe almost dropped her coffee cup.

"Shona writes about *me* in her letters?" she exclaimed.

"Every time." Dorothy reached forward and put her wrinkled hand over the top of Chloe's trembling one. "I just wish you could get rid o'that asshole Kyle who keeps sniffin' round you. And your father, he needs to step down and stop bullyin' people! There's a lot goin' on that you don't know about Miss–"

"I know. I'm sorry for that. It's difficult for me too. I'm working on making it better for her, and the others."

"Do y'know how little they're payin' Shona, Cuban and Elbie?"

"I got told all the workers are paid the same. They're not?" Chloe's eyes narrowed.

"Oh no, dear. They pay them less than half what the others get! Shona's on such a low wage that I don't know how she manages to save a *nickel* once she's paid her rent to Tom and Ruby, then sent me a bit too."

"So Shona sends you money every time she gets paid?"

"Yep, regular as clockwork. I've tried sendin' it back three times, but she just puts it in an envelope and sends it back to me with the next batch. It's that poor child who goes without, not me! No, it's time she had some happiness for herself with what she's been through and how she's been treated by people who she trusted, who supposedly loved her. Right now, if you told me she'd found love with somebody of her own *kind*, you know what I'd say?"

Chloe shook her head as the old lady took an excruciatingly long sip of her coffee, the cup shaking in her arthritic hand as it rose and fell from her lips.

"I'd say, that woman better love Shona the way she *deserves* to be loved." Dorothy pointed her long fingernail in front of her.

Chloe bit the insides of her cheeks, her thoughts clattering into each other like fireflies on a warm summer's night.

∽

"My goodness, it's so late, I'd better be getting to my hotel."

It was nearly 10 o'clock when Chloe finally checked her watch, after being completely engrossed all evening in Dorothy's tales about Shona. She rose off the worn, gray armchair and offered her arm to help the old lady as she struggled on her walking stick.

"It's been an absolute pleasure talking to you. You're one special lady. If there's anything I can help with–" Chloe said.

Dorothy walked up to her, touching Chloe's elbow softly. "There is somethin' I'd like very much–" she began. "I'd like to have your company again, maybe tomorrow?"

"I'd love that. Shall I bring anything?"

"Just yourself, that's more than enough," the old lady replied.

As she reached the front door, Chloe turned back and smiled.

"Shona *really* talks about me in her letters?" Her cheeks reddened.

"You've been in every one since she started working there. I was hoping I'd meet you one day, to see what all the fuss was about!" Dorothy winked playfully at Chloe. "Thinks a lot of you, she does. She wouldn't make somethin' as special as that pretty necklace for just *anyone*!"

The old lady's blue eyes twinkled.

The next evening, as promised, Chloe returned to Dorothy's house. She spent hours chatting with the old lady and reminiscing about Shona, but when she finally plucked up the courage to ask Dorothy to tell her the story about the basement, she broke down in tears hearing in graphic detail what Shona had gone through.

As it was almost time to get back to her hotel again, Chloe remembered she had one more thing she wanted to ask.

"Sweetheart, of course you can see Shona's room."

"You sure that would be OK?"

"Yes, dear, I haven't changed a thing. Come on up."

Dorothy struggled with the rickety stairs as they made their way up, then along the landing.

"Here it is," she announced, opening the old wooden door. On the wall, Chloe saw pictures of mountains, beaches and rivers. Shona loved the outdoors and it was evident to see why. *How could anyone feel trapped if they had the open plains to look at every night?*

One picture immediately caught her eye, not least as it was the one nearest to her pillow and had the most pin holes in it, the sharp corners of the card now blunt. It was of a little white beach house with cornflower blue window shutters and a white painted veranda. It sat beside the bluest of oceans, the clear water lapping against the golden yellow sand.

"May I?"

Dorothy smiled as she watched Chloe sit down on Shona's bed. She held her palm flat against the soft covers, knowing Shona had laid there in the dark of the night confused and feeling so alone in the world. The nightmares Dorothy told her about earlier that evening sliced through her thudding heart like a hot knife. The times Dorothy had woken to hear Shona's anguished screams and rushed in to comfort her. Chloe's eyes brimmed with angry tears as she felt Shona's heartache channel up through her flattened palm.

"I'll give you a moment," Dorothy said, shuffling out onto the landing and down to her little bedroom.

∼

Chloe recoiled as she sat up and looked at her watch, astounded to see that she had spent forty of the quickest minutes of her life in Shona's room.

"Will you stay the night? It's been a long time since I had company in this house. It's too quiet." Dorothy appeared in the doorway.

Without needing to think it over, Chloe agreed on the spot.

"You can sleep in here if you like?"

She stood up and gratefully wrapped her arms around the old lady.

∼

"Can you put me through to Miss Chloe Bruce's room, please? It's her father. What? What do you mean? Can't you tell me anything useful at all?"

Bruce growled as he slammed the phone down and drummed his heavy fingers on his office desk.

"What is it? Where is she?" Kyle frowned.

"Apparently, she came back briefly yesterday afternoon, got her things and then left."

"So where in the goddamn hell did she spend the night? And who with?"

Kyle banged his fist on the desk.

Chapter 59

"Hello? Yeah? Simms, how are you?" Bruce spoke loudly into the phone.

"Hey, Larry. Listen, m'wife told me she loved the fete, great event and all, but she said she caught sight of that damn colored you got workin' for ya 'round back of the stables. Damn son'bitch knows what my lil' girl looks like now. I'm scared for her safety. What if he sees her in town? I'm sorry, Larry, but I just can't see me investing in your business after all. It sends out the wrong message havin' coloreds representin' us, y'hear what I'm saying, Larry?" Tony Simms's voice echoed down the receiver.

"You know it's Ellis who's the stumbling block; he wants to give 'em all a chance. I want to send them back where they belong, so you can see my dilemma here. You and me, we're on the same page, Tony."

Bruce ran a hand through his thinning hair, trying to convince one of the richest men in Daynes not to take his money elsewhere.

"I understand what you're saying, Larry. Ellis is the past, just biding his time and all. I know his wife ain't well, so he won't want none of this bullshit! But I don't wan' be associated with giving work to no coloreds. Until then, I'll be holding back on my investment. I'm sorry."

"Tony, I hear you. You have my word. I'll deal with the situation. You understand me, don't you?" Bruce clenched his fist.

"Look, let me know if anything changes, OK?"

Bruce slammed the phone down and glared at Kyle.

"We need to deal with the nigger. Once and for all."

Kyle nodded compliantly, a sly smile creeping across his handsome face.

"I got an idea."

"Damn it!"

Shona cursed as she dropped the last of her clean cloths into a pile of oil on the ground by one of the trucks. It was Wednesday morning, and she hadn't seen Chloe for a couple of days now.

Why isn't she back from Mississippi yet?

Inside, she was terrified. The longer Chloe was away, the more the coyotes lurked, watching and waiting. Shona and Cuban needed her there to protect them.

"Cuban, y'got any more o'these over there?" She held up the oily cloth.

"Nope, but I got a coupla clean ones in my locker you're more than welcome to."

"Great, thanks. Hey, Cuban...you're a real pal, y'know that?"

"Well, lil' lady, the feeling is entirely mutual! I just got to unload this delivery or Deputy Paul will be on my ass! Here's my key. They're at the back on the right."

Shona made her way into the cramped cupboard space, immediately taken aback by the pungent smell of damp. Cuban definitely did have the worst of everything, but before she left for Mississippi, Chloe had at least seen to it that the *random* locker searches inflicted on him had been put to an end and, finally, he had been given a new one.

Shona opened his locker and gasped, coming face to face with a picture of Cuban's wife and children stuck to the inside of the door. She ran a careful finger over it and smiled; they truly were a fine looking family. Mindful of not invading Cuban's valuable privacy too much, she resisted the urge to go through his personal effects and reached back to the right to feel for the spare cloths she'd come for.

"What the hell are you doing in here?" A gravelly voice pierced the silence.

Shona spun around. Kyle stood before her, his venomous, jet black eyes pulsating through her head. He was holding two bottles of beer, a Rolex watch and an expensive-looking flick-knife.

"Me? It's you that ain't got any right to be in here!" Shona stuck out her chin and raised herself up to her full height.

"Get the fuck out an' get back to work, do you hear me?" Kyle whispered, the shadow of his six-foot frame looming over her as he approached.

"Not until you tell me what y'doing in Cuban's changing space!"

"This is no concern to you, so get the fuck out!"

Kyle put the bottles and watch on the side, then clicked the tiny release catch on the hilt of the flick-knife. Shona's blood ran ice cold as she saw the four-inch blade coming towards her. Before she could react, Kyle thrust his left hand out to cover her mouth as the knife in his right was then held to her neck. With her feet almost completely off the ground as he pinned her up against the wall, she gasped a large, muffled intake of breath.

"Do you understand me now, bitch? When I tell you to do something, you fucking do it. But then again, I heard that you weren't wired up in the head right, so you don't listen, do ya!" He squeezed Shona's mouth shut even tighter as she squirmed.

"It's a real shame you walked in on me just now. Planting a few items of interest in Cuban's locker would've been a real neat plan. I go to Ellis, say he's been stealin' and off he goes. He won't last more than ten fucking minutes in this town. But you? You have to be there, getting in my way...again!"

Kyle lowered the knife from her neck and began to press it into Shona's stomach. She winced, waiting to feel the blade pierce her denim shirt.

"You won't get away with this." She forced the words through his closed palm, tears streaming down her blood-red cheeks.

"Really? Why's that? Because Ellis is gon' save you? He's out of town today. And Chloe? She's out of town too. Left you all alone 'cause she thought I was playin' nice with you now! *Hi Shona, how's your day?* That's all I had to say to convince her you'd be safe!"

Kyle was enjoying every sordid minute of Shona's torture, glaring into her incandescent blue eyes as they blazed pure hatred at him, the whites started to fill with blood.

"It's so easy for me! All I have to do is put these things in his locker and conduct a random search. Chloe won't be around to save him *this* time." Kyle's sweaty face pushed in closer to Shona's, his grip tightening.

"You're a fucking *animal*." She tried to free herself, knowing any moment he could plunge his knife deep into her. Spots formed in front of her eyes as she struggled to stay conscious, desperately gulping for air.

Whistling absent-mindedly, Randy rounded the corner by the canteen when a loud crashing sound drew his attention away from the sandwich he was picturing. He carried on walking until he heard it again. Curious, he followed the trail of noise, leading him into the small room Cuban used as a locker space. Opening the door, he stopped, horrified by the scene he'd stumbled across.

"Woah, what's going on here?"

"Help me, Randy! PLEASE!" Shona could barely breathe, her boot limply kicking against the locker to hopefully raise the alarm.

"Mr. Chambers, sir?"

"Randy, this is no business of yours. Now turn around and don't say a word, understand?" Kyle glared at him.

"No, Randy, please," Shona begged, rapidly losing her strength as Kyle clamped his hand over her mouth tighter.

"Shut the *fucking* door, Randy!" he snarled.

Shona was powerless as the cold steel of the knife pressed harder into her soft flesh. Randy stared blankly at her for a moment, then, to her complete horror, turned and left, shutting the door firmly behind him.

"Now there's nobody here that knows, or cares, what the fuck happens to you. You're a white nigger lover, which makes you quite unpopular. Mixed with that, those rumors 'bout you–" He sneered at her as he lifted his eyes upwards over her heavy toe-capped boots, baggy work pants, then lingered on her tight-fitting white undershirt, through her now-open denim shirt.

"You know nothing about me," Shona seethed through her tears.

"What frustrates me is you're actually quite pretty for a... well, what the guys say you are! When you first arrived, you drove them nuts! They put bets on who would get to fuck you first! But they tell me that not one of them can fix a date with you! You're not interested in any of 'em! My guys not good enough for you, bitch? Fuck, I bet you ain't never even *been* with a guy...or have you?"

He moved his left hand from over her mouth and caressed

her neck roughly, his booze-soaked breath getting noticeably heavier and deeper the more aroused he was getting.

"I'll be honest. It's driving *me* crazy I haven't fucked you already! Women throw themselves at me day in, day out–but you didn't and I ain't used to that. You know what, though? I just can't help but wonder what it feels like to fuck you! You secretly wonder the same about me, don'tcha?"

He pressed his nose against the side of her face, his left hand now cupping her breast, his right still holding the knife against her stomach as she felt him get hard up against her.

"Go fuck yourself," Shona spat back at him.

"Oh, it's like that, is it? Y'know it actually turns me on more when I gotta work for it!"

"Cuban! CUBAN!" Randy raced over, as fast as his squat legs could shift his bulk.

"You OK, Randy?"

"Cuban. Your locker room. You need to go. Now," he blurted out between rasping breaths.

"What? What you talkin' 'bout?"

"Your girl's in there...with Kyle. She needs you. NOW!"

Cuban dropped the box he was carrying and ran as fast as he could.

"Come on, Shona, put your hand on me. You wanna touch it, don't you?" Kyle was grunting heavily in Shona's ear, but her lack of oxygen from his hand over her mouth minutes before had sapped her strength.

She couldn't fend him off any longer.

"I've waited a long time for this. C'mon, undo my pants and

feel how much you've got me goin' here!" He held her limp hand against the front of his pants and manipulated her fingers around the buttons, then onto his fly, groaning as he felt it unzip. "Just relax. If you let me fuck you, you'll keep your job and I won't say a thing."

"Get the FUCK off her, you animal!" Cuban roared, nearly kicking the door off its hinges.

Kyle spun around, losing his grip on Shona who slid to the ground.

"Trust me, for your own sake, walk away. Now!" His eyes were fixed on Cuban, daring him to make his next move.

"Shona, you OK?" Cuban called out, his eyes wild. She nodded weakly.

"I'm warning you. I will fuck you up! GET OUT!"

He pinned Shona back against the wall, sliding his left hand under the waistband of her pants. She looked over his shoulder at Cuban, her eyes pleading for him to help her.

Cuban needed no encouragement. He'd wanted to unleash his strength on Kyle for weeks, and now, with Shona at his mercy, he was unstoppable. Launching himself at Kyle, his hands clawed at his suit jacket, almost ripping it off his back. He tossed him to the cold stone floor like a rag doll, the flick-knife he'd been holding in his right hand clattering to the ground. Cuban reached down for it, but Kyle twisted his torso and got to it first, wrapping his fingers around the ivory handle of the knife. With his other hand, he gripped Cuban's standing leg and, with a mighty heave, plunged the blade deep into his ankle.

As he screamed out in pain, Cuban's legs buckled underneath his massive frame. Blood spurted out of the wound almost instantly, his peroneal artery severed. Kyle twisted the knife sadistically, scraping it against the bone and glaring at Cuban's wide-eyed, anguished face. The white-hot pain was blistering. Through her blurry vision, Shona could see her best friend writhing on the ground and holding his ankle tightly, the blood draining out fast.

Kyle dragged himself up off the floor, Cuban's sticky red blood perilously close to smudging on his expensive gray flannel suit. He straightened his jacket and saw to his open fly. Shona lay propped up against the wall, dazed and exhausted.

"Jeez, darlin', you sure do know how to make a guy work for it. You better be good!"

He wiped his mouth with the back of his bloody hand and swaggered back over to her, the adrenaline coursing through his veins and arousing him more.

As Kyle stepped over him, Cuban stuck out his uninjured ankle, taking his legs from underneath him and dumping him in a heap on the ground for the second time.

"What the...YOU SON OF A BITCH!"

He reached out to grab Cuban, but the bigger man dodged out of the way and struggled to his feet. Balancing on one leg, he stood over Kyle, the pain slicing through him.

"NO, CUBAN! Leave him! Just go...RUN!"

Shona knew he only had a head start of a few minutes at best. Once Kyle raised the alarm, Cuban didn't have a hope in hell.

"I can't leave you. I won't leave you," he yelled back.

"I order you, GO!" She screamed with all the fight she could muster, dragging her shattered body as far away from Kyle as she could manage.

But he was no longer interested in *her*.

"HELP! SOMEBODY, PLEASE HELP ME! GODDAMN IT! THE NIGGER'S GOT ME!"

Kyle's strangled, begging voice was incongruous to the psychopathically calm and still man who was lying on the floor, unimpeded, calling for help. Cuban's heart stopped when he realized his intention.

Within seconds, the stomping of boots thundered outside

the room. Confused cries reverberated along the corridor as the men asked each other if they had *heard that shout*.

"You better run! This'll be a pleasure to them when I tell 'em what you did!"

Kyle's voice was eerily calm, his mission almost accomplished.

"Cuban...RUN!" Shona ordered, tears streaming down her cheeks.

As their eyes met for the last time, a moment of profound sadness and regret passed between them. They knew deep down that this day was always going to come. All plans for the future were just pipe dreams.

They knew it was goodbye.

Outside the room, Cuban moved as fast as he could in the opposite direction to the approaching lynch mob, heavy drops of blood trailing behind him as he hobbled along.

Kyle clambered to his feet, waited until the angry crowd passed him down the corridor, then turned the opposite way to find the nearest telephone.

"Larry, it's me. Call the boys *now*! It's time."

Chapter 60

The gas station at the end of the driveway to Ellis and Bruce had been in the Bullen family for over fifty years, passed down from generation to generation. It'd started life as a simple convenience store but when the Ellis and Bruce plant arrived on the scene, the Bullen family realized they were sitting on a goldmine. Their store sat next to a busy crossroad, a few miles out of town–with no other gas stations for miles. When Larry Bruce partnered up with Jeffrey Ellis, he brought with him his fleet of trucks to be the distribution side of the partnership. As soon as Bullen senior had spoken to Larry Bruce, the deal was done. They offered the cheapest gas around, providing that the company sent their trucks there every time they were sent out on delivery. Bullen senior had the underground storage tanks fitted that same month. Gas, however, was not the only thing that brought money into the Bullen household.

Bullen senior had three sons: Earl, Ernest, and the runt of the litter, Billy. Earl took over the family business when his father died five years ago, leaving Ernest to be his second-in-command. Billy, the more sensitive one, kept to himself, choosing to spend his time fishing and playing with his Alsatian dog.

That afternoon, Earl Bullen sat on his porch swing, staring into the distance. He blinked as a black speck running into the field just opposite the gas station caught his eye. Across the other side of the field was the main building of the Ellis and Bruce site. The black speck slowed down, then dropped to the floor.

"Hey, Ernest, come here a minute, will'ya–" he drawled, scratching his head.

"What the hell's the matter?" Ernest Bullen emerged from the side door to the gas station, his grubby, white-stained undershirt riding up over his noticeable beer belly. He was twenty-seven years old, five years younger than his older brother and six years older than Billy.

"Over there." Earl nodded his head to the black speck which had started staggering again across the adjoining field.

"What th'hell is it?" Ernest said, squinting as he reached over to grab the binoculars constantly resting on the veranda banister. He let out a burst of excitement as it dawned on him what it was.

"NIGGER ON THE RUN!"

Ernest grinned at his older brother and reached over for his shotgun as if he'd just seen a prize turkey released into the open.

"Wait!" Earl grabbed his arm. "You know the drill. We wait for the call, remember? We don't do nothin' till *they* got our back!" He bit down tightly on his cigarette.

Ernest lowered his shotgun and frowned, but he knew his brother was right. They had to be smart. It had to be clean.

The telephone inside the office rang loudly. Moments later, a young man stepped out onto the veranda. His thick black hair was combed to the side, his bangs hanging heavily over his right eye. He wore ratty overalls covered in muck from doing the dirtiest jobs around the garage and couldn't have been more than a hundred and forty pounds dripping wet. His faithful Alsatian dog stood calmly by his side.

"Earl? That was Mr. Bruce. He said to tell you that *it was time*," Billy Bullen said meekly. His eyes lowered as he addressed his older brother.

Earl Bullen looked at Ernest, a slow grin creeping over his stubbly face as he removed his half-smoked cigarette.

"Well, I guess that's our cue!" He gestured towards Ernest, who began loading his shotgun.

"Billy, you get in the back with the dog. Ernest, in the front with me."

They climbed into their green Ford pickup truck as Earl crushed his cigarette butt underneath his heavy boots.

"Let's go catch ourselves a colored, boys!" Ernest Bullen cried as the truck engine roared, heading straight to the field, bypassing the formality of the driveway altogether.

The long rope they carried every time dangled ominously from the tailgate.

Ready as always.

~

Bang.

A perfect shot, expertly fired from a Remington 870 shotgun, exploded into Cuban's lower leg. They'd had lots of practice. Hitting him just above his knife wound, though, it at least gave him the use of his other leg to desperately try and drag himself onwards.

Not far behind him, he could hear the baying mob's angry jeers catching on the wind. Another shot whizzed past, a clean shot that would have gone right through his arm if he hadn't dropped to the ground as quickly as he did. With the long grass of the field acting as a kind of cover, Cuban crawled as fast as he could, spotting the Weaver up ahead. If he could just catch the current, he might have a chance.

"CUBAN!"

Shona screamed at the top of her lungs, doubling over as she bent forward as if it would somehow project her strangled voice further. She'd run out of the locker room and fought her way through to be at the front of the crowd. Scanning the field desperately to see her injured friend, she'd jumped as she heard the first gunshot, then saw Cuban fall to the ground.

It was hopeless.

Helplessly, she watched the wretched figure of Cuban rise and start limping again. She could see he was heading for the river. *Please just make it!*

"Whoa! Where d'you think you're goin', missy? Tryin' to help your lil' friend?" Kyle whispered in Shona's ear as his strong arms grabbed her from behind and held her chin up towards the field. "Let's watch, eh? Let's see if he can outrun...a dog."

He yanked her head in the direction of the Bullens' rusting green truck as it flew across the field chasing down a desperate Cuban.

"NO, SHONA, DON'T RUN AFTER HIM! YOU MIGHT GET HURT AS WELL!" Kyle shouted, inches from her ear.

The crowd watching Cuban's escape turned around and stared as Kyle restrained Shona, each man nodding in admiration at his heroic gesture. Shona's lungs burned as she squirmed in his tight grasp, screaming her friend's name over and over again.

Cuban could hear the water as it rushed downstream. He reached out, grasping for precious handfuls of earth to pull him closer and closer to the riverbank. Cruelly, he was only a few yards away when he felt the jaws of the snarling Alsatian, let off its leash to finish the kill. He tried to shake it off, feeling its teeth puncture his cotton shirt as it latched onto his forearm.

Another gunshot zipped passed Cuban's head, taking his attention away momentarily from the slavering dog. The Alsatian then released its grip on his forearm and bit down hard on his wounded leg, causing him to let out a fresh blood-curdling scream.

The Bullens' truck thundered up behind Cuban, swathing him in dust as the tires skidded to a stop. For a few seconds nothing happened, the men in the truck only too happy to watch the dog rip lumps out of his mangled leg. He was barely conscious now, dark red blood dripping from his mouth. Ernest Bullen leaped out of the truck and bounded over to Cuban, kicking him squarely in the stomach. He coughed up more blood, a gurgling sound bubbling up in his throat.

"Are you watching, Jackson? We're gettin' to the good bit now!" Kyle said as he held Shona's face in his cupped hand, forcing her to watch as the dust settled to reveal Ernest Bullen by the tail of the truck, his hands gripping the dangling rope. He walked towards Cuban, kicked the dog off, then looped the rope around his bloodied leg. Cackling over him, he dropped a huge globule of spit on Cuban's face, slowly letting it fall to prolong the humiliation.

"Hit the gas, brother. We bagged ourselves a prize!"

Jumping back into the truck, Ernest whooped as it roared to life once more. Then, with grim inevitability, the handbrake was released, and Cuban's fate was sealed.

Shona watched helplessly, the rope taking an agonizing six seconds to become taut as the truck gathered speed. With one mighty heave of her leg, she kicked Kyle hard in the shin and released herself from his grip. Running as fast as her trembling legs could carry her, she knew she only had seconds to get there.

The rope twanged as its slack ran out. Shona was less than five yards away when her friend skidded from her and his broken body was dragged over every bump, his skin ripping off more with every foot of ground. They picked up speed as they reached the road, totally out of Shona's reach now.

"Cuban! Cuban! I'm here. I'm here!" she screamed.

After less than a minute, Cuban's flailing arms became limp.

~

Shona screamed, put her hands on her knees, then vomited several times. Through her tears, she watched the truck stop at the top of the road. Laughing like hyenas, two men got out and dragged Cuban's lifeless body off the ground, dumping it on the back of the truck like a butchered pig.

She felt the world spin around her. Then she then felt nothing as darkness engulfed her and she hit the ground.

Moments later, Elbie's truck whooshed up to find her lying prone on the dry yellow grass. Jumping out of the cab, he ran over to her and gathered her up in his arms, trying desperately to shake her into consciousness. Eventually, she came to her senses, her eyes darting wildly.

"Elbie! They got Cuban...I need to get to the sheriff, NOW, goddamn it! Lemme go!"

"No, don't you realize? It was a setup! You won't get anywhere with the sheriff. He's on the payroll. You must know that by now!" Elbie's own eyes were filled with angry tears.

"What are you saying? That I'm not supposed to do anything? I just saw my best friend get murdered right in front of me! Chambers is gon' pay for this!"

"Shona, wake up! D'you think anyone is gon' believe you over *him*? He's standin' over there tellin' everyone he just saved your ass from the same fate! He's a goddamn hero to them now!"

"WHAT?" she raged. "Then I'll tell the sheriff it was Bruce! He musta ordered it!"

Exasperated, Elbie grabbed her face in his trembling hands. "Are you SERIOUS? Larry Bruce OWNS THIS TOWN!"

Shona wrestled her body out of the old man's weakening arms and stared at him for a moment, apoplectic with fury.

"ARGH! Those fucking bastards won't get away with this, I goddamn swear it!"

Dizzily, she dragged herself off the ground and looked around for a second. Elbie clambered to his feet also, then put his arm around her and guided her back to his truck.

Back at the site, the crowd was still staring in awe at their boss, who was recovering himself after his *heroics*.

"Sir, are you OK? You got blood on you...are you hurt?"

Kevin, the delivery guy, stared down in concern at Kyle as he watched him rub his bruised shin bone.

"I'm OK, thank you, Kevin. Jeez, that damn colored went straight for me! He was outta control! Caught him in the locker room attacking young Shona, then he went for me when I tried to intervene! Everyone told me he was a violent son'bitch, but I wanted to give him a chance, you know?"

Kevin nodded and offered his arm to help his shaken boss back to his office, the rest of the dissipating crowd smiling sympathetically at them.

It took a performance of monumental proportions to stop Kyle Chambers from screaming out with elation at his masterstroke.

Chapter 61

"Calm down, dear, calm DOWN! What on earth's happened?!"

Dorothy begged the distraught young woman on the other end of the phone to slow down. She could barely get a word in edgewise.

"Oh, my sweet Lord, I'm so sorry, darlin'! I know how fond you were of him. What happened? Oh my, those ANIMALS!"

The conversation ended. Chloe sat perched on the sofa, sipping her coffee.

"Who was that? I could hear crying," she asked, something instinctively panging inside her.

"That was Shona." Dorothy was ashen-faced. "She said her friend Cuban's been murdered! Something about a green truck...and Kyle?"

The old lady told her everything she'd been able to make out from Shona's garbled call.

"Oh, sweet Jesus, no!" Chloe shot up out of her seat, dropping her coffee cup, smashing it to pieces. "I have to get back. I have to be there!" She ran into the hallway to collect her coat and handbag.

"You look after my girl, y'hear me!" Dorothy ordered. "Don't you let anythin' happen to her as well, OK? You promise me?"

Chloe kissed her on the cheek and hugged her tightly. "I promise. Thank you for everything."

She raced to her car, fired the ignition and roared away, looking in her rearview mirror at Dorothy who wiped her damp eyes with her handkerchief as she waved her off. With her eyes fixed on the long, straight road ahead, Chloe dug her foot hard down on the gas pedal, doing everything in her power to do the two-hundred-mile drive home in the shortest possible time. Every passing minute was excruciating.

The thought that Shona would be next on the hit list filled her with gut-wrenching dread.

∼

Shona lay in the dark of the barn, with no idea how long she'd been there. She'd watched the day darken, the burning sun replaced by the pale coolness of the moon. She felt numb, dazed and utterly exhausted. The hard wood of the bench she'd been carving with Cuban only yesterday was the only real indication of the physical world around her, rough and unforgiving against her crumpled body.

Elbie, equally distraught and angry, had driven her home, with Shona heading straight for the barn, leaving him to explain to the Birds what had happened.

She traced her fingers over the smooth, planed edges of the handrail, remembering her chat with Cuban as she was shaping them. He'd been her best friend, the only man she had ever trusted with her secret. Now he was gone and she was completely alone in the world once again.

In the distance, the dull hum of a car engine caught the breeze, getting louder as the car drove nearer. Shona began to drift in and out of consciousness, with everything around her meaning little to her right now.

A light tapping on the door to the barn jolted her briefly from her daze.

"Shona? You awake?" Ruby's soft voice called through a tiny crack in the door. There was a muffled conversation with a second person, but Shona didn't have the strength to play detective.

The barn door opened a few inches, letting in a shard of light which flashed across her tear-stained face. She squinted and let out a murmur as a figure approached, their silhouette outlined by a halo of moonlight. As they got closer, a familiar sweet scent wafted over Shona, who felt the most conflicting confusion of emotions she'd ever felt in her life.

"Are you awake?" The figure reached out to feel for the bench Shona was lying on, then sat down on the edge next to her.

"I'm so sorry. I heard about Cuban. Shona?"

She opened her eyes and, through her blurred vision, found herself gazing into Chloe's soft brown eyes.

"I couldn't save him! I couldn't reach him in time." Her strangled voice came out in pathetic sobs.

"Oh, darlin'."

Chloe scooped Shona's limp body up in her arms and held her close. All her pent-up emotions came flooding out as Chloe rocked her, comforting her as much as she could. Her heart thumped in her chest as she huddled Shona in her arms, who every few minutes succumbed to a fresh wave of grief and gripped onto Chloe's waist. Chloe held her tightly throughout and, even though Shona was a trembling wreck in her arms, the moment just felt right. She pursed her lips and laid a gentle kiss on Shona's crown to comfort her, feeling her soft blonde hair beneath her nose.

Placing light butterfly kisses on the top of her head, Chloe couldn't resist breathing in the scent of Shona's hair. She'd stopped crying now and was snuffling softly, buried in Chloe's arms. Slowly, she raised her head and looked deep into Chloe's eyes as she stroked long locks of blonde hair from her grief-stricken, wet face. Shona trembled at her feather-light touch, the haunting rumble of nausea throbbing in her stomach, but right now she was unable to muster any strength to count her way through it. Chloe held her body tighter with every spasm, shushing her and rocking her gently.

Neither of them noticed the barn door open and Tom and Ruby enter quietly.

"Shona? Tom and I think it's best you come stay in the house tonight. You shouldn't be on your own," Ruby said, her own eyes red from crying. She walked over to her bunk and collected up her nightshirt and washbag. Chloe shuffled aside as Tom reached over her and scooped Shona up off the bench. As he walked out of the barn with her in his arms, Shona looked over his shoulder, her tired eyes not leaving Chloe's gaze.

"Are you alright, Miss Chloe? You were always good to Cuban. He spoke very highly of you–" Ruby broke off to dab her eyes, turning away as she did so.

"I thought very highly of him too, Ruby. I'd better be getting home. Please tell Shona she doesn't have to worry about work for at least a week, OK? Promise me you'll take good care of her. Make sure she eats and gets lots of rest."

Ruby promised and walked Chloe to her car. As she turned the key in the ignition, she looked up to the top window in the house and watched as the light was extinguished, then broke down into uncontrollable sobs of her own.

Chapter 62

The following Thursday morning, just over a week after Cuban's death, was Shona's first day back at work. Chloe caught a fleeting glimpse of her as she scanned the assembled workers from her usual position on the balcony during briefing. She looked hollow, her usual sparkly swagger missing. By the time the meeting had concluded and Chloe had managed to race down the balcony steps, Shona had disappeared.

Elbie finally caught up with her on their 10 o'clock break.

"Hey." He sat down, not sure what to say to her. "I haven't seen you eat yet. You gotta eat."

Shona stared blankly at the cold coffee in her mug.

"OK, Shona. Listen to me." Elbie moved the cup out of her eyeline, causing her to glare at him through bloodshot eyes. "You were the best damn friend he ever had and he was yours. I bet he'd want you to get out o'this dump and leave for the coast as soon as possible, like you always wanted. What the hell'ya waiting for? I'm retiring soon and the Birds have each other. Your friend Chloe? Well, let's face facts here, she'll be married off into a rich family soon and will never need to work again, just sit back and enjoy the profits from this place. It's all coming to a new junction. Shona? You hear me?"

One of the passing workers accidentally clipped Shona's back with his tray.

"Watch what you're fucking doin', asshole!" Shona slammed her fists down, sending her coffee cup skidding across the table. The whole canteen hushed and watched open mouthed as she stormed off, kicking the trash can over by the exit.

∼

"You wanted to see me."

Later that afternoon, Shona appeared in the doorway. The bags under her eyes were the first heartbreaking sight Chloe saw when she looked up from her desk.

"Yeah. I, um...take a seat. Please." She gestured towards the comfy chair she'd deliberately placed opposite her. "How are you?"

Chloe watched Shona's reactions, unsure if she'd calmed down from the incident in the canteen earlier that she'd been told about.

"With all due respect, ma'am, why d'ya call me up here? I got work to do." Shona looked down at her boots, her red eyes stinging.

"It was just to check on you. I haven't had a chance to speak to you properly yet." Chloe fiddled with her pen.

Shona swallowed hard, a lone tear dripping onto her hand.

"Can I go now that you've checked?" Shona hated being so cold with Chloe, but right now she had no idea what was going on between them. She had hazy memories of that night at the barn after Cuban's death. She stood up and walked over to the door.

"Of course. But...I know now why you left Wreckers."

Shona felt her blood turn to ice. She turned around slowly.

"What?" Her voice was eerily quiet.

"I spoke to your old boss." Chloe bit her lip.

"Do I still have a job here, now that you...know?" Shona swallowed hard again.

Just as Chloe was about to reply, Kyle appeared in the doorway, holding two cups of coffee and waiting patiently for the nod to enter. Receiving it, he placed the cups down on the desk pushing one over to Chloe, who left it untouched.

"Good afternoon, Shona, how are you feelin'? Terrible news about Cuban. I'm just glad I was there to stop you gettin' hurt too!"

"Can I go now? Please?" Shona bit down hard in frustration, wanting to get as far away from him as possible. Chloe nodded again.

"Poor kid. She really cared about that crazy friend o'hers. Just a shame he turned out to be just like all the rest of 'em!" Kyle sighed.

Chloe watched Shona leave. Stroking her pebble necklace, she was completely oblivious to every single word Kyle had said.

~

At the Copperpot Inn that Thursday evening, Shona was immediately escorted to the VIP area where Chloe already had a drink waiting for her.

"Sorry I'm a little late, wasn't sure if I was gon' come or not–" Shona apologized as she sat down.

Chloe had found her a few hours after she'd left her office. They hadn't finished their conversation and she wanted a proper chance to explain her reasons for going to Wreckers. She couldn't leave things the way they were and meeting at the Copperpot was perfect. It gave them the privacy they needed under the guise of just another one of her many business meetings.

"Well, I'm glad you did. Oh, I got the bartender to rustle you up a strawberry shake."

"This ain't the sort of place that does strawberry shakes, ma'am." Shona's confused voice was barely above a whisper.

"I know, but I'm a *very* good customer, so the bartender was delighted to oblige! And I did promise you one, remember?" Chloe smiled as she saw the tiniest flicker of light in Shona's tired blue eyes.

Even with the soft tones of "Blueberry Hill" playing in the background, as the night wore on there was a palpable feeling of tension in the air that no amount of small talk could break.

"I wish you would open up to me. I want to help! I can't stand to see you so sad," Chloe said tenderly, wanting to reach across the table to hold Shona's hand.

"I just miss him, you know. It's not so much that he's gone, it's how. I was so powerless. Cuban was trying to help me...it's all my fault." Shona's eyes were welling up for the hundredth time that week.

"What do you mean, *your* fault?"

"Nothing," Shona replied, looking into her glass. She blinked hard, trying to erase the memory of Kyle's leaden body pressed up heavily against her in the locker room, and the knife he threatened to plunge into her. She knew it was pointless saying anything. It was his word against hers.

Chloe watched Shona closely for a few moments, then reached over the table to the napkin holder, an idea of how to lighten the mood crossing her mind.

"Here, what d'you think? I've been practicing." Chloe clumsily tried to make a swan by folding a napkin several times, then presented it to Shona, who couldn't help but smile her approval even though it was terrible. She wiped her eyes and reached over.

"OK, well, just fold this bit over here, that bit there...see, perfect." She fixed the wings on the swan, accidentally hooking her fingers around Chloe's hand.

"Perfect." Chloe smiled, trying to hold on a second longer, but Shona broke away and put her hands on her knees.

"You don't have to be afraid anymore," Chloe murmured across the table.

"I was scared when I heard you'd gone to Wreckers," she replied quietly, circling the top of her glass with her finger, unable to meet Chloe's soft gaze.

"Why?"

"I'm…different." She felt her throat sting as the word caught in her throat.

But Chloe didn't flinch.

"Not to me."

Shona's eyes connected finally with Chloe's, both their hearts pounding like jackhammers.

"What exactly did you find out?" she asked, terrified of the answer.

"I know why you left Mississippi," Chloe replied, watching for her reaction.

Putting her hands underneath the table again, Shona clenched her fists tightly, trying to control her breathing, her head spinning. *She doesn't know about Louisiana, though*, she thought. That was at least some comfort.

"I'd better go. Thanks for the shake."

"You're welcome. You know you can talk to me about anything, don't you? I'll understand. You can trust me." She reached over again for Shona's hand, but she stood up to leave. "Hey, you don't wan' go see a movie with me, do you?" Chloe blurted out, desperate not to let her evening with Shona end too soon. "It might help take your mind off things for a little while?"

It felt like an eternity before Shona replied.

"Sure. OK."

Chloe beamed as she picked up her purse, left a few dollar bills on the table and led the way outside to her car.

They arrived only a few minutes before the start of the movie, and the usher showed them to their seats near the back of the theater. Sitting between Chloe and the wall, Shona was trapped, but for the first time in her life, she didn't want to escape.

As the lights dimmed to near-darkness, both women shuffled in their seats to get comfortable, placing their elbows on the same armrest between them. Glancing down, Shona saw Chloe's fingers trace the armrest as if searching for something.

Biting her lip, Shona edged her hand ever so slightly nearer to Chloe's, moving her little finger a fraction closer each second.

"Here are your seats, sir, ma'am."

As the usher from before reappeared at her side with two more latecomers, Chloe dropped her elbow from the arm rest a split second after Shona, hoping Chloe hadn't seen the movement, whipped her hand away too.

"What did you think of the movie?" Chloe asked as they walked the short distance back to the car.

"It was good. I feel for anybody bein' judged by others. Just don't seem fair to me," Shona replied, her hands rooted in her pockets as she kicked at a tiny piece of gravel.

"Wanna grab a bite to eat at Ed's?" Chloe asked as if it were the most normal thing in the world to do.

"Best not, it's gettin' real late and I gotta be up early for work. Mr. Ellis won't like it if I'm late." Shona's lips briefly allowed a flicker of a smile to cross them.

"I'd better get you home, then, Miss Jackson," Chloe sighed as she opened up the passenger side door.

She had really missed seeing that smile.

Chloe put her key in the door and opened it as quietly as she possibly could. Tiptoeing to the stairs, she lifted her foot to the first step but was stopped in her tracks as a lamp clicked on in the living room.

"Good night, was it?"

Eleanor Bruce rocked back and forth in her chair, her mouth set firmly as she stared at the little carriage clock on the mantelpiece. It was nearly 12 o'clock, and her daughter had only just got home.

"Yes, it was, actually. Why are you still up? It's late."

"Your father and I have been talking." Eleanor's facial expression was impossible for Chloe to read.

"OK?"

"The business could be in trouble."

The enormity of the words that came out of Eleanor Bruce's mouth was completely incongruous with her closed body language.

"In trouble? How?" Chloe entered the living room and perched on the end of the sofa.

"Investors. You know what they're like—they want a sure thing."

"I don't understand."

"Business insight's not really your strong suit, is it?" Eleanor said scathingly.

"Get to the point, Mother," Chloe replied, her tone equally acerbic.

"Well, earlier this evening, a rich young hotshot was in town for one night only on business and called an impromptu meeting with the management team. Your absence tonight did not go unnoticed," she added. "Anyway, after the usual talk about Jeffrey and your father getting older, the conversation naturally drifted towards the future of the business."

"*And–*" Chloe pressed, pursing her lips.

"And...there's concern with your lack of focus. They haven't seen you at events lately, you weren't there tonight...Can you understand why they have concerns, Chloe?" She turned to stoke the fading embers of the fire.

"How did the conversation end?" Chloe stared at her.

"They wanted assurance," Eleanor replied, spinning her chair around to fully face her daughter.

"What kind of *assurance*?"

"They want to be sure that when Jeffrey and your father are long gone, the business will be in safe hands. You haven't given them that impression." Eleanor paused. "But they seemed to like Kyle."

"*Kyle*?" Chloe screwed her face up.

"He's shown commitment to the company and a willingness to potentially take over one day. He also mentioned that he'd take care of you, which your father and I were naturally thrilled about, especially as you've been a little...*distracted* lately."

"*Meaning*?" Chloe replied, clenching her teeth.

Eleanor fixed her cold stare onto Chloe. "Meaning that if you and Kyle showed a united front, the old investors are likely to stay and this hotshot will be sure to invest his newfound wealth with us. You know as well as I do there have been new companies shooting up all over the place lately. He could easily go elsewhere, no doubt to one of our competitors, and put us out of business. You understand what I'm saying, don't you, dear?"

"What are you *really* asking of me, Mother?"

"It's no secret, he adores you and your father likes the idea of the business being in Kyle's hands. You two together make a great team."

"For who exactly?" Chloe felt her tenuous grasp on her temper slipping.

"For *all* the employees. You see, if you don't like the idea, the business may have to lay off some staff. It would be starting with people like, for example...Shona. She was the last one in. The old man too, he won't be needed anymore. They'll have to try to find jobs elsewhere, but I can't think of another place around here that would take on a female mechanic and an old man." She shook her head with fake pity.

"That's blackmail!"

"That's *business*, sweetie. We have to do right by our men and by our livelihoods."

"So, what you're saying is I have to get together with Kyle for Shona and Elbie to keep their jobs, right?"

"It's hardly a chore, darling. I mean, look at him! He's handsome, comes from wealth...why, he's the most sought-after man around! What's not to like?"

Chloe recoiled in horror as she turned away and headed upstairs to bed, feeling sick to her stomach at her mother's cold-blooded proposal.

Chapter 63

"Well, would'ya look at *this*!" Deputy Paul grinned as he prized open the window blinds in his ground floor office to watch the very late worker race to reach the reception to sign in before the buzzer sounded. Kyle walked up behind him and stared in disbelief at who it was.

"Come on, just one minute late! That's all I need you to be. One *tiny* minute and you're gone!" He held his breath, hoping the sprinting worker would stumble and fall—anything that would cost them valuable seconds.

Shona had woken up that Friday morning half an hour later than she would usually set off for her normally leisurely stroll to work, her late night with Chloe taking its toll on her punctuality. She'd raced to put her clothes on, grabbed her bag and run as fast as she could, darting down any shortcut she could find and hopping over every fence. Judging by the trucks that were already making their way down the driveway to go out on their deliveries, she guessed that she was already late. If not, then any minute she could claw back was crucial. They needed no excuse and she couldn't lose her job now—not when she was so close to having enough money saved up to afford her one-way ticket to California. Her lungs burned as she ran the last hundred yards down the driveway.

"Mornin' all, I got those figures tha–" Ron Black stopped in mid-sentence as he popped his head around the door on his way to his office upstairs. "What you guys looking at?" he asked, sidling over to the window.

When he looked out of the window and saw who it was, he doubled back and headed outside to the main entrance, almost running into the sweaty, exhausted wreck launching herself at the sign-in log at reception.

"Shona! Hey, calm down!" Ron caught her as she fell into his arms, just as the buzzer sounded. "I ain't ever seen you late once and you made it in time, OK?" He smiled as he watched her regain her composure. "I gotta say, though, I can't fault your commitment! I should ring Guinness and tell'em to put you in that new world record book they got!" he joked.

She smiled back, mouthed a *thank you* as he left her to sign in and headed up to his office.

"Out late last night?" Kyle drawled, appearing by the door with his arms folded.

"Pardon me?" she panted, still trying to catch her breath.

"You were lucky this time. You won't be lucky again. It'll be my pleasure to shut that door in your pretty lil' face, got it?" Kyle hissed at her, then swaggered off down the corridor.

For the rest of that morning, Shona struggled to concentrate. Her late night with Chloe had been the reason she nearly didn't make work on time, but she didn't regret it. It just made her want to spend more time with her. As the 10 o'clock buzzer sounded, she ran to the bathroom to smarten herself up in case she saw Chloe on the balcony, then raced to the canteen to catch the last ten minutes of break.

"You OK?" Elbie asked as she sat down next to him with her tray.

"Y'seen Chloe anywhere?" she whispered, smoothing the sides of her hair down.

"Yeah, 'bout an hour ago. You haven't touched your food yet, c'mon, you need to eat!" he coaxed.

"I'm not hungry." Shona pushed her plate away, her restless foot tapping on the floor. She had far too many butterflies in her stomach to care about eating. It was a welcome change, though, to the usual churning feeling in her gut she used to get. This reaction to her feelings for Chloe had become less frequent lately. The more she concentrated on her breathing and keeping calm when she was around her, the quicker the spasms subsided.

"There's a damn work drinks thing tonight at the usual place, you goin'?" Elbie asked, looking nonplussed himself about it.

"Don't know, maybe," she replied, her untouched food sitting in front of her as she gazed hopefully at the balcony.

That Friday night, the Copperpot was packed to the rafters with workers from Ellis and Bruce. The air was filled with laughter and the smell of beer as people stood around talking and listening to the music playing in the background.

"I'll just have a glass of water, please," Shona asked the barman, who looked confused, then reminded her politely that it was a free bar.

But Shona wasn't there for the party.

She searched the bar area and tables beyond. To her left, she saw Deputy Paul leering at two waitresses, who were only putting up with it in the hope of separating him from the dollar bills he was holding. Over on the other side of the room was

Ron Black, chatting happily to one of the new drivers. Somewhere in the bar was Larry Bruce, his bellowing laughter resonating loudly across the space—he was clearly enjoying himself, no doubt on his umpteenth whiskey neat.

And then, directly in front of her as Shona turned, around twenty yards away, was a sight she did not expect to see—one that filled her with happiness and revulsion simultaneously.

"My God," she murmured to herself, her eyes unblinking.

Over by the jukebox was Chloe wearing a dark green cocktail dress, effortlessly fitting her as if she had been poured into it. She was picking out the next few songs and smiling *that* smile, the one that sent electricity up Shona's spine. Seconds later, the color faded from her daydream when a smartly dressed man sidled up behind her and threaded his arms around her waist. What sickened her was that Chloe didn't even seem to flinch. She actually looked to be encouraging him.

"Son of a bitch!" Angry, hot tears pricked her eyes. The times they'd shared moments together, their chats and little looks to each other. They were all false.

Shona had yet again read a situation completely wrong.

"Oh my God, no! It's not what–" Chloe said to herself as she turned around and caught Shona staring across the distance at her. Realizing what she must have seen, she broke herself free of Kyle's cloying arms and swam through the crowd to where Shona had been standing seconds before. But it was too late, the damage had been done and Chloe, in her five-inch heels, was never going to catch up with Shona, who had fled full tilt out of the Copperpot and into the darkness.

"Hey, where you going? Ellis is just about to make a speech, then we gotta do one each too, remember?" Kyle caught up with her in the parking lot and, holding her arm firmly, walked her back into the bar, droning on about the finer point of the speech he had perfected last night in front of the mirror.

Chloe closed her eyes as she walked, just wanting to jump in her car to find Shona.

∼

Tom looked out of the kitchen window, alerted to the car thundering down his driveway by the headlights blaring against his kitchen blind. He strode over to the door just as the driver stepped out of the car and ran up the steps.

"Miss Chloe? Everything OK?"

"Hi Tom, sorry it's so late. Is Shona here?" Chloe turned her gloves over and over in her sweating palms.

"She is...well, she *was*! Came back around twenny minutes ago. I ain't see her like this for a while, thought she was startin' to deal with losin' Cuban, but she came back with tears in her eyes, stomping around like a bear with a sore head...and to top it off now, she's gone out on that lunatic horse! That's like suicide, I tell ya. That horse feels every single emotion Shona feels, you know! Tenfold!"

Chloe's face blanched.

"Tom, where did she go?" she asked, panic rising by the second within her.

"To the river, no doubt. It's her favorite place. But riding Storm, with how she's feelin' now? She'll end up breakin' her damn–"

Chloe didn't wait for him to finish. She flew to her car and sped off towards the river, her heart beating wildly. It wasn't too long before she spotted a rider galloping at crazy speed along the bank parallel to the road in the fast-fading light. Chloe slammed her foot down on the gas pedal, trying to catch up with the manic horse, which seemed to be a near impossible task.

Shona yanked hard on the reins and galloped towards the road. In her blind rage, she continued rapidly towards the one car that happened to be on the road at the same time. She didn't care—she would ride straight through it if she had to. As the car got closer, Shona's resolve got weaker. At the final second, she pulled the reins in and turned the horse, flying over the top of Storm's head and landing on the ground below.

"My God, Shona!" Chloe skidded to a halt and jumped out, rushing towards her.

The rider groaned, but she was moving. She punched the ground and sat up.

"What the *hell* you doin' here? Pulling out in front of my horse like that? AGAIN!"

"I'm so sorry...It's just, you left so suddenly, I wanted to make sure you were OK–" Chloe rambled, reaching down to help Shona to her feet.

"I'm fine. You didn't need to come out here and *run me over again* to check I was OK!" She screwed her face up, shrugging Chloe's hands off her.

"What you saw with Kyle wasn't–"

"I didn't think you liked him," Shona interrupted, trudging over to settle Storm who was dragging her hoof through the dust and snorting.

"You don't understand what it's like for someone like me–"

"Why? Because I'm not smart? Or because I'm not rich?" She stroked the mare's head, switching between whispering in her ear to reassure her everything was OK and turning to Chloe to scold her.

At that moment, Chloe wanted, more than anything in the whole world, to swap places with Storm.

"That's not what I mean. I have to *behave* in a certain way. I can't just do what I want."

"WHY? Who's stoppin' you? You're free! You wanna drive to the coast with the roof down? Y'can do that. You wanna paint? Y'can do that too. Because THAT makes you happy! Those who don't wanna see y'do that stuff obviously don't give a rat's ass about your happiness, so why would you care what *they* want?" Shona's eyes were ablaze.

"It's not as simple as that! Please...just try to trust me on this one." Chloe reached out to Shona, who again dropped her shoulder and rested her hot cheeks against Storm's mane. Shona clenched her teeth and sighed deeply, terrified of the answer to her next question.

"Do you like him? You think you can...*love* him?"

Her words hit Chloe like ice water.

"I don't know...I don't know. It just has to be this way," she replied unconvincingly.

"For who? Him? Your parents? Who you doin' it for?"

Untangling the reins, Shona climbed back on Storm.

"Let me ask you one thing, Chloe."

She nodded, gazing up at Shona through her glassy eyes.

"If he's where your future's gon' be..." she paused, feeling a stab through her heart as she noticed the diamond necklace Chloe was now wearing, which matched so damn perfectly with her expensive green sequined dress. "Then why the *hell* are you all the way out here, tryin' so hard to justify it to ME?"

She turned Storm to face the way she was heading and galloped off, leaving Chloe to mouth the answer to that question into the night air.

An hour later, after redoing her smudged, tear-stained make-up in the car, Chloe walked back to the Copperpot from the parking lot, wanting to be anywhere else instead.

It was all going wrong.

Her mother beckoned her over as she traipsed through the door.

"We have a driver taking me and your father home, darlin'.

The night is still young; you two kids have fun," Eleanor said, winking at Kyle who did the same back.

Chloe sighed heavily. This wasn't who she wanted to be alone with right now, but as the crowds staggered off home in their various states of drunkenness, Kyle placed his jacket around her bare shoulders and grasped her hand in his.

"I'd be very grateful, ma'am, if you could drive me home," he slurred as they reached her car.

Chloe didn't reply. She dumped him in the passenger seat and started the engine robotically as if she were a cab driver who'd just picked up a fare.

"By the way, you look delicious in that dress. I know I've had too much to drink, but I'd say it anyway. Every man alive wants to be where I am right now," Kyle drawled, walking his fingers up Chloe's thigh.

"You're drunk," she replied flatly. She stared at the road up ahead, trying to ignore his wandering hand as it stroked the soft skin of her inside leg for the next two miles.

"Y'know I've wanted you for a long time now. I'm gon' make you real happy." His fingers drifted higher.

"Alright, here we are," she announced as she pulled into his driveway.

"You're takin' me in, aren't you? Can't expect me to look after myself tonight? I'll hold you responsible if anything bad happens to me," Kyle chuckled as he hit his head on the doorframe getting out of the car and fell onto the grass. Chloe couldn't remember him being this drunk. He'd seemed perfectly lucid in the bar when she'd returned. She rushed around the car to pick him up off the floor and hooked his arm over her shoulder, practically dragging him to the front door.

"I promise not to bite–unless you want me too!" He looked at her, sniggering at his own joke.

He handed Chloe his key and, after carrying him to the living room, she flung him like a sack of potatoes into the nearest chair. Hands on hips, she looked around the room in disgust. The place was a pigpen. All around, there were boxes of possessions and pictures that hadn't been hung. Reams of paperwork, receipts, letters and scrunched-up pieces of notepaper were strewn about, covering the old mahogany coffee table in front of the blue Palomino plastic couch. It was the stark opposite of the office he kept immaculate at work.

As she began tidying up, Kyle heaved his inebriated body out of the chair and stumbled over to the well-stocked portable bar.

"See, the most important things I *have* unpacked!" He grinned, poured a large whiskey and downed it in one. "Want one?" he asked, remembering his manners.

"No, thank you. I'd better be getting home."

Chloe turned to head towards the front door, not wanting to stay a moment longer. She had done the decent thing by getting Kyle home safely, but his company was grating on her.

"Why? Your parents know where you are and have encouraged us to *have fun*, remember? Stay. We could have a *lot of fun* together!"

He lunged over to plant a wet kiss on her powdered cheek, his stubble grazing against her soft skin. She pulled away, turning her head to the side.

"No, Kyle, I don't want *that*. Look, I'll fix you some coffee before I go, OK?"

She smiled sweetly and hurried away from him, trying to remain calm.

Slowly, he followed her into the kitchen, eyeing every movement she made in her tight dress, the thought of her gorgeous body underneath driving him wild with desire. As the kettle began to boil, he slunk up to her and draped his arms over her shoulders, running his hands down her body and over her tiny waist. Holding her hair back, he kissed her heavily on the neck, the odor of whiskey catching in Chloe's throat.

"Kyle, I said NO!" She spun around and pushed him away from her with both hands. He sprawled backward on the kitchen counter, a look of surprise on his face.

"Hey, I'm sorry. I thought..." He held his hands up, trying to apologize, but Chloe was in no mood to listen.

"Look, go sleep it off, OK? I'll see you at work on Monday,"

Chloe straightened her dress, picked up her purse and left. She sat in her car for ten minutes, holding a trembling hand to her knees as she fought to control her shaking legs until she felt calm enough to drive the three miles home, blinking continuously to clear the shocked, angry tears from her exhausted eyes.

Chapter 64

"Nice evening?"
Eleanor Bruce smiled as she stared up the stairs at her daughter, who was standing in a daze at the top. It was 11:30 a.m.

Chloe faked a smile, but inside her emotions were swirling.

"So? You gon' see the *dashing* Mr. Chambers again?" Eleanor clasped her hands together.

"Of course. I'll see him at work, won't I?" Chloe knew she was being flippant.

"Oh, you *know* what I mean! They'll all be talking about your big date by now. I've told quite a few of the women in town this morning, and they were real jealous! There's a long list of women who'd jump to be in your position."

"Mother, why would you tell everybody?"

"Oh, I know, but I couldn't help myself. You know I like to gossip." She chuckled, thinking nothing of her indiscretion. "Anyway, you don't need to worry, dear. You got no competition! Apparently, Mr. Handsome has been telling everyone about how much he adores you! Says there's no other girl on his radar!"

Chloe stared openmouthed at her mother. *Was it possible I'd misread the situation last night?* She thought. Maybe he was just so consumed with lust for her that he couldn't help himself. She had no experience at all with men; maybe this was just how it was? *Did Kyle really love me after all?* Her head was buzzing with confusion.

"I'm gon' go to my den for a bit," she said.

"Well, don't you spend too much time on those silly paintings, I mean, not now you're part of the hottest couple in town. You have events to go to and clothes to pick out, you ain't got time for all that," Eleanor said, wagging a finger at her. "Oh, by the way, Kyle is coming over for dinner tonight. We want to welcome him to the family properly."

Chloe nodded impassively as she headed down the basement steps to her sanctuary.

~

"Hey Elbie."

Shona walked over to Elbie's farmhouse on the same Saturday morning. It was only a mile or so from the Birds' farmhouse, south of the river. He looked up at her from underneath the hood of his beloved truck.

"Shona, what a lovely surprise. Come in, and I'll make us a drink."

Elbie poured her a glass of sweet tea and sat down with her at his kitchen table. After a few minutes of small talk and closed answers, his intuition told him that something was bothering her.

"Come on, talk to me. Ain't no point keeping this all in, you hear?"

He squeezed her hand gently.

"I just really miss Cuban and I...um...miss Chloe too." Shona's eyes started to harden. "She's with that creep, and there's nothin' I can do about it. I don't expect you to understand, Elbie, but Cuban told me he'd confided in you about my feelings for her." She sniffed and wiped her eyes with the back of her hand as she finished her sentence, staring nervously at the old man as she waited for his response. After a few moments, he cleared his throat and chose his next words wisely.

"Listen. I might not understand what y'have going on with Miss Chloe, but I know it can't be easy for you," he said, holding Shona's hand. "Yeah, Cuban did come see me, told me everything. He was worried that he wasn't able to help you, said that you'd saved him, given him a shot at life when everybody else shut their doors on him." Elbie's kind eyes sparkled as he cleared his throat again. "Look, I don't care who it is you have feelings for, I just care that you're happy. You're one o'the special ones, girl. One o'life's very rare gems."

Shona couldn't hold in her emotions a single second longer. She hugged Elbie as if he were the only person left in the world she could anchor herself to.

"What do I do now? It's all such a mess!"

"You wait." He drained his glass and smacked his lips.

"Wait?"

"Yep. You'll win her by just bein' you. That's what made her come to you in the first place, wasn't it? *You* are what she's been searching for all these years. I see things others don't see; I can tell when there's a glint in somebody's eye for someone. I had it for my darlin' wife. You two both have it for each other."

"Yeah? But she's with him! She doesn't know the half of what a monster he is," Shona said, fiddling with her glass.

"She will soon enough. And when she does, you'll be there for her."

∼

Later that Saturday evening, the doorbell to the Bruces' mansion chimed.

"That's him!" Eleanor chirped as she skipped down the stairs, almost barging Antonia out the way.

Chloe sat upstairs, frozen with confusion in her room. Downstairs, she could hear muffled voices of greetings and her mother doting on Kyle, hanging on his every word.

"Chloe, honey. Come down here," Eleanor called up the stairs.

Taking a deep breath, she turned the doorknob and sidled down the staircase.

"Hello, my sweetness! Gosh, you look amazing!" Kyle grabbed her shoulders, pulling her in to kiss her lavishly on the cheek. She wrinkled her nose, smelling the fresh alcohol on his breath. This clearly hadn't been his first port of call that evening.

"Kyle, m'boy!" Larry Bruce extended his huge hand.

The two of them shared a moment of backslapping and complimenting each other on the latest deals they had pulled off, with Kyle bragging to Bruce about the two-hundred-dollar prize he had won at poker earlier that week at Red's.

"Men, eh? You'll get used to it, Chloe," Eleanor said, smiling wearily at her daughter.

Just as the four of them were about to head to the dinner table, Kyle remembered something he'd left in his car. Moments later he returned, a wide grin spreading across his chiseled features.

"For you, my angel," he purred, handing her a flat rectangular box with a black ribbon wrapped around it, held in place by a small bow.

"What is it?"

"Open it," he replied, his coal-black eyes fixed on her.

She pulled at the ribbon and took off the lid, then peeled

301

back the tissue paper. There inside was a lacy black sequined cocktail dress.

"Um. Thank you," Chloe held up the garish, extremely low-cut dress by its thin straps.

"Thought you might wanna wear it for dinner? Then I can see how gorgeous you look in it!" Kyle stared at her, as did her parents who seemed to delight in his expensive gift.

"What? Now? But I'm wearing this." She smiled nervously, smoothing down her casual white pencil skirt and loose-fitting peach blouse.

"Darling, Kyle has gone to the trouble to buy you a gift and it would be rude not to go try it on," Eleanor coaxed diplomatically, but her eyes flashed fire at her insubordinate daughter.

Realizing she was outnumbered, Chloe trudged back upstairs with Kyle's gift draped over her forearm. She pulled off her comfortable clothes and squeezed herself into the scratchy dress. It looked perfect on her, as all clothes did, but she felt sick to her stomach as the reflection of somebody she no longer recognized stared back at her in the full-length bedroom mirror. She stopped adjusting herself, hearing muffled voices from below and the mention of her name.

"I don't know what's got into her, but y'have our blessing to sort that mixed-up head of hers out." Eleanor laughed as Kyle replied with his typical *knight in shining armor* repertoire, then excused himself to stand at the bottom of the stairs.

"You OK, honey? Need me to come up and help?"

"No. I'll be down in a minute." Chloe finished getting herself ready in front of the mirror and sighed deeply as she descended the staircase.

"Wow!" he breathed.

"It looks lovely on you, see? Now, I better get changed. I don't wanna spill anything on it." Chloe turned to head back up the stairs, but Kyle gripped her arm tightly.

"Keep it on," he said, clenching his teeth.

Leading her back into the dining room, he pulled out Chloe's seat and sat her down.

"Aren't you lucky!" Eleanor gushed as she and her husband looked over the table at their daughter in unison and smiled.

"Trust me, this is just the start," Kyle said, his menacing glare going unnoticed as he fixed it on Chloe, who sat silently staring at her soup.

Chapter 65

Resting her weary head in her hands and rubbing her throbbing temples, Chloe narrowed her eyes, trying to make sense of the paperwork in front of her late that Monday evening. Her agitated mind was already full to bursting. She knew she had to try harder with Kyle, for the sake of the business, but it wasn't *his* face she saw in her dreams, not his hot breath she wanted to feel all over her body. She sat in her dimly lit office, daydreaming about how different her life could be if only she were brave enough to say the words.

As the day began to darken, she packed up her things and grabbed her keys. Kyle and her father had left an hour earlier to attend a *business meeting* at Red's, or so they called it, and Ron Black had been summoned to the Copperpot by Jeffrey Ellis. This left Chloe to lock the place up, which she didn't mind doing as it meant she got some peace to think, without Kyle swanning around.

With her head bowed as she locked her office door, she turned on her heels, walking straight into the quietly approaching worker who had been tasked to deliver a pile of forms to her. With paper flying everywhere, she bent down instinctively to help the poor worker pick it all up.

"Oh my, I'm *so* sorry! I–" Chloe began, before raising her head and locking eyes with the worker. A pair of gorgeous blue eyes gazed back at her.

"That's OK. You alright?"

"I'm fine. I'm just leaving for the night. I guess I was in too much of a hurry." Chloe flashed a lopsided grin as she fumbled with the papers.

"No harm done. Mr. Black asked me to give these to you as he was leaving. I just had to wash up, then bring them straight to you. Didn't wan' get no oil or grease on 'em!" She chuckled.

Chloe lowered her eyes to Shona's hands, which she saw were now impeccably scrubbed clean, only a tiny remnant of the day's hard work now visible beneath her nail beds. She felt a strange flutter as her eyes wandered over Shona's long, perfectly shaped fingers, which she had unwittingly begun brushing against her own in her attempt to help collect the dropped forms. Shona's gentle touch sent shivers up Chloe's spine, her soft skin intriguing her. Her heart thudded in her chest, her eyes searching for some kind of sign that Shona was feeling the electricity between them too.

Clutching the collected papers, they both stood up. Chloe had never felt so scared in all her life but she knew that Shona was the safest person in the world she could be standing with right now. But her eyes were giving nothing away. It was as if they were the loyal gatekeepers to her heart, deciding whether or not to let Chloe past them and access her soul. As long as the moment felt, it was still over far too soon.

"Well, I guess I'd better be gettin' home now. I got loads of stuff to do–" Shona lied.

"OK, well, I'll see you tomorrow then?" Chloe replied, trying to mask her disappointment.

"Bye." Shona lingered for a second, then turned.

"Bye, Shona." Chloe watched as she disappeared down the balcony steps.

"What am I doing?" she whispered to herself. Shona had no *special* feelings for her. She clearly only saw Chloe as a friend, someone she could talk about in her letters to Dorothy, another female to chat with when the conversations with the men at work became too lurid. Walking over to her car, she wished that Shona could have shown her something tonight, some nugget of feeling.

Little did she know that all her confusion could have been solved by one confession Shona had been too petrified to make. Shona hid behind a bush watching Chloe's car until it was out of sight. Mercifully, her stomach lurches were absent again, replaced by an unfamiliar fluttering sensation. She felt the moment she'd been waiting for, the moment to tell her how she felt, had completely eluded her. There was something in Chloe's eyes before that had given her a glimmer of hope and with no one else around, it surely would have been safe. But if she'd said those words to her tonight, she couldn't be totally sure they would be reciprocated.

She'd felt safe the last time.

Chapter 66

Everyone was in a jovial mood that Friday evening, apart from Chloe, who sat quietly on the sofa next to Kyle. He popped the champagne cork and cheered as the first flushes of liquid spilled through his fingers and onto the Persian rug. They were celebrating after Jack Edwards had visited the site earlier that week and, after an impressively exuberant performance by Kyle, made good on his promise from the fete to go ahead with his investment in the future of Ellis and Bruce.

"Here's to us all! Edwards loves us! I can smell the money already." He clinked glasses with an equally ebullient Larry Bruce.

"Here you go, darlin', not too much for you though, you know how it goes straight to your head! I don't want no woman of mine embarrassing me," Kyle said in a low voice, only pouring a token amount of champagne into Chloe's glass. She smiled meekly, gritting her teeth as she suppressed her outrage at his condescension.

"Well done, boys." Eleanor raised her glass. "Oh, I forgot to mention at dinner, I went into town today to get my dress altered for the gala next week and I saw those two filthy, disgusting animals outside Stella's shop again. I think they're

Charlie's friends. Eurgh, it makes my skin crawl." She shuddered, clasping her fingertips to her neck.

"Pete and Ronnie? They still in town?" Bruce exclaimed, lowering his champagne flute.

"Walking 'round together without a care in the world. They're giving this town a bad name. We all know they're together, living in sin! No children, no wives! It's the worst kept secret in Daynes!" Eleanor scowled at the thought.

"Do they look happy?" Chloe asked quietly, staring down at her untouched champagne.

The room fell deathly silent.

"Excuse me, dear, I didn't quite catch that?" Eleanor replied coolly.

"Pete and Ronnie...do they look happy together?" Chloe repeated.

Eleanor grunted dismissively as Larry Bruce guffawed at his daughter's simplistic attitude. Kyle drained his champagne flute, his eyes not leaving his insubordinate girlfriend's questioning face.

Chapter 67

"Shona!"

Ron Black walked up behind her quietly. It was a week later, and that Friday morning Shona was hard at it, scrubbing the tool room floor.

"Sir," Shona replied, placing her hand over her heart as she stood up. "You made me jump!"

"I just wan' say well done! Some damn good ideas you had there." He slapped her heartily on the back. She froze in bemusement as he went on his way.

"Did you see that, Elbie?" Shona exclaimed.

"Sure did! What in the hell's he talkin' bout?"

She shook her head just as the morning break buzzer honked. They smiled, only minutes earlier remarking to each other how hungry they were.

"Our prayers have been answered! Now we can go rejoice in the *slop* Lou decides he wants to delight us with," Elbie said with a wry smile.

As they walked through the corridors towards the canteen, they were stopped every few feet by back-slaps and looks of admiration towards Shona.

"Has everyone had their head tested?" Elbie screwed his face up, dumbfounded at the positive cheers and handshakes Shona was getting from every man she passed. As they walked into the canteen, one table even clapped in her direction.

"This is freakin' me out now. What the hell's goin' on?" she asked, bewildered.

"No idea," Elbie replied.

Shona headed over to the serving area but as she looked over the counter and into the kitchen behind, her confusion took on a whole new level. Chef Lou was stirring a pot of delicious-smelling soup with pleasure and singing loudly, his raspy voice squeezing out the lyrics to "Roll Over Beethoven." His pudgy hand was clenched tightly around the wooden spoon he was intermittently using as a microphone. Opening his eyes, he turned to see Shona standing in front of him blank-faced.

"Shona! Well, bless your heart, I had y'down as nothing but a nigger lovin' lil' tramp. But I see you as so much more now. Hell, anything you want, I'll cook it for you!" He planted both palms face down on the counter, eagerly waiting for her request.

"Can I ask why?"

"Well, darlin', whoever makes it so that I get a pay raise, I get Friday afternoons off to go take my little girl to dancing lessons, I get a better uniform *and* I get better quality food to cook is more than alright with me!"

Shona was none the wiser. She pointed at the eggs in front of him and put some toast on her tray, then nodded a thank you to Lou, who grinned as she walked back to her table.

"Randy, can I borrow you a second?" She beckoned him over after seeing him wave at her.

"Hey, Shona!" He gave her a side-on hug, his heavy bulk almost squashing her.

"Everyone's being real strange to me today. What's goin' on?"

"You don't know? Oh, of course, you didn't go last night, did you? Well, we had some drinks at the Copperpot, organized by

Miss Chloe. Her father and Kyle couldn't make it; I think it was something to do with another meeting they had to attend at Red's. But Miss Chloe wanted to show her gratitude to the workers so paid for the free bar out of her own pocket. We'd just got the news about the big new investment from Mr. Edwards, y'see? She got up and did a speech and–" Randy paused.

"And? Come on, Randy," Shona said, impatient for him to get to the point of his meandering story.

"She said there was gon' be some immediate changes 'round here and they were all *your* ideas, so we have you to thank for them." Randy beamed at her.

Shona looked over at Elbie, who raised his eyebrows.

"So, what ideas did she mention?" she pressed.

"I can't remember all of 'em, but there were a lot! We're all getting a pay raise with immediate effect and she's ordering better quality overalls. Oh, and we're all gon' finish at 12 o'clock on a Friday, startin' from next week! You really are a miracle, girl! How in the hell d'you pull that off? Don't even think she listens to Mr. Chambers the way she listens to you."

Shona's brain whirred as she sat down at the table with Elbie.

"Quite the hero 'round here, aren't you?"

A dulcet voice purred into Shona's ear as a faint shadow fell across the table in front of her. She spun around, the beautiful face she had completely and utterly fallen for now only inches from her own. Breathing in her intoxicating perfume, Shona couldn't stop herself from smiling when she noticed Chloe's shiny pebble necklace was once again sitting proudly in its former position. It was clear from the blush pink blouse she was wearing that she'd deliberately picked her outfit that morning to compliment it.

"Yeah, seems like it! All thanks to you, I hear." She beamed as Chloe stood up straight.

"Well, I just listened."

"I appreciate it. So do the guys. But, how did you get it past Kyle and your father?"

"I have my ways." Chloe suddenly looked a little uncomfortable.

"Thank you...for listening." Shona fought to hide the blush that had crept upon her cheeks. "Hey, would you like to go see a movie again tomorrow night?" she said, unsure as to where she'd found the courage to ask.

"Oh, Shona, I'd love to...but I've organized a little fundraiser of my own this Saturday. I found out from Ron, when he was doing the accounts, that some of the people in town didn't seem to receive any share of the money we raised at the fete last month." She paused, noticing that Shona hadn't registered any surprise on her face at this. Thinking for a minute, her eyes glowed. "Hey, why don't you come help me? I can't be everywhere, so I'm gon' need people I can rely on...and trust...to help the evening run smoothly—"

She barely reached the end of her sentence before Shona nodded her answer.

"I'd be honored to help you, ma'am. What would you like me to do?" Shona's hands were shaking so much, she had to hide them under the table.

"Leave it with me," Chloe replied cryptically.

She flashed a smile at both of them before turning to leave. Elbie shook his head affectionately at Shona, who began to cough when she realized she hadn't taken a breath for at least ten seconds, completely entranced by the departing figure of Chloe walking back up the steps to her office. She turned to the old man and punched his shoulder gently, her cheeks burning at being busted by him.

Randy, however, saw everything from his table. Although he was out of earshot of their conversation, he hadn't missed the look on Shona's face as Chloe left her table. Like most of the workers at Ellis and Bruce, Randy was quite a simple being. He didn't look for trouble, but his weakness in wanting to please, to fit in, was his Achilles' heel.

"Kyle won't be happy with this," he said to himself, secretly ecstatic that he finally had something worthwhile to offer his boss in his *weekly update* with him after lunch.

∽

"Who the hell does this WHORE think she is, manipulating my girlfriend? I'd never have agreed to the changes if I'd known! Jackson's made a fool outta me! What, she some white Rosa Parks now, messing up the system?"

As expected, Kyle was enraged by Randy's report informing him about the impromptu drinks reception ordered by Chloe and her speech to the workers, while he was at Red's capitalizing on his lucky streak in poker. Larry Bruce had just left for his weekend away at Jack Edwards' ranch and had told him he was *not to be disturbed*, no doubt so he could concentrate fully on getting as much money out of him as possible. He'd put Kyle in charge in his absence, and he'd wasted no time in getting comfortable in Bruce's luxurious leather office chair.

But Randy still had the most interesting part of his report left to relay.

"Sir, that's not all. I think Miss Chloe's bein' led astray. You shoulda seen the look Jackson gave her as she walked up the balcony steps. I wouldn't feel comfortable with her looking at *my* girl like that. I think Jackson's got in her head. Miss Chloe might be in danger!" He twisted his cap over and over in his pudgy, sweating hands as he embellished his tale shamelessly in the hope of impressing his boss and gaining a break temporarily from being the focus of the workforce's highjinks.

Quietly dismissing Randy after telling him he'd *done an excellent job* and to *keep him updated,* Kyle softly closed Bruce's office door. Unable to contain his fury a second longer, he pounded the desk so hard that the objects on the highly polished mahogany surface continued to shake for at least five seconds later.

Recovering himself, he began considering his next move.

Chapter 68

The bright pink and blue neon OPEN sign in the window of the most decrepit drinking joint in Louisiana crackled and faded every few seconds, only springing to life when the bartender reached over to give it a whack. He grunted under his breath at the crappiness of his sign, plucking the half-smoked cigarette from his lips.

The drunk in front of him lifted his head groggily, just long enough to order another shot. Seven other empty glasses littered the sticky bar, even though it was only early that Friday afternoon.

"Don't you think you've had enough, Mike?" the bartender asked dryly.

"Listen, I've had enough when I've had enough. My money no good here?" Mike slurred, pointing messily at the bartender, who reluctantly poured him another shot. He swallowed it in one gulp, then reached over to an old beer-soaked newspaper someone had left on the bar, and clumsily pawed at the pages.

"What bullshit they printin'?" he muttered, bringing the newspaper closer to him, hardly able to make out the small print due to his degenerate eyesight. He prodded each article with disgust as he turned the pages. "He's a liar, and he talks shit, she needs a good time...from me, they all need lynchin'." After a dozen or so pages, his eyes landed on a story with a huge picture that took up a quarter of the page. He blinked several times, not quite believing what he was reading.

Daynes Community Fights Back After Storm

But it was the picture that captivated him.

He rubbed his eyes and refocused on the names printed underneath, then cross-referenced each name against the figures from left to right. As he checked the name against the picture of the person on the far end of the line three times, to be sure his eyes weren't deceiving him, his mouth fell wide open.

"Man, that's disgusting," the bartender said, squinting in revulsion as the drunk man dribbled all over the newspaper.

Mike wiped his slobbering mouth with the back of his dirty hand and glared at the bartender.

"Give me a phone...I need the phone, NOW!"

"Sorry to bother you, sir, but there's a man on the line who's insisting on speaking to *the man in charge*...now! As Mr. Bruce is out of town all weekend, I...No, sir, he didn't give his name—"

Linda held the phone a few inches away from her ear, well used to Kyle's angry tirades when he was disturbed. With begrudged permission, she patched the call through.

"Who the hell is this? You sound drunk," Kyle roared.

"I *am* drunk, but I ain't blind. I seen the picture of your lil' fete last month in the paper! You *really* know who y'got employed there?" the man's voice slurred back.

"What you talking about?" He stood up in annoyance at having to go around in cryptic circles with this strange caller, still seething from his meeting with Randy an hour earlier.

"The girl in the photo...the one holding the horse."

"What about her?" He slowly sat back down again.

"Well, I don't know what she's been tellin' *you*, but I guarantee it's all a pack of lies!" the man goaded.

"Spit it out, for fuck's sake."

"Let's put it this way. She's *dead* if she comes back to Louisiana and once you find out why, you'll understand!"

"Who are you?" asked Kyle.

"The name's Mike. I'm her father. Oh, and another thing...*Shona Jackson* ain't even her real name!"

Kyle sat back in Bruce's leather chair, not quite believing the strange turn of events of that Friday afternoon. He'd gone from wanting to tear the office apart in his rage, to complete elation in now having the perfect opportunity to rid himself—and Chloe—of *Shona Jackson*, or whoever the hell this woman really was.

He knew he couldn't ring Bruce so, calmly, he picked up the phone and dialled a different number.

"Kyle. What can I do for you?" Jeffrey Ellis answered the call on the tenth ring.

"Sir, I'm sorry to bother you, I know your wife is sick, but I have some new information about one of our workers and I thought you should be aware. Shona Jackson has been deceiving us all! I've got no choice. I'm gon' have to fire her."

There was a lengthy pause.

"Really? Why?"

"Well, for starters, sir, *Shona Jackson* isn't actually her real name. She's been lyin' to us all about that!" He spoke with as much indignation as he could muster.

There was another long pause on the line.

"Is that all?" Ellis replied, annoyed he'd been called away from administering his wife's medicine for this.

"Sir?" Kyle recoiled in surprise, confused as to why his bombshell hadn't caused the ripple he was expecting. He heard Ellis take an exasperated breath on the end of the phone.

"Tell me, Kyle. Has she ever stolen anything?"

"Well, no, sir, but—"

"Has she ever been late?"

"No, sir, the point is—"

"Has she ever refused *any* kind of work?" Ellis was rapidly losing his patience.

"No, sir, she's just lied about who she is. She's given us a fake name!"

"Now you listen to me, Chambers. Shona Jackson is the best worker we have there. You're tellin me that the person who's raised morale, encouraged new ideas *and* charmed Jack Edwards into investing a massive chunk of his inheritance into the business should be fired? Just because she decided one day she wanted a different name?"

Realizing the conversation wasn't going according to his plan, Kyle played his trump card.

"But sir, I don't think you understand. There are things you don't know about her. I'm worried she's a bad influence on Chloe. She's getting in her head, manipulatin' her—"

"Oh, I see. Well, that changes things. Has Miss Bruce made a complaint about this?" Ellis asked, seeming genuinely concerned.

"Erm, well, no sir, but—"

"Look, I'll be honest. I was at the Copperpot last night and I heard the way Chloe spoke about Shona and her ideas. Oh, that reminds me, I didn't see *you* there supporting the company? You have somewhere else y'had to be that was more important?" Ellis questioned.

Kyle swallowed hard, mystified as to how his plan had gone so wrong.

"Anyway, Chloe seemed pretty in control, and it didn't look to me like there was any *manipulation* there. In fact, she seemed to really respect Shona's ideas...as do I."

"Sir, I really think—"

"I don't have time for this. Unless you tell me she's broken any of my rules, then I don't care if she calls herself *Marilyn Monroe*–she stays! You seriously think that *everyone* in that place is using their real name? Some people have things in their background they're not proud of, don't they, Chambers?" Ellis's tone sharpened.

Kyle's blood ran cold.

"Let me be crystal clear. If I find out Shona's been fired then YOU'RE next, understand?"

Jeffrey Ellis hung up the phone, leaving Kyle in complete shock. He had to think of another plan.

Fast.

"I need to speak to you. It's urgent," Kyle announced as he flew through Chloe's office door.

"What's the matter?" She looked up from her desk, startled at his unusually concerned voice.

"Jackson! She's been lying to us all! I've just had her father on the phone; he saw the picture from the fete in the paper. There's a lot of stuff you don't know about her. She's been leadin' you astray, targeting you 'cos you're so kind and soft. She's probably just tryin' to get money out of you! I didn't want to be the one to tell you this but—"

"What, Kyle? What is it?"

"*Shona Jackson*...ain't even her real name!" His eyes blazed with fake concern.

The expression on Chloe's face was unreadable as she leaned back in her chair, running her fingers over the pebble hanging around her neck.

Chapter 69

The venue of the fundraiser that Saturday night was the country club in the next town. Chloe had thought better of holding it in Daynes now that she knew how *choosy* some of the people who attended the fete were about where their raised funds should go. Even Tom and Ruby Bird were shunned now that word had spread that Cuban had stayed in their barn for the few months before he died, receiving nothing to help them with the costs of repairing their barn roof.

Arriving at the country club at 8 o'clock, she was dressed in her best red velvet ball gown. Touching up her make up in the rearview mirror after pulling up in the parking lot, she breathed deeply to steady her nerves. She'd given Shona the address on Friday and told her to be here at 5 o'clock to meet her master of ceremonies who would give her her uniform and tell her which tables Chloe had set aside for her to be in charge of looking after.

The ballroom had been decorated beautifully. Tables had been decked out with the finest crockery and crystal glasses, with the most exquisite red silk tablecloths draped over them. The band Chloe had arranged was all set up on the stage, the guests all milling around ready to take their seats for dinner.

She looked around to find the master of ceremonies, to check that Shona had turned up.

"Why, of course, ma'am, Miss Jackson turned up just before 5 o'clock. She's already over with the other waitresses. I did exactly as you said and I don't mind saying, that girl looks just breathtaking tonight. That dress coulda been made for her—"

Chloe had been smiling all the time Bob, the master of ceremonies, was speaking, but one word he'd uttered had made her face drop.

"*Dress*? You put Shona in—"

"Of course, was that not what you wanted? Oh, look now, there she is, don't she look a picture? I was so glad to get her out of those unflattering, manly clothes. Her figure was just *wasted* underneath them!"

Chloe whirled around to face where Bob was pointing. Standing over by the bar area with the other waitresses stood a woman she barely recognized. She was dressed in a silver sequined cocktail dress and four-inch heels, her blonde hair matted down, her face made up like a cover girl. She was holding a tray laden with drinks, her expression blank as she served the guests. As Chloe raced over, the glamorous waitress turned around robotically and stared at her.

"They put me in a dress. Did *you* ask them to put me in a dress?" Shona looked at her with tears in her eyes, the anguish on her face indescribable.

"Oh my...NO, of course I didn't. I would *never* do that! All I said was for you to look smart. I would never want you to feel like this. Please believe me."

Chloe was mortified at what had been done to Shona. There was no denying that she looked stunning, her blue eyes accentuated by the dark mascara she was wearing, her clear skin flawlessly made up.

But it looked wrong.

"Chloe, I'm sorry, but I can't wear this. I just—"

"Come with me," she ordered, leading Shona firmly by the hand backstage to the little changing area the workers were using that night. "Go in there. I'll just be a minute." Leaving her in the staff bathroom, Chloe then searched around the changing room for anything that would be more suitable.

"Excuse me, Miss Bruce, are you OK? You lookin' for something?" the young waiter asked as she rifled through all the clothes hangers, mindful that her opening speech to the guests was due in less than ten minutes. She turned to the waiter and smiled; the answer to her problem was right in front of her.

"Say, would you like the rest of the night off? On full pay, of course."

"Why, yes, ma'am!" The young waiter's eyes lit up.

"Alright then. Just one thing...can I have your pants?"

Standing in the bathroom, Shona stared vacantly into the mirror. Wearing a dress for the first time in her life, she felt completely exposed.

Empty.

The figure in the mirror stared back at her, its hair flat to its head, its mascara streaked from the desolate tears that had rolled down its face. Shona closed her eyes tight shut, hoping that when she opened them, the figure would be gone.

"Shona, here, put these on!"

Out of breath, Chloe ran up to her, holding the young waiter's black tuxedo, and locked the bathroom door behind them. Shona turned around, just as a bundle of clothes was thrust into her hands. She opened her eyes and looked down at the pile.

"You mean...you don't want me to wear this...*thing*?" She looked down at her scratchy silver dress, then back up at Chloe, her eyes glassy.

"No, I would NEVER want you to wear something that made you feel like this!" Chloe looked at Shona's head and, without thinking, reached her hands up and combed her fingers carefully through her matted-down hair.

"I can't believe they did this to you. I told them not to make you feel uncomfortable!" Her fingers ruffled Shona's blonde hair back into its regular choppy style. The hairspray that the stylist had soaked it in made it a challenge, but eventually it fell back into place. Reaching over to a pile of cloths, Chloe ran one under the faucet.

"Now, let's get this off too. I can't see you properly under all this muck!" She ran the cloth over Shona's heavily made-up face, holding her chin tenderly as she concentrated. Several wipes later, Shona's natural beauty was restored.

"There we go. You look like you again now!" Chloe said triumphantly.

Shona smiled back as if it were the most perfect thing she could've said to her at that moment.

"Ma'am, we need you on the stage for the opening address," Bob called out from outside the bathroom door.

"I gotta go. Will you be OK?"

"I will be now," Shona replied as Chloe smiled at her, unlocked the door and turned to head off.

"Chloe—" Shona called after her.

"Yes?"

"Thank you. For the clothes. And for understanding."

"You're welcome. Now SCOOT! I need you out there, so get ready!"

∼

Chloe was halfway through her opening address to the guests when a figure appeared at the back of the ballroom, completely distracting her. The waiter that had caught her eye was captivating, their aura filling the room with light. Dressed smartly in a black tuxedo and balancing a tray of drinks on one palm, the waiter flashed an infectious grin at everyone they passed; men and women alike raising their eyebrows in surprise at how natural the figure looked. Just then, the waiter ran a tanned hand through their long blonde bangs and lifted up their piercing blue eyes to meet Chloe's gaze, hypnotizing her completely into forgetting every remaining word of her speech.

~

"So, the first lot of the evening is this magnificent beast. Do I hear two dollars?"

As the auctioneer started off the night's main fundraising event, a flurry of offers was fired at him with five dollars becoming six, then ten. Chloe stood at the edge of the stage, still mesmerized by Shona's movements around the ballroom, watching her effortlessly charm everyone she came into contact with. Her gentleness when seating some of the older guests made Chloe's heart ache with affection for her, so much so that she'd taken her attention off the auction and completely misheard what amount they had reached.

"I'll bid FIFTY dollars for the cow!" She raised her hand to stunned gasps.

"SOLD! To Miss Bruce. Wow, I thought it was only gon' go for *fifteen* there! Thank you, ma'am!"

After rushing to sign the sale document, Chloe then darted over to Shona, taking advantage of the first opportunity she'd had since seeing her emerge from the bathroom. Walking up to her, she couldn't help but notice the strange look spread over Shona's face.

"What? What is it?" Chloe asked, her eyes wide.

"What in the blue blazes you gon' do with a COW?" Shona replied, shaking her head.

~

As the night wore on, it was clear that Shona had become the most popular waiter in the room, even challenging the others to a juggling competition to entertain the more jovial of the guests.

"I got two bucks says you can't juggle three, girl!"

"Easy!" She grabbed three oranges from the fruit bowl on the bar and tossed them into the air, catching them expertly over and over again. Her smile faded moments later, though, as she saw Chloe approach looking stern faced.

"Shoot, guys. Think the boss just busted us foolin' around!" one of the waiters panicked.

Chloe stood in front of Shona, her lips pursed in thought. With a glint in her eye, she reached over to the fruit bowl and picked up another orange.

"FIVE bucks says you can't juggle four!" She held the orange out to Shona who grinned.

"You're on!"

Shona tossed the oranges in the air and, with impressive ease, juggled them perfectly, even picking up a grape simultaneously and catching it in her mouth, to rapturous cheers from the onlooking crowd.

"Now you're just showing off!" Chloe yelled over the noise.

After she'd finished and taken her bow, Shona held out her palm playfully for the five dollars Chloe was holding, then popped it in her top pocket with her other tips from the evening.

"Excuse me, Miss Bruce, but I would like to donate one

hundred dollars to your fund in exchange for the first dance of the night with you."

Chloe turned around to see an old man standing behind her, leaning heavily on his stick. She had known Chester for years, as well as his grandson Matthew, who'd escorted him over.

"Well, sir, that is mighty generous of you. Matthew, shall we?" She gestured towards the dance floor.

Shona watched, her heart aching when she saw Chloe standing next to Chester's incredibly handsome grandson.

"What? Hell, NO! I want your first dance to be with ME! Here, young lady, put this in the pot, will you!" Chester handed Shona the hundred dollars, which she placed securely in her top pocket. He then waved his stick at Matthew, who bowed graciously at Chloe and backed away, leaving her to gently walk her dance partner over to the middle of the floor.

Feeling strangely relieved seeing a forlorn Matthew traipse back to his table, Shona couldn't help but watch in awe as Chloe twirled around the dance floor, gingerly moving the elderly man with typical care and grace.

Suddenly she felt as if the whole world, apart from the movements of Chloe Bruce, had stopped. Her red crushed velvet dress caressed every curve of her body, her sheer beauty completely mesmerizing to Shona, who hadn't until that very moment properly registered how breathtakingly gorgeous Chloe looked that night.

And with that recognition, she felt something irreversibly change within her.

∼

Chloe had searched everywhere. In the half an hour since she'd finished her dance with Chester, her panic had grown worse.

"Excuse me, ma'am, but are you lost? This is the staff area, no place for someone as important as you!" The young waiter who had sidled up to Chloe looked embarrassed as he tried to coax her back to the ballroom.

"Do you know where Shona is, please?"

"I think she went home, ma'am. She wasn't feelin' so good."

Chloe's heart raced. She searched the piles of clothes lying around, a single thought hammering around her brain. But she couldn't let herself believe that Shona would do such a thing. Next to the back door, she finally found what she was looking for and picked up the tuxedo jacket, her heart in her mouth as she rifled through the top pocket.

Nothing.

Reeling, Chloe felt her head spin. *Kyle had been right about Shona all along!*

"Oh, Miss Bruce, there was one thing. I was told to make sure you got this." The waiter reached over to her and dropped a wad of dollar bills in her hand. She counted slowly, then counted again. There were one hundred and twenty dollars.

"Hey, there's more here than I was expecting," she said to the bemused waiter.

"Oh, yeah. Shona said something about wanting to donate her tips from the evening to the fund. Said she just wanted to help. I told her she was crazy, but she insisted!" He shrugged.

Chloe stared down at the huge sum of money in her hand, open-mouthed in horror at what she'd allowed herself to briefly consider and almost believe. Kyle had been so determined to convince her to mistrust Shona and now, as she ran her shaking fingers over her bare neck and around the hollow space that was normally filled by her precious pebble, Chloe vowed to herself never to take it off again.

Determined to find Shona, she made her excuses and ran to her car.

Meanwhile, stumbling through the darkness, Shona felt dazed. Tears were streaming down her cheeks as she bent over, thrusting her fingers down her throat. She dragged her flailing body along the road, screaming at the moon, trying to somehow instigate the retching she'd come to expect when thinking *that way* about Chloe.

"What's the matter with me? Come on! Do what you usually do, COME ON! It's wrong to have these feelings, IT'S WRONG! GODDAMN IT! What the hell do I do? I don't know what this means now!"

No matter how hard she punched herself, her stomach felt unnervingly settled.

Calm.

~

Chloe flew down the driveway of the Birds' farmhouse, having seen no sign of Shona along the way.

"Miss Chloe, whatever's the matter?" Tom asked as he opened the door.

"Is Shona here? Is she home OK?"

"She's home, but I'm not sure if *OK's* the word I'd use. She was in a real state. I didn't wanna ask, I just left her to go straight to the barn. She looked exhausted."

"Can I go see her? Please?"

"Best leave it for tonight. Let her calm down," he replied.

"OK, well, tell her I said thank you for tonight and I'll see her Monday."

"Will do, Miss Chloe. Goodnight."

Chloe left, but she was surer now than ever about what she wanted and it terrified and exhilarated her in equal measure.

Chapter 70

Kyle charged into Bruce's office on Monday morning and slammed the door almost off its hinges.

"What in God's name's the matter with you?" Bruce's head shot up from his desk.

"The matter? That broad is what the matter is! I've had a call from her father. She's been deceiving us all and Ellis won't fire her 'cos she's so damn perfect. We need to get rid of her, fast! She's sniffin' around Chloe too much. She'll brainwash her, mess with her head. That's why she's on the run from Louisiana. She's a fucking dyke!"

Bruce saw the opportunity as clear as day in front of him.

"I'm gon' call in the Bullen boys. This is beyond scaring the bitch now; she needs to be taken out. Permanently."

All of a sudden, Kyle's fury subsided. He stood still, a thought crossing his red-misted mind.

"Wait a goddamn minute. We might not need to get our hands dirty on this one. Her father said she was a *dead woman* if she ever set foot back in Louisiana–" His brain was processing the finer points of his plan.

"Yeah?" Bruce was trying to keep up.

"So why are we gon' get blood on our hands when there are others only too willin' to do that for us?"

"What d'you mean?"

"Gentlemen!" Jeffrey Ellis burst in through the slammed door and smiled. Kyle and Bruce swiveled around, panicking that he'd heard every word.

"Jeffrey!" Bruce's voice quivered with surprise.

"Great news! We've had more donations pour in after Chloe's fundraiser Saturday night! That's great for Daynes, isn't it?" Ellis glowed.

"Really great, sir," Kyle replied through gritted teeth. It was the first he'd heard of Chloe's little side project.

"Right, well, I'll leave you two to it. I'm just gon' have a quick chat with Ron, then I'll be off, gentlemen." Ellis headed back out of the office door.

"Sir–" Kyle quickly called out.

"Yes, Chambers?"

"I was thinking about what you said on the phone on Friday, and you're right–"

"About what?" He turned back to fully face Kyle.

"Shona Jackson? She is making an impression here, regardless of her past. She's really thriving," Kyle continued robotically. Even Bruce looked confused as to what he was going to say next.

"So that's why I think she'll be great to help other companies, spread good vibes about our place and also get some inside information on our competitors. Like you said, she has a way with people, even those high up."

His plan was hovering into view.

"Go on." Ellis was intrigued, glad to hear Kyle being more positive for once.

"I propose that she ventures out as soon as can be arranged. Strike while the iron's hot, as they say! Let's call it a *promotion* for all her hard work here. I've got some contacts I can call on if you like?"

"Great idea! Where were you thinking of sending her?" Both Ellis and Bruce were intrigued as to what he was going to say next.

"Louisiana," Kyle grinned.

Genius! Bruce thought.

Chapter 71

Shona had been quiet all of that Monday so far, even though Elbie had tried to coax an explanation out of her for most of the afternoon. She hadn't seen Chloe since she'd left early Saturday night and was still trying to get her head around what had happened on her walk home. Thoughts raced through her head. *Why has the sickness completely stopped now? What did that mean for my feelings for Chloe?*

"I'm gon' jump right in that ocean when I get to the Californian coast, I tell ya, clothes and all!" Shona said, trying to distract herself.

Elbie smiled back at her as he hung up the last of his tools in his workshop.

"Good luck to ya, girl! I'll be taking my granddaughter to school. I can't wait! Just a few more weeks to go! Now things have smoothed over here, it might even be a pleasure," he replied.

"Shona?" A soft voice rang out from the doorway behind them.

Elbie instinctively placed his foot over the thin piece of broken floorboard underneath him as Chloe walked into the tool room.

"Will you meet me, tonight?"

"Where?" she replied, taken aback at Chloe's forwardness.

"The riverbank. You remember?"

"Course I remember. What time?"

"8 o'clock. Sorry, gotta go." And as quickly as she'd arrived, Chloe disappeared down the corridor, looked around to see who was watching her.

"What was that all 'bout?" Elbie asked.

"Beats the hell outta me!" Shona replied, shaking her head.

Her heart thudded against her ribs, the waves of uncertainty crashing around inside her.

The evening was bright and balmy, the fresh water of the Weaver lapping against the bank. Storm was busying herself eating shrubs, safely tethered to a tree as her rider breathed deeply to calm her fluttering heart as she waited. 8 o'clock came and went, with Shona kicking the dusty ground out of sheer frustration, spooking Storm momentarily until she lost interest and continued to snuffle at the bushes.

"What now, girl? Do we wait?" Shona patted the mare's flank.

After another couple of minutes, she jumped up to take a slow trot back to the barn when Storm nickered loudly, startled by the dull roar of a car approaching them. Fighting to get her errant horse under control, Shona saw the familiar red Deluxe speeding down the road parallel to the river.

"Come on." She kicked her heels and rode Storm over to where the car had pulled up in a turnout on the side of the road.

"Shona." Chloe strode towards her, breathing heavily and looking over her shoulder. "I'm so sorry I'm late–"

"Kyle, right?" she guessed intuitively, climbing down from her horse.

"Something like that."

"Does he know you're meeting me? 'Cos that man hates me with a passion. He'll go nuts if he finds out and make my life hell again. Just when, if I'm bein' honest, it's started to be kinda alright."

Chloe's face dropped, her well-rehearsed explanation falling apart in her head.

"I told him I was meeting one of the girls from the Copperpot."

"Uh huh. That seem right to you, though? I mean, it ain't my business n'all, but don't you think it's strange y'have to lie?"

"I know, I know!" Chloe ran her hands through her hair, then over her face. There was something openly agitating her, but Shona unwittingly carried on with her lecture.

"I don't know if you know what that man's capable of but–"

"I do know," Chloe blurted out, her eyes brimming with tears.

"Sorry," Shona replied, shocked to see her in such a state. Her arms ached to wrap themselves around Chloe, to comfort her friend, but she stuck her hands deep in her pockets to resist the urge. "Chloe, can I ask why you wanted to meet me here tonight?"

Not able to hold on a second longer, tears cascaded down Chloe's cheeks like rushing waterfalls as she crumpled to her knees on the ground. Instinctively, Shona bent down and threw her arms around her.

"I feel so trapped. I don't know what to do."

Her pitiful sobs were heartbreaking for Shona to hear. She cradled her gently, remembering how Chloe had done the same to her the day Cuban died. Resting her full body weight in Shona's strong arms, Chloe gripped on tightly to her checked shirt, her head lying in her lap.

"Shhh, it's OK, I'm here, I'm here...It's OK..." Shona murmured as she tenderly stroked Chloe's soft brown hair.

Doing her best to soothe the ebb and flow of tears, Shona sat on the soft grass with a helpless Chloe lying draped across her. She'd once dreamed of the moment she'd have Chloe wrapped up safely in her arms, but the sadness emitting from her made the scenario bittersweet. She let Chloe cry for as long as she needed, while inhaling the painfully beautiful scent of her freshly-washed hair.

As her sobs turned to snuffles after a few minutes of comfort, Chloe raised her head and looked deep into Shona's eyes. They were like shimmering pools of calm blue ocean, making all confusion and doubt wash away from her.

"You don't know what it's like for me, having to be a certain way, dress a certain way, be with a certain man who *has* to be wealthy," she blurted out between sniffs.

Silently, Shona stroked her hair. "I know," she replied, though her mind stirred at Chloe's cryptic words.

"The dinners, the parties, the fake people, my family! If only they knew the truth about my feelings!" She buried her head in Shona's lap again and clung to her knee as fresh sobs vibrated through her petite frame.

Shona held her tightly through every tremble.

"Could you not just tell 'em all that you and Kyle have split up?" she asked innocently. Chloe's head shot up, a look of pain and confusion etched on her mascara-streaked face.

"What?"

"You and Kyle? I mean, I know it probably made good business sense you two bein' together, but if he don't make you happy, to hell with what folks think. People split all the time–"

"You don't get it, do you?" Chloe interrupted.

"Get what?"

"It's YOU I'm talking about! The truth about my feelings for you, Shona. I can't keep them inside me a second longer!"

"Hi, Cindy? It's Kyle, how you doin'? Listen, could you ask Chloe if she could pick me up some Lucky Strike's on her way home? What's that? Ain't seen her all night, huh? OK, sorry, my mistake. Bye."

Kyle hung up the phone, his pen almost ripping through the notepad as he crossed off the fourth name he'd rung that night. Tearing the page out, he screwed it up into his fist, his face red with fury.

Where the hell are you?

～

Shona was thunderstruck.

"Wait a minute. What you saying?" she croaked, jumping to her feet, trying to process Chloe's bombshell.

"You *know* what I'm saying. It's like, I wanna scream but I feel so damn trapped all the time. Yet what I feel for you makes me feel so right, so complete. It always has. From the first moment I saw you. But you were always so quick to get away from me, though, every time I wanted to speak to you. But then, when I met you properly, my heart just knew. I tried to fight my feelings, but—"

Chloe tailed off as Shona paced the dirt in turmoil. She'd fantasized about the moment she would hear these words. But right that second, all she could focus on was the terror of people finding out. Chloe's feelings for her were all she'd ever wanted to be real, since the day she first saw her on the balcony. It should have been the perfect thing to hear, but right now her confession hit her like a freight train. Dreaming of this moment was one thing, but it actually coming true felt like a thunderbolt to Shona. The grim reality was that in this town, or any town for that matter, it could never work for them to be together. She'd already been run out of one town for who she was, and beaten half to death because of it.

And what about when Kyle found out?

He'd already arranged for Cuban to be killed, nice and clean, she was sure of that. She didn't stand a chance once he knew. With her heart twisting in her chest, she crouched down on her haunches to face Chloe, who was still half-lying on the ground.

"That kinda feeling is dangerous in these parts, you *know* that," she half-whispered. "Not to mention that Chambers is the nastiest piece of work I ever met. Do you know how many days and nights I've begged God for you to say those words to me—?"

Tears of frustration welled up in her eyes as Chloe stared at her, hanging off her every word, hoping her next words were the ones she longed to hear.

"—but when I saw you with Kyle at the Copperpot that night, and you hugging him back? It actually made *sense* for you to be with him. What kinda life could we have together? It's just pipe dreams, Chloe. I've been runnin' all my life to stay alive. If folks around here knew about about us, we wouldn't survive the week. I'm goin' to California soon and for once in my shitty life I wan' leave a town behind that ain't gon' chase after my blood. I'm terrified, Chloe! I don't wan' have to look over my shoulder anymore. I can't do it!"

Hardly believing the words that were pouring through her trembling lips and unable to look Chloe in the eye any longer, Shona stood up and stepped a few paces away, staring at the horizon as the sun started to sink below it. Biting back the tears, she uttered the words to Chloe that she never thought would cross her lips.

"I can't do this right now. I don't know what the hell I'm feeling! It's all mixed up!" She held her hand to her fluttering stomach as she walked away. "I need to think."

Chloe climbed up off the ground and dusted herself off. "I told you before that I knew what happened in Mississippi...but I didn't tell you *everything* I found out when I was away. I *know* now why you're scared!"

"What are you talking about?" Shona stopped dead in her tracks.

"I found Dorothy. I *know* about Louisiana now too."

Shona's mouth dropped open. Her secret was out.

"I asked Dorothy about what happened to you," Chloe continued. "I know why you had to leave Mississippi. I know about you being set up that night with that hooker and everybody finding out. I know about your father, your mother and how she died. I know about the treatment they gave you in that basement–"

"STOP! PLEASE!" Shona yelled through the tears at Chloe, who staggered back, almost knocked off her feet as Shona accidentally shoulder barged past her. "You know NOTHING about me!" Her eyes blazed at a bemused Chloe, who didn't see her confession ending like this.

"I know that *Shona Jackson* ain't your real name!"

Her words struck Shona like a bullet. She froze on the spot, turned and stared at Chloe in complete horror.

"Your father rang Kyle last Friday and he wasted no time in coming in to tell me the truth. Thought it would change my opinion of you, that I'd hate you for lyin' to me. But you know what? He was wrong. I understand why you did that! You were scared. I don't give a rat's ass what your name is; you'll *always* be Shona Jackson to me...the Shona Jackson I have fallen in lo—"

Shona blindly staggered over to Storm, her head crushed, her world spinning. Without even a look back, she kicked her heels into the horse and galloped off into the distance, her eyes streaming with hot, salty tears.

Chloe stared after her and screamed into the air until she

felt her lungs burn. Embarrassment, confusion, and the rawest pain she'd ever felt in her life coursed through her veins like acid.

~

Parking in Kyle's driveway, Chloe felt emotionally drained. Halfway home, she'd remembered the paperwork she'd accidentally left at his house and reluctantly turned left instead of right at the crossroads, huffing with annoyance that she would need it for the usual Tuesday morning investors' meeting. Seeing that there was no car in the driveway and no lights were on, she smiled, relieved that he wasn't home yet. She picked up the spare key from under the mat and slipped inside the front door.

A dark silhouette stood in the living room, the outline of a glass of whiskey in hand clearly visible in the light that shone through a crack in the drapes.

"Which friend did you see tonight?" The voice was deep and gravelly, the whiskey obviously not the first that had been downed that night.

"Um...Cindy," Chloe replied, quickly scanning the coffee table for the paperwork she'd come for. "I didn't see your car in the driveway. You get a cab home?"

"Cindy, huh? You sure?" He ignored her question and stepped closer, the whites of his eyes glistening.

"Yeah, you know, she works at the Copperpot?" She reached down to the coffee table to search through the piles of paper, but quick as a flash Kyle grabbed her arms, digging his fingernails into her wrists as he threw her up against the wall.

"What the hell are you doin'?" Chloe gasped in shock.

"Cindy, huh? Well, we both know that's a fucking lie. I called your friends tonight, all of 'em! None of 'em know a single fucking thing about your lil' play date tonight, so where the fuck were you?"

"Kyle, you're hurting me, please–" she cried out, her skin pinching against his rough grip.

"You seein' somebody else? After everything I've done for you, for us! You've been leadin' me on for months and I've waited for you like a good lil' boy, then you go out there acting like a whore and makin' me look like a damn fool? You know how much I want you, and you're goin' out and givin' it to every *other* man out there but keep denyin' me MY right?"

He dragged her back to the couch and pinned her down underneath his heavy, sweating body. His groans began to get louder in her ear as she clawed at him with all her might.

"NO, Kyle, STOP! PLEASE!"

When it was all over, Chloe lay motionless on her side with her knees hugged into her chest. The pain she felt inside her was almost too much to bear.

Chapter 72

"So? How'd it go last night?" Elbie asked a distant-looking Shona.

It was early Tuesday morning in the tool room and she had barely said two words to the old man who was itching to know what happened at the river bank.

"Chloe told me everything. She has feelings for me too, Elbie," Shona replied, her voice eerily quiet for someone who should have been bouncing off the walls with this revelation.

"Well? That's *great*! Ain't it?"

"I don't know anymore," she said sadly, her face pale.

Elbie dropped his wrench and stared at her, his wise eyes flashing disbelief.

"Are you kiddin' me? Y'been borin' the pants off me for weeks now 'bout how much you like that girl and now she says it back to ya, *you don't know how y'feel?*"

Shona looked startled at the old man's outburst.

"Elbie, when they gave me all that treatment to make me sick when I saw those pictures, they *knew* how it'd affect me. I started to get used to it. It was predictable, like in a weird way it was keeping me safe from gettin' hurt again. But now, the sickness has gone away! *Now*, when I'm around her, my heart just feels still, like it ain't even beatin' no more. What the hell does that mean, huh? That mean I don't feel *nothin'* special for Chloe anymore? That we're just friends now that I don't feel the sickness. Am I cured now my heart don't race no more when I'm near her?"

Her searching eyes implored Elbie to explain her raging confusion, but his face broke out into the most joyful smile she'd ever seen.

"Child, I hate to be the one to break this to ya, but you're in trouble, girl! I had that exact same feelin' for my wife. When we first met, I couldn't even speak to her without getting tongue-tied, I thought my heart would explode right outta my chest! But after I realised she was *the one*, well, I just felt so damn calm around her. She was where I felt most at home. Shona, your heart only races when you're not sure of someone, when you're anxious around them, wary of 'em even." He chuckled as a light seemed to switch on in Shona's mind.

"Elbie, that's it, isn't it? Those doctors tried to force me not to feel lust, but they couldn't ever find a treatment to stop me falling in...love!"

He smiled as the truth finally dawned on her. "Nope, what you're feelin' now? There ain't no cure for that! Your heart ain't racin' no more 'cos to you Chloe feels like home."

Shona stared at the old man, her eyes wide with a mixture of elation and terror.

Chapter 73

Elbie walked past Chloe's open door after lunch, stopping as he heard her wince in pain as she struggled to lift a file box onto her shelf.

"Here, let me help, ma'am!" He darted into the office, just catching the box in time before it slipped out of her hands.

"Thank you," she croaked.

As she reached up, with Elbie taking most of the box's weight, her blouse's long sleeves rode up. Her wrists were red as fire, dotted with what looked like fingernail imprints. Elbie gasped.

"Miss Chloe? Are you—?"

"I'm fine. Now, if you'll excuse me, I have to be getting to my meeting." She gingerly slid her sleeves back down, walked Elbie to her door and closed it behind him.

"Enough is goddamn *enough* now! It's time." Elbie stormed into his workshop, red halos circling his watery eyes.

"For what?" Shona replied, scrambling off her stool.

"To expose that bastard Chambers," he roared, tearing the

floorboard up and ripping the top off his escape box. He grabbed his diary and opened it up to the next clean page. Taking the pencil from behind his ear, he scribbled furiously.

"What you talking about?"

"I've just seen Miss Chloe. Got nasty marks all over her wrists and looked mighty embarrassed that I saw 'em too. Poor girl didn't look too comfortable walkin' either. What d'you suppose that means, huh?" he asked rhetorically.

"Oh no," Shona felt her whole body freeze as Elbie's words sliced open her heart.

"No woman deserves that. That no-good animal! I'm goin' to the damn newspaper and tellin' 'em everythin'! I don't care anymore, I got years of dirt, stuff I can prove, times and dates, you name it! And when it all blows up, I'll be long gone!"

He strode towards the telephone in the corridor, taking out a scrap of paper from his top pocket and carefully dialing the number scrawled on it.

"Hello? Gimme the editor. Hello? You got someone there who's lookin' for a big story? 'Cos I got one! Right, OK. What time can you meet me?"

Shona stood motionless in the tool room, her mind a maelstrom of emotions. Elbie trudged back in, his fists clenched.

"Listen, Elbie, do you really need to go to the *papers*? It's dangerous! Just tell Ellis! Surely he can put a stop to Kyle?"

"Ellis is *one* man! You ever tried gettin' to him on your own? I tried that twice already! Chambers is *always* nearby. I did think of tellin' Chloe once, but I seen the way that animal treats her, the injuries he's inflicted. He's torn her down, broken her spirit, and her father doesn't even give a damn. Too scared of losing his prize asset – the one who's bringin' in all the investors. He won't rock the boat, even if it *is* his daughter who's collateral. No, Shona, I got one shot at this, and it's gotta be big. We need the whole town on our side, not just one man. When that story lands, Larry Bruce and his thugs will be history!"

"Larry? It's me. Yeah, listen, who *you* been upsetting? This old guy, Elbie, has apparently been keeping some secret diary that he's gon' bring with him tonight. Yeah, been keeping it years now, all the bad shit that's goin' down over there! He's got names, dates, all the stuff sheriffs like to make a case clean. What d'you want me to do 'bout it?"

"You leave him to me."

Larry Bruce sat quietly in his chair for over an hour after he'd hung up on Sam Lewis, hatching a plan as he fought to control the seething fire that was raging through his cold heart.

Elbie patted his pocket to reassure himself that he hadn't lost his precious cargo on the way to his meeting with Sam Lewis that Tuesday evening. He surveyed the empty street in front of him surreptitiously before crossing over next to a run-down diner on the edge of Daynes. The last thing he wanted was to be followed. Just as he was about to cross the road, a dark green truck rounded the corner. Out of nowhere, he felt his jacket collar tighten as his body was yanked out of the road and back to the safety of the sidewalk.

"Jeez, old man—you alright? Truck missed you by a whisker!" The young man who saved him wiped his brow and smiled at a shaken Elbie, who stared after the truck as it sped away down to the other end of the street and out of sight. "Strange thing, though, I coulda sworn that truck was speeding up, not slowing down!"

He blew his cheeks out and shook his head at Elbie, who was shaking uncontrollably with delayed shock.

Chapter 74

Shona found Chloe sitting at her desk the next morning, staring into space as she stirred her coffee.

"G'mornin', may I?" She gestured towards the open door.

"Of course." Chloe half-smiled, but her eyes couldn't mask her pain.

"Elbie told me what he saw yesterday? I tried to find you, but you'd already left for your meeting. I waited for you to come back but..."

Shona stepped closer to Chloe's desk, biting her lip as she saw tears prick the corners of her tired brown eyes. She went back to close the door, then gently perched on the edge of the desk directly in front of her as Chloe slowly folded her blouse sleeve upwards.

"My God!" she gasped, the fury for Kyle incinerating her insides. "Do your parents know?"

"I haven't told them. My mother believes certain things about a woman's role at home. She stays quiet, does as she told and she gets looked after by my father. Her life is as simple as that." Chloe's weak voice trailed off as her eyes lowered.

"That is not how *your* life has to be, do you understand? What he did to you was wrong. You don't do *that* to someone you love." Shona whispered intently, leaning forward, her face only inches away from Chloe's.

Chloe lifted her weary eyes and lost herself completely in Shona's gaze.

Both their hearts were as calm as a millpond.

Chloe had been thinking about Shona all day. Avoiding any interaction with her parents when she got home from work that evening, she slipped upstairs for a long, hot bath. It seemed to take forever for the tub to fill, but when she finally slid into the soapy water, she gasped as its warm caress completely enveloped her aching body.

Her mind started to drift as she lifted droplets of water and cascaded them over her body, feeling their erotic touch as they warmed, then cooled on her skin. Instinctively, she knew Shona would always be gentle with her, her feather-light touch the complete opposite of Kyle's brutality that night. What would it be like to feel her soft, silky skin against her own, in a place where they were undisturbed?

Lying back in the tub, her hand slipped beneath the surface of the water. As she closed her eyes, Chloe pictured Shona's beautiful face and played out the scenario she'd imagined every night in her head. Totally engrossed in her fantasy, she didn't hear the creak on the staircase a few minutes later.

"Sweetheart, Kyle's on the phone. Hurry up, don't keep your man waiting!" Eleanor hammered on the bathroom door. Chloe's hand splashed from between her legs and back to the surface of the water, her cheeks reddening.

"Just a second," she called back, lifting herself out of the tub and wrapping her robe around her, the unsatisfied tingles between her legs driving her crazy.

With her daydream last night still thundering through her mind, Chloe raced to the tool room early Thursday morning, a clipboard full of official-looking papers tucked snugly under her arm.

"Shona," she called out, the expression on her face serious as she breezed through the door. "Here. Just some jobs I need you to do, OK?"

Chloe looked at her for a second too long before turning on her heels and striding away. Opening the paperwork, Shona saw the words as clear as day on the page:

I love you.
There, I said it!
C x

With every nerve ending in her body tingling, Shona rushed into Elbie's workshop to find some paper and a pen, then sneaked up to Chloe's office. Seeing her in-tray outside, she placed her folded note underneath the few bits of paperwork already in there and scampered away before anyone noticed her.

Returning to her office that afternoon, Chloe sank down heavily in her chair, weary from the tedious meeting she'd endured with Kyle. She sat staring blankly at him as he leaned against the doorframe, and refused to invite him in.

"Kyle, we're not backtracking on the new ideas. They've really boosted morale!"

"Morale? That ain't important. It's profit that'll make this business thrive!"

As he outlined all the reasons why she was making a mistake, Chloe began sorting through her mail. Picking up the third envelope, she froze, then slammed it back down on top of the swan-shaped note she'd uncovered. Carefully, she folded back one of the swan's wings to read the writing underneath.

> What you said,
> Me too
> S x

"What's that?" Kyle asked, not able to see properly from where he was standing.

"Nothing. Just something I thought I needed to deal with, but it's old news so...anyway. I need to get back to work." She shuffled her papers and eyeballed him until he tutted and slunk away.

Her heart thudded hard in her chest as she read Shona's words back to herself for the fourth time. Even though her pain-ravaged body still ached, inside she felt reborn as she pressed the note to her lips. Rushing out of her office and down the stairs, Chloe knew that it was the same time every day Shona was tasked with washing down the floor of the tool room. Kyle, catching a glimpse of her blurry outline rushing past his window, watched her disappear through the canteen, then down the corridor. Racing back to his desk, he picked up his phone.

"Randy, see where Miss Bruce is heading, will ya. Let me know who she talks to."

~

Staring fondly for what seemed like ages through the doorway of the tool room, Chloe's feelings of love for Shona almost overwhelmed her.

"Ahem." She cleared her throat as gently as she could.

"Hi! Um." Shona spun around in surprise, dropping the mop and tripping over her bucket.

"Oh my—!" Chloe rushed over to try and save her from the lake of dirty water that had gushed all over her clean floor.

"Son of a–" Shona cursed, then looked up to see a pair of soft brown eyes gazing down at her.

"I got your message," Chloe said, kneeling down to be at eye-level with her.

"I got yours. What in the blue blazes do we do now?"

"Oh God, I don't know. It's so dangerous. I just wanna be alone with you, Shona, without us having to watch our backs, you know?"

Shona nodded. "It was kinda brave what you did, giving me your note first," she smiled.

"I *had* to do something. You didn't believe me when I told you at the river, so I needed to *spell* it out!" Chloe replied.

"What kills me is that we can't go anywhere. We can't be seen talking, or laughing..."

"It won't be for much longer. I just need to work out a plan. Kyle will suspect something if I'm not careful."

"I *hate* you bein' around him. The thought of what he's done to you breaks m'heart," Shona replied through gritted teeth. "I'll kill that bastard if he touches you again, I goddamn swear it!" She smacked her hand down hard on the wet floor.

"I won't let him. He's not the one who has my heart, you just remember that! We'll figure out a way somehow, I promise."

"People get hurt in this town for being like us! I'm scared," Shona sniffed.

"Then we won't stay in this shitty town." Chloe's eyes radiated determination. Desperately trying to resist embracing

Shona, a noise outside the door brought them both back to their senses.

"I better go," Chloe whispered.

∼

Outside the doorway, Randy had strained his ears to hear the conversation inside, but the two women were speaking too quietly. All he could report back was that Chloe had met with Shona, but he sensed that it was good enough for Kyle, who'd gone back into Chloe's office and sifted through her in-tray. In her haste to get to Shona, she'd left the swan hidden in her paperwork and, after reading the words written inside, Kyle screwed it up tightly in his clenched fist.

∼

After bumping into Randy and receiving his report, Kyle marched into Larry Bruce's office, his face like thunder.

"This is out of hand now, Larry. After everything I do for your daughter! I treat her like a princess, buy her gifts and how does she repay me? She's off hatchin' plans with that no-good whore, Jackson! Probably to get more brownie points with the workers, make me look like the hard bastard that's makin' them work. She's way too close to my girl, writing her goddamn love notes now! As if Chloe would be swayed. She knows when she's got it good with me!" He stalked around the office, banging on each surface in rage.

"I know, son. We just gotta hang in there. That guy at the site in Louisiana is still on vacation, but once he's back, Jackson's gon' find herself on a lil' *exchange program*! He's had the payment from us, so I know he won't let us down," Bruce replied calmly.

"Yeah, you're right, Larry. It's a shame we have to pay; it's making it more difficult for us to filter out money. Ellis is bound to start asking questions soon when he realizes profits are low, but productivity is high."

"Leave it with me. Jackson's getting her *promotion* and going to Louisiana very soon—I'll make GODDAMN sure of it!"

∽

Shona arrived early to work on Friday, before everybody else. Dropping her satchel down in the tool room, she looked around to see what needed doing for the day.

"Who the *fuck* do you think you are, bitch?"

Kyle emerged from the doorway looking dishevelled. Through quietly raging eyes, he squinted at her, his mouth curled into a snarl.

"What?" Shona recoiled.

"*You* heard me, bitch." He advanced towards her, slamming the door to the tool room behind him.

"I don't know what you're talkin' 'bout." Shona felt behind her, but found only the edge of the workbench blocking her path.

"THIS!" He held up the now-grubby, screwed-up paper swan.

"I don't know what that is!" she lied, swallowing hard.

Kyle lunged at Shona, pinning her against the wall, his hand clamped around her throat in a horribly déjà vu fashion.

"Listen here, you fucking dyke. You stay the fuck away from Chloe, you understand, Shona? Or should I call you...*Kathleen*?" He pressed his unshaven face into hers.

"You're an asshole. You're a fucking coward! Look at you, manhandling a woman!" Shona was half-choking as she spat out her hatred towards him while he squeezed her neck even tighter. "How's your car, Kyle? Been repossessed yet? Or you hopin' your luck'll hold out on the cards? Yeah, that's right, I know all about you, you bastard! Go on, do your worst to me, but you leave Chloe alone. She's way too good for you and you fucking know it! It eats you up at night, don't it! That's why you're so fucking insecure, you piece of shit! Deep down, you KNOW she don't love you. And she NEVER will!"

"Quiet!" Kyle slapped Shona so hard she fell to the floor, hitting her head hard on the concrete.

"You can beat me all you want, it ain't nothin' I ain't had before, but my words will burn your insides every time you close your fucking eyes at night." She glared at him, her head pounding.

Kicking out viciously at her, Kyle caught Shona full in the stomach. She curled up in pain, recoiling from the blow and gasping for air. Furiously, he spat on the floor next to her, yanked open the door and slammed it behind him.

Chapter 75

"Shona, you got a visitor," shouted a voice from outside the tool room where she was stacking some boxes. It was later that afternoon, the heat of the day stifling.

"Who is it?" Shona called back as she opened the back door to the tool room. She squinted, her eyes adjusting slowly to the intense sunlight. As her eyes focused, she looked in horror at the face of the smiling young man in front of her.

"*Jonny?*" Shona gasped, her throat dry.

Jonny Pearson had worked with Shona at Wreckers. He was twenty-eight years old, tall and quite good-looking. His dark brown hair flopped over his well-proportioned face, and his affectionate smile when he saw her standing in front of him after all this time affirmed the soft spot he'd always had for her, even thinking one day of asking her to be his girl. Even after what had happened to Shona back in Mississippi, he still cared about her.

"I'll be damned, you really *are* here!" he exclaimed, his green eyes like saucers.

"What you doin' out here?" Her hands clenched tightly in her pockets.

"Had to deliver some parts. Y'needed 'em as soon as possible, and we were the only ones who had what you needed spare so, here I am." Jonny flung his arms out wide.

"How is everything...back there?"

"Great, well, apart from renewed gossip about you," he grinned. Shona folded her arms and nodded, prompting him to continue. "Yup, since a certain *Chloe Bruce* came to visit, people been talkin' and things...um...things ain't looking good for you."

"Why?"

"Why? Folks are wonderin' if you're up to your *old tricks* again, setting your sights on Miss Bruce. I gotta be honest, girl, don't think it'll be long before people start venturing out this way to find you. There are a lot o'angry people you left back home who feel you was lyin' to 'em."

"Lyin'? Jonny, do you think it's easy being...*me*?" she snapped.

"Listen, Shona. Before I found out you were one of them *kind*, I thought you were the best worker at Wreckers!"

"What changed?" she interrupted.

"What changed? Do y'know what they do to people like you?"

"Course I do!"

"Do y'know what they do to people who *help* people like you?" Jonny whispered the end of his question.

"Yeah," she replied.

"And I got my family to think about, Shona. I don't believe that you're bad, you're just unwell or wired up wrong. Ain't there no *cure*?" He wrinkled his nose.

"Cure? I've had treatment, Jonny, electric shocks all over me! Do you really think I wanna feel like this?"

"Listen, Shona, you're a real pretty girl, you know. Can't you just, I don't know, find a man, settle down, have kids if you want and just bury these feelings? Pretend, even? I mean, it's safer that way." Jonny stepped closer to her.

"Safer? So, I just get together with any man? Marry him,

maybe have kids with him? Just to throw everybody off the scent, right?"

"Yeah. Pretty much." He nodded gravely.

"Who wins then, Jonny?"

"You don't die," he said matter-of-factly.

"I don't *live* either," Shona fired back, wiping her nose on her sleeve.

"Listen, Shona, I gotta go. But my advice, if it's worth a dime, is start packing up from this place. Won't be long before it gets out here too. And for God's sake, if you're even thinking about Chloe Bruce in any other way than as your boss, well, I hate to be the one to say it but your days would be numbered." He tipped his hat, headed back to his truck and roared away up the driveway.

She coughed and wiped her face, Jonny's warning resonating in her mind.

Chapter 76

"Miss Bruce. What a pleasant surprise!" Charlie gushed as he looked up from the dress he was altering on the counter of Stella's Boutique that Saturday morning.

"Charlie, how are you?"

"I'm fine. Oh, let me be the first to offer my *sincerest* congratulations." He clasped his hands to his chest and beamed.

"Congratulations?"

"Yeah, you know. On becoming the future *Mrs. Kyle Chambers*."

Chloe's mouth went dry.

"Charlie, what are you talking about?"

"Your *lovely* fiancé came in here two days ago, with your mother."

"What? Why?"

"*Why*? They were looking for your wedding dress, of course." Charlie threw his arms out wide.

Chloe rocked back on her heels and gripped the edge of the counter, the color draining from her face.

"What else did they say?"

"Just that he's told everybody in town that he's gon' make an honest woman o'you and what kind of dress he'd want you to wear. I thought you knew! *Everybody* knows. Oh heavens, have I spoiled the surprise?" He clamped his hand over his mouth.

"Did Kyle say anything else?"

"Just that in the next few weeks he'd announce the news."

Chloe nodded her head thoughtfully.

Time was running out.

After some small talk and Charlie showing her some new fabrics that had just come in, Chloe asked if they could talk somewhere quiet.

"Of course. Juliet, can you mind the register, please?" he called out to his fellow shop assistant, holding the door open as he took Chloe into the back room.

"Right, what can I do for you? Charlie smiled.

"Well, I mean, I'm asking this for a...friend. And you're an understanding man. You know a lot of people in this town and she feels a little *different*. She'd like to go somewhere to socialize where she can be comfortable around people of her own *persuasion*," Chloe said intently, hoping that he was catching her drift.

His face turned more serious. He straightened his shoulders and brushed his eyebrow with his little finger. "And why would y'think that I would know anything about this *affliction* your friend has?"

"Oh, I don't mean to cause offense—"

"With all due respect, Miss Chloe, your father has made a lot of folks scared in this town, especially since you went away five years ago. A lot has changed–"

"I know, Charlie! But you're talking to *me* now, not him. Please trust me."

"What exactly are you asking, ma'am?"

"Is there a place that people who can't be open in town can go? You know what I'm saying, Charlie, don't you?"

Her eyes pleaded for him to understand.

"I think I do."

"Can you help me?"

"This can't get out, Chloe, for obvious reasons. This place is a haven for a lot of people." His eyes moistened.

"What *can't get out,* Charlie? I need to use the bathroom. Could you come back out, please?" Juliet, the middle-aged shop assistant, sauntered into the back room, curious as to why the two of them were whispering.

"I'll be right out," Charlie said as politely as his shaking voice would allow. *Did she overhear anything?* His mind was whirring. Juliet tutted loudly and returned to the shop floor.

"Your secret is safe with me, I promise."

"OK. You need to ask for Sidney at this address." He scribbled on his notepad.

"Thank you." Chloe tucked the address in her pocket.

"Please, not a word about Sidney. He means a lot to me."

"I promise, I won't tell a soul."

"So, this *friend*, she close to you?" he probed gently.

"Yes. *Very* close." Chloe blushed.

"I won't say a word. I'll go to my grave with half this town's secrets. Trust me, you'll see!"

With her hand on the door handle, Chloe turned and smiled.

"So, was it love at first sight for you two?"

"I love him more now than ever," he replied, his voice quaking with pride.

"That's beautiful, Charlie. I look forward to meeting Sidney, and thanks so much."

"Goodbye, Miss Chloe."

Charlie rejoined his snippy colleague on the shop floor.

Slipping the piece of notepaper back in the pocket of her new green dress, Chloe lightly tapped on the nondescript wooden door, checking behind her to see if anybody had followed her. She felt like the butterflies in her stomach would fly up her throat any minute, and swallowed hard every few seconds to keep them down.

"Hello?" came a man's croaky voice from behind the door, his face hidden.

"Hello. I'm looking for *Sidney*?"

"Who sent you?" the old man replied sharply.

"Charlie."

"What's your name?"

"Chloe."

The old man appeared from behind the door. He was tall and well built, wearing a red and navy checked shirt. His jeans were spotlessly clean, his gray hair neatly trimmed. He searched Chloe's face with suspicion in his eyes, but she understood why he had to be so cautious.

"I trust that given who your father associates with, you won't tell a living soul about this place? This place is all we got...All *they got*," Sidney said, cocking his head.

"Of course, I trust that you'll also not tell anybody about me being here?" Chloe winked.

"Sweetheart, we call it *The Shelter*. I'll take those secrets to my grave," he replied, reminding her of Charlie's words earlier.

"Thank you. Where is this place?" she asked, looking over Sidney's shoulder and into his modestly-sized farmhouse.

"Well, I wouldn't want it to be *too* obvious, now would I? It started as a little room just inside the storm shelter, then year after year, I extended it underground to what it is now. You wan' go take a look?"

Chloe nodded excitedly. He led the way around the perimeter of the farmhouse and to the storm shelter door.

"After you, ma'am." Sidney yanked open the heavy door.

Walking down the steps in near pitch black, Chloe couldn't help but feel a little underwhelmed. The walls were cold and damp, the odd drip of water the only sound.

"Made it like this to throw 'em off the scent. Smart, eh?" he whispered behind her, holding a flashlight as if reading Chloe's puzzled mind. "By the way, I know you're probably worried about people recognizing you, but everybody is sworn to secrecy. Go on, don't be shy, open the door."

Chloe pushed open the door at the bottom of the stairs. Instantly, she was bathed in warm light, the cold and damp darkness evaporating around her. The inside had been heavily soundproofed, with swathes of black duct tape around the frame to block out any giveaway chinks of light. The room was expansive. There were scores of people drinking and laughing as they danced to the smooth jazz playing on the jukebox. Every face she saw looked completely relaxed in their surroundings.

"Can I get you a drink?" Sidney asked.

"Yes, please. Just a soda." The bartender heard and poured her one right away.

Women sat with other women, some locked in an embrace, others were just talking. A small group of men were holding hands and laughing on the other side of the bar area.

"Sidney, this place is incredible!"

"I couldn't have done it without my Charlie. He's the one who put the money behind it and then I built it."

"Sounds like you're the perfect team," she said, smiling as she sipped her drink.

"We are. Only ever been him for me, since we were kids." His voice cracked as he spoke of his love for Charlie. "Just wish we could live together properly, but we'd be pistol-whipped before the end of the first day if we were seen out together."

Chloe's smile vanished, knowing he was right. It gnawed at her heart, recalling her mother's revulsion for Pete and Ronnie who were there at The Shelter, pointed out by Sidney as she stood at the bar.

Meandering around The Shelter, Chloe smiled at every face she came across, recoiling slightly in surprise at the amount of townsfolk she recognized. Even the local judge was there, stroking the back of a man's head. He nodded at her, in equal recognition, but all now duty bound to keep it a secret to keep themselves alive.

Wandering around for the last time after checking her watch and seeing that almost two hours had flown by, Chloe found a door leading to another room. It was slightly ajar and, curiosity getting the better of her, she peeked inside. As her eyes adjusted to the dim light inside the room, she stepped back in shock, recognizing a face. She knew who it was immediately.

It was Billy, the youngest Bullen brother.

Not only that, his arm was draped over a young black man in a tender embrace. Their faces registered pure bliss, entirely comfortable in their surroundings.

Still in shock at seeing one of the town's thugs in a place like this, Chloe took a deep breath to steady herself, then headed for the exit door. But as she did so, two women, a little worse for wear, bumped into her, sending their drinks flying. The loud smash of breaking glass on the concrete floor startled the two men she had just been watching.

She looked back to see both of them now staring at her open mouthed.

"Miss BRUCE! I...What are *you* doing here?"

Billy Bullen looked mortified to see the daughter of his family's *employer* bearing witness to his deepest, darkest secret.

Chloe stumbled over herself, trying to politely leave the two men to their evening, shocked and surprised at the reality that anyone in Daynes could be lying about who they truly were underneath. She couldn't work out if she felt comforted or scared by the tragically necessary dishonesty she had witnessed that evening as she drove home.

Chapter 77

Monday morning, Larry Bruce leaned back triumphantly in his leather chair.

"You got it, thanks. Bye." Replacing the receiver and taking a long puff of his cigar, Bruce grinned, his smugness palpable.

"You done it?" Kyle asked, his eyes wide.

"Of course I have." Bruce stubbed his cigar out and took a swig of whiskey.

"What'd I miss?" Deputy Paul strolled in, catching the last part of Bruce's phone conversation.

"A friend of mine's back from vacation and, after a little *persuasion*, he's willing to take one of our best employees to pass on their excellent ideas." Bruce couldn't hide the smirk crossing his face as he spoke.

"Right, so?" Deputy Paul frowned.

"So, that employee would be a certain broad! Ha, Ellis said we can't fire her—so we'll *promote* her!" Kyle sniggered.

"OK, I get 'cha now. Where you sending her?"

"Louisiana! She won't even make it to my guy's place. Way too many enemies there, more than willing to get her blood on their hands. And the best part? Nobody suspects we know about her bein' on the run, so *imagine our heartbreak* when we discover we sent her there in good faith and it's all her own fault for lyin' to us about where she came from. It's all coming together nicely, gentlemen! She goes next week. Just another employee on an outreach program—and who better than our *star* pupil, eh, boys? It'll be nice and clean!" Bruce clinked glasses with an equally jubilant Kyle.

"Paul, I want you to do the honors. Give her the news that she's going in a week's time," Kyle said.

"With pleasure."

"Randy, let me help," Shona offered as he struggled with the huge delivery he'd just taken.

"Thanks, Shona," he said nervously. Randy never knew how to talk to her now, in his new role as chief spy for Kyle. Guilt was eating him up inside, especially when he saw her black eye. But he was in an impossible situation, with Kyle knowing about his young family and how much he needed his job.

"Jackson!" Deputy Paul yelled across the yard.

Shona strode over and was ushered into a damp side room in the garage.

"Can't believe I'm saying this, but you been doing good lately."

"*Really?*" she stared at him, mystified.

"Yup, I mean, I know y'have it tough here, being the only broad and all, but y'got our respect now, after you saw to the changes around here gettin' made."

"OK. Well, thanks."

"So, what we thought was that you could...*share them.*"

"Share what? With who?" Her brow creased as she tried to follow what Deputy Paul was getting at.

"Your knowledge. Your ideas."

"I'm sorry, sir, I don't understand."

"Well, Larry Bruce himself wants you to train guys at other places."

"Other places? Like here in Daynes?"

"Oh no. In Louisiana!" Deputy Paul said inching closer, enjoying his moment.

"*Louisiana*?" Shona's world began to spin as she tried to keep a lid on her panic as best she could. "No, sir, please, not Louisiana."

"Why, what you not telling us?" His rancid breath filled her nostrils, causing her to gag even more.

"What? Nothing, I just–"

"You start in a week. End of discussion." He kept his face straight for the few steps he needed to, but then broke out into a loud cackle as soon as he was out of earshot.

Shrinking to the ground, Shona's face contorted in shock.

It was after 8 o'clock that Monday evening and Chloe was still in her office, begrudgingly catching up on her paperwork, when Kyle casually strolled past.

"Workin' late?" he asked, looking behind him to see if anyone else was around.

"Yes. Father's gone home and Ron's downstairs. What do you want, Kyle?" Chloe couldn't stand the sight of him now.

"Just to let you know, you got a call this morning, while you were out...from the dry cleaner. Something about a piece of paper you left in your dress pocket?" He waited for her reaction, not taking his eyes off her.

"Yeah?" She continued to stare blankly at her paperwork.

"They weren't sure whether it was important or they should just toss it out." He stepped forward into her office.

Chloe felt her blood turn to ice.

"*Which* dress?"

He paused, knowing the impact of his next three words.

"The *green* one," he confirmed nonchalantly.

The lead point of the pencil Chloe was writing with splintered. She looked up at him, trying to mask her inner panic.

"Okay, well, I'll ring them first thing." She smiled at him, her face as calm as she could muster.

"No need. I picked it up this afternoon for you."

He cleared his throat and curled his fingers around the edge of the door. Closing it gently, he turned the key in the lock.

"Who's *Sidney*?"

The room began to spin for Chloe. She sat in silence, unable to break the intense stare Kyle had fixed on her. After a few unbearable moments, she opened her mouth to speak, but this was too much for him. His calm facade slipped as he strode across the floor and grabbed Chloe's throat, squeezing her windpipe.

"Kyle, stop, get off me," her strangled voice croaked.

"WHO IS HE? You'd better tell me, goddamn it, or I SWEAR to God, I'll–" he hissed into her ear, flecks of spit landing on her neck.

"Let me go, Kyle, let me go!"

"Why can't you just answer me? Who's Sidney?" he repeated, squeezing tighter.

"He's a friend. I haven't done anything wrong." She could feel her strength slipping away from her as his grip tightened around her thin neck.

"I'm gon' pay this *Sidney* a little visit, to make sure his story matches yours." He released her from his sweaty grasp finally and reached over her to the phone, dialing the number he knew by heart.

"It's me. Got a job for you and the boys. Get down here now." He replaced the phone, his eyes blazing with adrenaline as he pressed his face back into Chloe's.

"Kyle, who did you call? Where are you going?" Hot tears streamed down her terrified face.

"Well, I got an address right here. I might start with that!" He pulled out the piece of notepaper that Charlie had given to Chloe that day at Stella's. "I can't believe I was wrong about Jackson all along! When I found that fucking swan in your tray, with the letter S on it, I thought it stood for *Shona*! I just figured she was sniffing 'round my girl. But now I see it stood for Sidney. I shoulda known you weren't no dyke! You liked it that night, didn't you? The feel of a *man* inside you?" He pressed his face into her menacingly, his hands on the armrests as she sat pinned back in her chair. "What a shame we've already arranged to have your lil' friend sent away, but who the fuck cares?"

"Shona? Sent where?" Chloe swallowed hard, trying to clear her throat enough to make her voice audible.

Kyle sniggered loudly, still reveling in his triumph over the one woman to ever reject his charm. He looked away, his attention drawn to the dull roar of the Ford pickup that had just pulled up outside.

"I'm gon' pay Sidney a little visit and I don't want you following me."

He reached over into Chloe's purse, taking out her car keys, then left her in her chair in paralyzed shock at what had just happened.

"Um, what we doing here, boys?"

Billy Bullen wiped his brow nervously as they pulled up to the location written on the note Kyle was holding.

"Good question. Boss?" Earl Bullen directed his confusion towards Kyle.

"I need to know if a guy called Sidney spent the evening with my Chloe last night." His voice was eerily calm.

"Wait, we sure it's here? I mean, I can't see Miss Chloe comin' all the way out *here*?" Billy shook his head, desperate to get them to leave. He shrank into the back of the truck.

"The name and address said here. Let's go." Kyle jumped out and marched towards the farmhouse. Ernest hopped up the steps and hammered on the heavy wooden door.

"Hello?" an old man's voice sounded from behind the door.

"Open up!"

Sidney opened the door slightly. Spotting Ernest Bullen, he panicked and tried to shut the door, but Kyle wedged his foot in the way.

"What do you want?"

"Did you see Chloe Bruce last night?" Kyle yelled through the crack in the door.

"What?" Sidney yelled back, feeling his strength drain away.

"I said, did you fucking see her last night?" Kyle booted the door as hard as he could, knocking Sidney crashing to the ground inside his house. He stepped over the threshold and grabbed the old man, throwing him outside onto the ground at the bottom of the three steps leading from his porch.

"Wait. Yes, I did bu–"

Not waiting for him to finish his sentence, Kyle punched Sidney so hard that his nose exploded, caking his wrinkled face in scarlet blood. Collapsing into a heap on the ground, he held his hands up in surrender, but Kyle kneeled and grabbed him by his collar, his right fist drawn back ready to strike again.

"What the fuck is a withered old bastard like you doing with her?" His eyes were wild with fury.

"It's not like that–" Sidney began, realizing his explanation was futile as Ernest Bullen appeared from the back of the truck brandishing a baseball bat.

"Then why don't you tell me exactly what it's like if it ain't you sneaking 'round with my woman?" Kyle screamed, nodding to Ernest who grinned as he pulled the bat back and struck Sidney across the legs. He yelped, a sickening crack emanating from his kneecaps.

"There's nothing going on, I swear," Sidney pleaded, trying to crawl away, his kneecaps shattered.

"Then what was she doing here?"

"She just came to chat."

"You're fucking lying!" Kyle nodded to Ernest, who waved his bat and struck again.

At that moment, Sidney raised his head up and caught sight of a smaller figure crouching in the back of the truck, almost out of sight.

"Wait. That boy, HE KNOWS ME!" He pointed his shaking finger towards Billy, crying desperately for him to save him.

"What the fuck's he talking about?" Earl stared over at his little brother, who had now shrunk completely out of sight.

"He knows for a fact there ain't nothin' goin' on with Miss Chloe and me! Please, ask him. ASK!" Sidney begged them, the blood spilling freely out of his quivering mouth.

Billy appeared from behind the truck and strode purposefully towards the group, his decision made. His face was pale as he reached into his pocket.

"What's he talking about, brother?" Ernest demanded.

With the last of his strength, Sidney sat up and looked Billy straight in the eye. "He knows me, he knows because–"

With tears in his eyes, Billy Bullen took his hand out of his pocket and pulled the trigger of the revolver he was holding. The bullet ripped straight through Sidney's heart, killing him instantly.

His older brothers looked at him with a mixture of shock and admiration on their dirty faces.

"WOW, brother! I never knew you had it in you–your first kill!" Earl slapped him hard on his back.

Kyle stared at the dead man on the ground. "Alright, now that that's taken care of, you boys know where to get rid of *this*." He kicked the body.

"Usual place?"

"Yeah. Make sure you get rid of that gun too!" Kyle nodded to Billy, who was standing motionless over Sidney's dead body, trying to hide the grief and shame he felt for what he'd just done to the man who had, for once in his miserable young life, been the only one to ever accept him for who he was.

~

"What are you doing here?" Chloe whispered as Shona appeared unexpectedly at her office door.

"I had to work late. I was just about to go home when I saw your car still here. I can't rest, Chloe. They're sending me back to *Louisiana*. I'll be killed the minute I set foot there!" Shona blurted out.

"Kyle's been gone half an hour now. He could be back any minute. I'm scared of what he's gone and done! I can't leave—he's taken my keys!" she replied, her blanched face still frozen in shock as she sat in her chair. She ran her shaking hand over her red raw neck, not registering a word of what Shona had said.

"What happened? Did *he* do this to this to you?" Shona asked as she bounded across the floor and kneeled in front of her, her eyes wide in horror as she saw the angry red handprint on Chloe's pale neck.

"Shona, I've gotta get away from him!" She broke down, terrified she would hear the growl of the Ford at any moment.

"Ssshhh, come here." Shona tried to pull Chloe into her arms, but she resisted.

"I can't. I want to be with you so much, but if Kyle comes back and finds you here, he'll finish us both off!"

"We'll think of something," Shona reassured her.

Just then, bright headlight beams streamed through the blinds. Chloe jumped out of her chair and stared down out of the window at the green Ford truck that had just pulled up outside, her face stricken with fear, realizing they had only moments.

"Go, NOW! I can't let him find you here–"

"I'm not leaving you here on your own with him!" Shona's eyes blazed.

"I'll be fine, Ron's downstairs. If I need him, I'll scream. Now, GO!" Chloe cried as she gently pushed Shona's arms away.

As Shona raced reluctantly away to find Ron, Kyle rounded the corner and headed up the balcony steps, missing her by milliseconds. He walked into Chloe's office and placed her car keys on her desk in front of her. She stared at him, petrified.

"Kyle, what the hell have you done?" Her voice was barely a whisper.

"Here are your keys." He fixed his cold stare on her and smiled, then left her alone in the semi-darkness of her office.

Chapter 78

Chloe found Shona the following morning in the tool room.

"You OK?" Shona asked wearily, looking as if she hadn't slept a wink.

"Yeah. Listen, give me a day or two to get some money together, then we get out of here, for good!" Chloe replied.

"You serious?"

"I mean it, Shona. I want us to be together. I'll get some money out of the bank at lunch, and I got more hidden away at my parents' house too. I'll see them tonight and I'll let you know what we're doing tomorrow, yeah?"

"OK," Shona replied, her stomach churning but with excitement this time.

"Shona?" Chloe turned around when she reached the door.
"Yeah?"

"Tell me you love me." Her eyes moistened.

Shona gazed at her, her eyes shining brighter and bluer than Chloe had ever seen before. The truth in them was unmistakable.

"I love you, Chloe."

Chloe smiled, the words landing safely in her heart.

"I love you too." She hurried away, still tingling.

"How much today, Miss Bruce?" the bank teller asked brightly.

"All of it," Chloe replied matter-of-factly, hardly even glancing up.

"Oh, I'm afraid our policy is that we can only give you half today and half tomorrow, would that be OK?"

"Fine, I'll come by in the morning and get the rest. I just wanna buy a few things, you know," she replied lightly, keen to play down her frustration at her plans being delayed.

After returning from her lunch break, Chloe walked along the balcony and knocked on her father's door.

"Chloe," Bruce said coolly.

"Father, I thought we could have dinner tonight?"

"Sure. Will Kyle be joining us?"

"No, he's out tonight at Red's, some business I think he said. I thought it would be nice to have just the three of us."

"OK." Bruce's mustache bristled nervously at her unexpectedly pleasant manner towards him. "See you at 7 o'clock!" he called after her as she left his office and disappeared down the balcony steps.

Sticking her head around the tool room doorway, Chloe whispered to get Shona's attention.

"Hey," Shona replied.

"I have a plan and a way out of here. Meet me at 10, at the statue in town. Can you do that?"

Shona didn't even need to think about her answer.

∼

"So, how's it going with Kyle, dear?" Eleanor Bruce's voice sounded hollow.

"Fine," Chloe lied, picking up her knife and fork.

"I've picked the wrong damn glasses up! Be back in a minute," Bruce said, dropping his newspaper on the table.

As he disappeared up the stairs and out of sight, Chloe saw her opportunity.

"Mother, I need to speak to you. It's important."

"About a certain wedding, giving me *grandchildren*?" Eleanor smiled coldly as she sliced through her beef.

"I'm not happy with Kyle." She tried to make eye contact with her mother.

"It takes work, Chloe, you don't just *give up*. Kyle's worried about you, he–"

"Mother, he doesn't treat me very good. He's often *physical* with me–"

"Now you listen here." Eleanor clattered her knife and fork down onto her plate, her patience finally wearing out. "Our job as wives is to support our husbands. It's that simple. You being with Kyle has attracted a lot of interest from investors and the wedding you'll have, my goodness, everybody who is anybody will be there! And you want to turn that down because it gets a little *difficult* sometimes?"

"Difficult? Mother, do you know what I mean by physical?" She stared at her mother in disbelief. "Has Father done it to *you*?"

"What happens between a man and a woman in the privacy of their own home is nobody else's business. Besides, overall, he's a good husband."

Chloe stared open-mouthed at her mother, who carried on eating her roast potatoes.

"Found them." Bruce joined the table holding his glasses in front of him.

After dinner, Eleanor and her husband retired to the drawing room, brandy glasses in hand.

"I'm just going to my den," Chloe said.

"I wish you'd grow out of that drawing stuff," her father called after her.

"Hey, can I come down too?" Antonia's gentle voice soothed Chloe's inner turmoil, as it always had done since she was a baby.

"Sure," she replied, smiling at the welcome company.

Inside the small, cluttered den, Chloe lovingly sorted through her sketches, a sad smile etched on her face knowing that she couldn't take them all with her.

"Miss Chloe, I gotta say, I've noticed that you ain't been the same lately. Something's changed, hasn't it?" Antonia probed gently.

"You don't miss a thing, do you?" Chloe answered, unsurprised.

"Nope, but I keep it all in here," she replied, pointing to her temple.

"I just wish I could keep these with me." She gestured towards the pictures piled up high on her easel.

"You could always draw *new* pictures? But I like these ones. Done with so much care and attention...and love."

Antonia pointed to a pile of detailed sketches Chloe had clearly taken the time to complete perfectly. Eyes had become faces, faces had become bodies, with each sketch lovingly finished off using her finest watercolors. Shona's beautifully painted face gazed back at her in every portrait, most of which showed her seated on or stroking Storm.

"Your father hasn't seen these. Don't worry, I kept them hidden away. But he doesn't come down here anyway."

"Thank you." Chloe was touched by her intuition. "I'm going to miss you, Antonia. Here, take this—"

She handed her a thickly stuffed envelope. "But don't open it until tomorrow, OK? And keep it to yourself, like all the other things I know you know." Chloe kissed her on the cheek. She looked at her watch. It was already 9 p.m.

"Shoot, I gotta go and get ready."

Chloe arrived in town with only a few minutes to spare, but Shona was already waiting patiently by the statue. She jumped into Chloe's car and beamed at her as she put her foot down and sped away.

"So, what's this plan?" she asked, her eyes wide with excitement.

"I want to spend the night with you, Shona."

Chapter 79

Chloe pulled up outside Fortua Hotel, just on the outskirts of Daynes. Rooms here were the most expensive in town, but she wanted luxury and nowhere else would suffice. Open-mouthed, Shona looked out of the car window at the stone pillars holding up the grand entrance to the hotel and the long red carpet leading up to the gold-embossed glass door.

"Wow," she said, blowing her cheeks out.

"I've booked the best room. I wanted our first night together to be special." Chloe switched the engine off and turned to face Shona, but as she did so, her eyes clouded with concern at the halo of sweat that had matted Shona's long blonde bangs to her forehead.

"What's the matter? Are you nervous?" She reached across and stroked Shona's face, losing herself once again in her blue eyes, the anguish in them almost unbearable to see.

"I've pictured this moment so many times in my head. I never thought it would happen, though," she replied softly.

"Surely you know my feelings for you are real by now?"

"Back in Mississippi, I thought that girl liked me then. But she tricked me. I was terrified it was gon' happen again. That's why I kept fightin' it with you. I couldn't let my heart fall for you 'cos I would've never recovered." Shona bit her lip. "I love you so much it makes me ache."

"Come on. Let's go inside." She jumped out of her car as Shona sniffed and wiped her face with both hands.

"Ma'am!" Chloe winked as she opened the passenger side door.

They walked through the opulent lobby together, side by side. Approaching the front desk, Chloe smiled confidently at the clerk.

"Hello, I have a booking for tonight and we would very much like not to be disturbed. I'm sure you still pride yourself on being the *soul of discretion* here?" she hinted, giving him her name without even blinking an eye, then sliding a ten dollar bill across the counter.

"Yes, ma'am." The clerk smiled back, understanding Chloe's subtle words perfectly. "Room 223 on the top floor. The elevator is just over there. I see you have no luggage, so I won't trouble the bellhop. Have a pleasant stay with us, Miss Bruce," he purred as he handed her the key, his open palm then gesturing towards the gold-plated doors behind them.

As the two women headed towards the elevator, the clerk stared after them. As he pocketed the bill, he walked to the other end of his counter and picked up the phone.

Chloe slipped the key into the door and pushed it open. The room was enormous, with a lush Persian carpet and azure-blue crushed velvet drapes. The gilt-edged furniture set the room off perfectly, but it was the huge king-sized bed that dominated the room. The navy-blue damask quilt was peeled back slightly to reveal crisp white sheets below. It looked achingly inviting as the two women stood inside the room together, alone and undisturbed for the first time. Chloe turned the key in the lock as Shona surveyed the magnificence of the gorgeously perfect room.

"Hey," Chloe said after a minute or two of silently watching her.

Shona turned around and smiled back nervously, her hands clasped over her fluttering stomach. "I can't believe I'm here with you." She lowered her head as her whole body began to tremble.

Realizing what was happening, Chloe moved towards her quickly and slipped her fingers underneath her collar. She caressed the back of Shona's neck, sending bolts of electricity down her spine. Shona held back for a split second, but Chloe pulled her in closer, trying to reassure her.

"It's OK. I know what happened to you, but what we're doing isn't wrong. You do believe me, don't you?"

Looking up at her, Shona's anguished eyes filled with tears.

"All my life I've been told it *was*. What they did to me...they made me feel so dirty, so ashamed of myself. And now I'm here with you and I never wanna be anywhere else," she whispered.

"Say them. Say the words to me. Say, *'it's not wrong'*." She cupped Shona's face in her hands, holding her gaze.

After all the years of pain, guilt and suppressing who she was all her life, Shona finally found the strength to squeeze out the words.

"It's...it's not wrong." She fell limply into the safety of Chloe's warm body.

Smiling proudly, Chloe wrapped her arms around the back of Shona's neck, stroking her hair and locking their bodies together. Shona lowered her face to rest on Chloe's perfumed neck, their faces inching closer. A fraction away from connecting, they both pulled back and stopped, savoring the longed-for moment.

Unable to resist a second longer, their lips finally met for the very first time.

Kissing tenderly and stroking each other's hair, their mutual arousal began to build inside them. Occasionally they broke away from each other in disbelief that the moment was real, that they were both with each other at long last, their eyes communicating every unspoken emotion they'd ever held in their hearts. In no time at all, their kisses had become hotter, more urgent, with Chloe nudging Shona closer and closer to the edge of the bed, unbuttoning, then peeling off her checked shirt and running her fingers over the warm skin of her shoulders. Feeling the soft material of the sheets graze the back of her legs, Shona froze, pulled her face away and looked down, trembling once again.

"What is it?" Chloe stroked the hair out of Shona's face.

"It's just...I've never actually done this...with another girl before."

Holding on to her chin delicately, Chloe kissed her.

"That's OK, me neither. But there ain't no rule book here. We just take it slow, trust each other and do what feels good, OK?"

Shona's skin tingled more each time she felt Chloe's fingers brush against it. Running her palms over Shona's bare shoulders, then underneath her arms to lift them, Chloe gripped the bottom of her white undershirt and slid it up over her head. Shona's bangs flopped over her face, obscuring her view momentarily until a giggling Chloe swept them out of her eyes again. Her smiling face darkened when she looked down onto Shona's bare chest and saw her pale scars for the first time.

"Is this where they–" she began, her voice cracking with anger.

Shona swallowed hard and nodded, the shame of her treatment still burning deep within her.

"I wish I could take away what they did to you," Chloe said

as she ran her fingertips over the scars, her anger subsiding with each butterfly kiss she then planted on each one. She lay Shona down backward on the bed and kneeled in front of her to untie her laces. Pulling them off with a heave, she threw her boots, then her socks out of her way and walked her fingers up the inside of Shona's thighs. Biting her lip, Shona waited for Chloe to touch her where she was aching to feel her the most.

~

Downstairs, the front desk clerk dialed a number without even needing to look it up in his Rolodex.

"It's me, Peter from the Fortua Hotel? Sir, you are never going to believe who has just walked into my lobby. No, she didn't give me the name of her companion. Description? Well, blonde hair...Sir? Hello?"

Peter replaced the handset, frowning as his line went dead.

~

Chloe lingered over Shona's pants buttons for a moment to ensure she was comfortable, then slowly picked them open, one by one. Shona's heart was beating out of her chest with excitement as she tried to control her breathing, but the throbbing between her legs was almost too much to bear. Gazing up, not wanting to take her eyes off her, Chloe wrapped her fingers around Shona's waistband and deftly slid her pants down over her slender legs, leaving her lying on the bed wearing just her underwear.

Smiling, she lightly planted kisses up the insides of Shona's thighs, but as she almost reached the top, she felt her flinch. Looking closely, Chloe saw more scars.

"They did it *here* too?" Horrified, she lifted her head up, her heart breaking with the thought of the intimate places Shona had been hurt.

Nodding, Shona instinctively tried to close her legs.

"If you want me to stop, I'll stop," Chloe said. Sensing her anxiety, she climbed back up Shona's body and lay next to her, stroking her hair.

"No, I don't want you to stop. I just don't know how to deal with what's happenin' in my body right now–" she buried her face into Chloe's neck.

"Is it a bad feeling?" Chloe asked, terrified of the answer.

"No. What you're doing...feels...it feels *incredible*," Shona replied, wiping the stray tear that had rolled onto her cheek.

"It's OK, I'm not going to rush you," Chloe reassured her as she waited a few moments for Shona's nervous heartbeat to calm. As it did so, Shona placed soft kisses on Chloe's mouth to let her know she was OK. Reading the sign intuitively, she crawled back down Shona's body to the end of the bed and stood up. Without taking her eyes off her, she removed her pumps and began unbuttoning her silk blouse, enjoying the thrill of holding Shona's undivided attention, finally having her entirely to herself after months of her dashing away all the time. Leaning back on her elbows, Shona was completely transfixed by the slow reveal of Chloe's breathtaking body as her blouse glided down over her smooth shoulders and onto the carpet. Chloe threaded her thin black belt nimbly through her fingers and inched the zip on her pencil skirt down. Gazing at Shona, she peeled her skirt agonizingly slowly over her hips and stood in front of her wearing nothing but her precious necklace and lace underwear.

"Is this OK?" Chloe bit her lip anxiously as she remembered what Shona had been forced to look at during her vile treatment. But there was not a flicker of doubt on Shona's mesmerized face.

"Come here," she breathed, feeling only the torture of not having Chloe in her arms right that second.

Chloe stepped forward and straddled Shona who held her carefully around her hips, mindful to avoid the dark bruises and fingernail dents still haunting her milky-white skin. Sitting up straight to be at eye level with her perfectly shaped breasts, Shona kissed them softly as she reached behind and unclipped Chloe's bra clasp, her fingers shaking with adrenaline as she freed her from the straps. Chloe arched her back at her soft touch, feeling the tingling sensations start to build between her legs. Shona gasped as she saw Chloe's breasts for the first time, her hands nervously exploring them as if they'd been sculpted from the finest marble.

"You are...the most beautiful thing I have ever seen!" Shona murmured as Chloe gently pushed her back down onto the bed. Closing her eyes, she moaned as she felt Chloe's lips brush over her neck and around her earlobe, then onto her collarbone, eventually moving lower and lower down to her chest.

"Is this OK?" she asked quietly, kissing the goosepimpled skin around her ribs and down over her hip bones.

"Uh huh." Shona's fists clenched around the crisp bedsheets as her head dropped back at the touch of Chloe's soft lips on her delicate skin. Trailing the tip of her tongue down lower and lower until it was nearly at the place Shona craved to feel it, Chloe savored every moment of the wait. Shona applied the lightest of pressure with her shaking hand on the back of Chloe's head, stroking the nape of her neck with her thumb, which just spurred Chloe on more as she breathed hot breath onto Shona's shivering skin.

"Oh God, Chloe, please don't stop," she groaned.

Unable to resist a moment longer, Chloe reached down and slid Shona's underwear off, impatiently throwing the cotton hindrance to the floor. She parted her quivering legs and kissed up inside them, higher and higher until she found the spot that Shona had been aching for her to reach.

"Oh...my..." She writhed on the bed as Chloe held on to her. The sensations rippled through her like wildfire as she fought to keep her eyes open, but the sheer pleasure of what Chloe was doing with her expert tongue was making it impossible for her not to clamp her eyes shut in ecstasy. Running her fingers through Chloe's silky soft brown hair, she held her head exactly where she wanted it. Needing no encouragement, Chloe sped up the movements of her tongue until Shona could take no more.

"Oh God...Oh my God..." she panted.

Suddenly, a massive wave crashed over her, exhilarating every nerve ending in her body, like electricity coursing through her. She cried out as Chloe's unrelenting tongue moved faster and faster until she felt the orgasm completely pass through Shona's convulsing body. Chloe lifted her head, then kissed her way back up to Shona's trembling face.

"Are you OK?"

"That was the most incredible feeling of my life," she said, looking deep into Chloe's eyes. Reaching up to dry Shona's tears with her own shaking fingers, Chloe cuddled up next to her, cradling her in her arms as both their racing heartbeats returned to their now-familiar calmness.

∼

After hearing the description from Peter, Larry Bruce slammed the receiver down with a crash. He let out a strangled roar, then swiped his arm over the surface of his desk, sending his work files and papers flying in all directions, his whiskey glass shattering into a million pieces against his office wall.

Sinking back into his chair, he knew what to do. He picked up the phone and dialed.

"It's Bruce. Find Kyle. Find him *NOW!*"

∼

"I don't know what happened there." Shona looked embarrassed by her tears as she lay in Chloe's arms, both of them now tucked underneath the warm blankets of their luxurious bed.

"I love you, Shona," Chloe said, scooping her face up in her hands.

"I love you too."

Shona began stroking the thin layer of skin around Chloe's bruised hip bone. Before long, her confidence began to grow as she watched her bite her lip with every circle of her fingertip. With one fluid movement, Shona slid her hand underneath the waistband of Chloe's underwear, edging the lace down over her thighs, then she lay on her side next to her. Hanging her right arm down over Chloe's navel, she draped her left arm above Chloe's head, interlocking their fingers. As Shona kissed her neck hungrily, Chloe's lips parted, her eyes closing as her arousal was building again. Shona explored lower and lower with her right hand until her fingertips were resting just between her thighs. But Chloe's body flinched, her legs twitching from the still-raw tenderness she felt down there since Kyle's brutal assault.

Shona stopped instantly.

"Because of him?" she asked.

Chloe, feeling her own shame now, buried her face into Shona's neck, confirming the answer.

Shona held her unconditionally. Time wasn't in the slightest bit important.

"I wish I could take back what he did to you," she murmured in her ear. She felt Chloe nuzzle in deeper, her damp eyes moistening Shona's skin.

After a few minutes of feeling their hearts beat in unison,

Chloe lifted her head out of Shona's neck and looked deep into her understanding eyes. Without a single doubt in her mind, she reached down to place her hand on top of Shona's, moving it back between her legs, not taking her eyes off her for a second.

"I trust you," she whimpered as she slowly placed Shona's fingers inside of her, feeling them slip in effortlessly.

In slow motion, their bodies rocked together in perfect rhythm, with Shona reassuring her every single moment by a kiss on her neck. Chloe's panting became more urgent, her heels digging into the bed as she writhed with pleasure. She closed her eyes and looked away, biting down hard on the back of her hand as Shona found her spot perfectly.

"Please look at me," Shona whispered as she locked the fingers on her left hand around Chloe's again, tighter this time as her right hand continued carefully working inside of her. Chloe's memory of how rough Kyle had been that night ebbed away with every second of Shona's sure touch. She'd taken the time to make sure Chloe was fully prepared for her and now, as Shona held her close to her body the whole way through, Chloe was finally ready to let go completely.

"Oh my...Oh, Shona!" Arching her back, she lifted Shona almost entirely off the bed with her, her toes tangling up in the sheets, calling out her name as her orgasm raged through her body. Shona slowed down her movements inside of her, kissing Chloe's forehead as she guided her back down to earth. Their heavy breaths returned to normal, followed by a few precious moments of calm.

"Shhhh...I'm here, I'm here...Shhh, it's OK," Shona whispered in Chloe's ear, wiping her stray tears away with her left hand. Waiting patiently until she was ready, Shona removed her fingers from inside of Chloe, letting her control the movement in her own time. They lay there in each other's arms, savoring every delicious second of what had just happened.

"Can I ask you something?" Chloe began as she stroked Shona's arm.

"Sure," she kissed Chloe's forehead and nuzzled into her.

"When did you first know? That you loved me?"

"When you first walked out on that damn balcony, I knew I was in trouble," she replied lazily, her eyes half-closed.

"Really?"

"Yeah, why? When did you?" Shona opened her eyes.

"That first day I saw you, rushing away. I knew right then I had to get to know you! I can't explain why, I just did. You can't help who you fall for, can you? It's just who we are. Then when you made it so damn difficult to keep up with you—"

Shona laughed as Chloe gently tickled her.

"I just wanted to know you more. I can't believe you didn't see that!" Chloe said, a little hurt.

"I'm sorry, I was just so scared after what happened last time, and what with the treatment I had an' all. I couldn't understand what was going on in my body. But I knew I loved you. I just never thought you'd feel the same." Shona's voice cracked with emotion.

"Well, I do, so now what? What happens now?"

"I just want to lie here with you tonight," Shona replied, a more serious tone in her soft, sleepy voice.

Shona's head was snuggled deep in her soft pillow when she felt a gentle kiss on her forehead. She opened her eyes a crack to see Chloe ready to leave.

"Whass'up, where'y'goin', it'sss late," she slurred, her body ravaged with exhaustion.

"Baby, I gotta go. I gotta get home before my parents notice

I'm not there." She stroked Shona's messy hair. "D'you want me to wait for you to get dressed so that I can take you home?"

"No, I don't want you to be late and get in any more trouble. Plus, I just wan' enjoy this room a bit longer! I never slept so good! This is the most luxury I ever had in my whole life!" she added, a contented grin on her face.

"I'll see you later, OK? I'll need a little time in the morning to go to the bank again, but then we're gone. Meet me at 10 tomorrow break time; people won't notice you going to the parking lot. Then we get in the car and drive, OK? I love you."

"I love you too. Don't worry, I'll leave here to get to work in plenty of time, *boss*," Shona added cheekily.

Chloe smiled, grabbed her bag and put her hand on the door handle.

"Chloe–"

"Yeah?" she replied, fondly rolling her eyes at Shona starfishing across the huge king-sized bed.

"That was the greatest night of my life. I just wanted you to know that," Shona drawled as she drifted back off to sleep.

"Mine too," she replied softly, closing the door quietly behind her.

Chapter 80

Chloe drummed her fingers on her office desk, the clock on her wall seemingly ticking down the minutes painfully slowly. It was 9:27 and a half exactly when she rushed through her office door, her handbag stuffed with the rest of the savings she'd withdrawn from the bank on her way in. The trunk of her car was packed with her suitcase and the few possessions she was taking with her. Now, it was just a case of waiting until the break time buzzer sounded and they could slip away unnoticed.

At 9:30, Chloe sighed, looking for a way to pass the next thirty minutes as quickly as possible. As if on cue, a knock on her door roused her back to reality.

"Hi Chloe, sorry to jump on you as soon as you walk in, but can you sign this order form, please?" Ron Black popped his balding head around her door.

"Of course, Ron. How's that lovely wife of yours doing?" Chloe asked politely as she took out her pen to sign the form.

"She's doin' OK, Chloe, thanks for asking. Well, I'll let you get on now, thanks again!"

9:35 a.m. came and went. The wait was excruciating.

∼

"Chloe, we have an emergency meeting, Larry's office, now. Some investors have just dropped in on us!"

Chloe's face filled with horror as she looked at the time. It was 9:45 a.m., and she had just finished tidying her desk for the last time.

"Sorry, but I can't–"

"What do you have to do that's more important than meeting with the people who ensure we get paid?" Kyle asked coldly.

"OK. I can spare ten minutes, then I have things to do," she replied, trying to control the adrenaline rushing through her as she looked again at the clock.

After time dragging so torturously when she was in her office, it now seemed to race by, five minutes disappearing as if they were seconds.

"So, what do you think, Chloe? You agree?" one of the investors probed.

"Um, can you explain again, please?" she said, shaking her head out of distraction. Kyle and Bruce quietly fumed.

"Honey, were you listening?" Kyle tapped his pen on the desk.

"Of course. Go ahead, I agree. I gotta go, sorry."

Chloe made her apologies to the investors and rushed out of the office, leaving them–and Bruce and Kyle–dumbfounded as to why she had left the meeting not even a quarter of the way through.

∼

9:55 a.m.

Chloe ran down the balcony steps, her heart beating the

samba against her chest. Barely able to control her excitement, she searched for Shona, checking all her usual work areas.

But there was no sign of her anywhere.

Bumping into Ron again in the canteen, she smiled, her heart in her mouth.

"Ron, do you know where Shona's working today?"

"She should be out in the fields today, finally on the machinery detail she's been yearnin' for. Jeffrey Ellis insisted on it after all her hard work around here." Ron grinned.

Chloe thanked him and darted out into the fields, spotting some tractors and trucks in the distance being tended to by the chief mechanic, Ray Brown.

"Ray!" Chloe called out breathlessly after running the thirty yards over to him. "Where's Shona?" she asked, trying to sound professional.

"If I knew, I'd tell you, ma'am," Ray said gruffly, not looking up from his clipboard.

"I'm sorry?" she stared at him, panic starting to rear its ugly head in the pit of her stomach.

"I ain't seen her, and I've got work backed up. The first time she gets put on machinery, and she lets us down! If you see her, Miss Chloe, can you kick her in the backside from me?" Ray barked orders to some guys in the distance.

"Wait, sorry, WHAT? Shona isn't here?" Her world began to spin.

"Yep, she ain't turned up to work this morning. I checked with the office, nothing! Looks like–" Ray trailed off as Chloe raced towards the front desk.

"You OK, Miss Chloe?" asked one of the clerks.

"Yeah...Um." Frantically, she rifled through the punch cards, finally finding Shona's. That morning's column hadn't been punched, and Chloe's worst fears began to manifest themselves.

"Mary, have you heard why Shona Jackson's not in?" Chloe drummed her fingernails on the counter.

"Nothing, and that ain't *like* her. Mr. Ellis ain't gon' be happy." Mary tutted as she adjusted her horn-rimmed cat-eye glasses.

Chloe searched everywhere, hoping Shona had arrived so late that she'd got straight down to work and not bothered to punch in, thinking there was no point. There was one person who must've seen her at some point that morning. She looked over at Elbie running an oily rag over a piece of truck engine.

Just as she was about to run over to him, a voice called her name. She turned to see Randy standing behind her looking as if he hadn't slept a wink, his clothes disheveled, his face shrouded by dark, bumpy stubble, his eyes red and raw.

"Randy, what is it? I ain't got time to–"

"Oh, Miss Chloe, I'm so sorry! Please, say you'll forgive me."

Elbie looked up and smiled, seeing Chloe heading his way. His smile turned to a confused frown when he saw her stop to talk to Randy, who seemed to be distraught about something. Throwing his oily rag down on his bench, he started to walk over to them, in case he could help.

"They only told me to give her a *lift!*"

Randy's words dribbled out of his mouth, along with globules of spit as hot, salty tears streamed down his pudgy red face. Chloe's panic was building by the second but, to extract some fragments of sense out of the man crumbling in front of her, she had to remain calm.

"Give who a lift? Who, Randy?" she demanded.

"Shona."

"Who asked you to give her a lift, Randy? Who?"

"Kyle. Your father was there too. Oh God, I'm a dead man now!"

"Randy, I swear to the Holy Ghost, if you do not tell me everything you know this instant, then *I* will kill you right now with my bare hands! Now, TELL ME, GODDAMN IT!" Chloe roared.

～

Elbie broke into a run hearing Chloe yell. In all the years he'd known her, he'd never heard her raise her voice.

～

"Miss Chloe, if I tell you, they will kill me! I got a family."

"Here, you see this? It'll keep you and your family going for over a year! Take it, then get outta here. Now tell me!"

She thrust an envelope stuffed with money into Randy's quivering hands.

"I was at home around midnight last night, and there's a knock on my door, so I answer and Kyle storms in with your father and the three Bullen brothers. Kyle demanded I go with them. I had no choice, I didn't want 'em in my house with my wife and babies asleep upstairs." Randy begged Chloe for some understanding of his predicament.

He received none.

"And?" Her eyes shot arrows of fire at Randy.

"I got in your father's car, sitting in the back, and I heard them say that you were with Shona in some hotel."

"Go on–"

"Then they gave me the address and said all I had to do was offer Shona a lift to work or I'd get the beating of my life."

"And *did* you?"

"I had no choice! At 4:45, I saw her walking down the road towards work, and I had to make it like I just happened to be driving past. I pulled over and asked if she wanted a lift, like I was told to."

"And? What did she say, Randy?" Chloe swallowed back the maelstrom of emotion inside of her.

"She got in. *She trusted me.*" He lowered his eyes.

"Then what happened?"

"We drove half a mile until I stopped where they told me to stop, somewhere quiet. Where *they* were waiting. They reached into the truck and grabbed her. She was screaming so much, punching and kicking at them, but they were too strong for her. Kyle told me to get the hell outta there. I ain't heard no screams like that in my life!"

Randy looked traumatized.

"What did you see?" Chloe whispered as she bit the the inside of her bottom lip.

"I looked in my mirror and saw her on the ground. They were beating the shit out of her, like a pack of wild animals. All that anger and aggression they'd built up against her! She was crying out for you, Miss Chloe, she sounded in so much pain! They knew they had to shut her up somehow, she was makin' too much noise!" Randy paused momentarily.

"And then I heard it."

Chloe swallowed hard, her heart disintegrating inside of her.

"Heard what? WHAT, RANDY?"

He paused again, this time for what felt like an age.

"The gunshot."

∼

Elbie was only a few feet away, hearing only a few scattered words coming from a distraught-looking Randy. He saw Chloe's body sway, then her legs buckle underneath her in slow motion.

~

Chloe held her hands up to her mouth and let out an agonized scream. Her world became blurry around her, her legs giving way. Elbie, who was only a few feet away by then, caught her just in time as her body collapsed into his arms.

"What in the GODDAMN hell, Randy? Did I just *hear* that right?" His eyes raged with fury and confusion as he struggled under Chloe's dead weight.

"I'm so sorry, Elbie, I'm so sorry." Randy turned and ran as fast as his enormous body could carry him, leaving the old man to hoist Chloe up in his arms and take her back to the tool room.

He placed her on his stool, her arms safely tucked over the bench. Grabbing his crowbar, he stomped into the workshop at the back of the tool room and thundered it down with all his might onto the floorboards below him, shattering them into tiny pieces.

He simply didn't care anymore.

Scrabbling around in the hole he had created, he pulled out his escape box, ripping the lid off to get to his hip flask. He poured a measure into a clean glass and gently tried to rouse Chloe, stroking her hair firmly as he sought to wet her lips with the strong liquor. She gasped and coughed, almost falling off the stool as the alcohol started to take effect. When she realized where she was, Chloe stared into Elbie's anxious eyes and begged him to tell her what she had been told by Randy wasn't true.

"I'm so sorry, but I haven't seen her all day either. It's not like her. I'm so sorry, darlin'." Elbie crumbled as he watched her release a fresh set of strangled sobs. He forced another few sips of brandy into her mouth to help calm her.

"Oh, Elbie, it's all my fault! If I hadn't got involved with her, then Kyle would never have–"

"Now, *you* listen to me, girl–" Elbie gripped her face in his hands firmly, his own eyes overflowing with tears. "Do you have *any* idea how much that girl loved you? She would've given up her life to spend just one single *second* with you, you know that?" The tears were streaming down the old man's face now. He had lost the last friend he had there.

"Oh, Elbie! What am I gon' do now? I can't live without her, I loved her so much!" Chloe's mascara-smudged eyes were heartbreaking for him to look at. Turning away, he caught sight of the answer staring him in the face.

His diary.

~

Kyle and Bruce clinked glasses, celebrating the successful meeting with the investors that had just concluded.

"We are covered, aren't we, Larry? The sheriff's on our side with regards to the *disappearances* around here?" Kyle asked quietly after the investors had left. "Now the broad is gone, people around here are gon' be asking questions."

"Well, that's where a lot of the money goes. Well, Ellis's money, you could say, but we're not gon' tell him that, are we? It's an expensive business keeping this town quiet."

Kyle nodded his head in agreement.

"Just one last loose end to tie up," Bruce added. "The old man and that fuckin' diary of his. I don't know what dirt he thinks he's got on us, but it's best for everyone if it, and he, disappears. Understand? Then we can all get on with our lives!"

Understanding perfectly, Kyle drained his glass.

"I'll go pay him a lil' visit."

∽

"What is this, Elbie?" Chloe asked, holding the leather journal in her trembling hands.

"I been keeping a log of every despicable crime that has happened in this place over the last few years now. There's dates, times, names. It's all in there, proof that can be checked up on. They ain't getting away with it any longer. I seen two of my friends die here. I'll be damned if I'm gon' go the same way."

Chloe held the old man's hand as he shook with years of pent-up anger at the treatment he had witnessed and not been able to stop.

"I was gon' give it to the press so they could blow the lid of this, but someone up top must have found out about it. Some truck near as damn ran straight into me the night I had arranged to meet a reporter in town. Put the fear of God in me at the time, but now, after Shona? Well, I couldn't give a damn anymore. It has to stop, NOW!"

"What are you going to do, Elbie?"

"I want you to have it. I'm gon' get in my truck and I ain't gon' stop driving until I get to my daughter's ranch. I don't know what the hell I been waitin' for. I told Shona a while back not to waste a single damn second of any potential happiness she could have with you, and there I was doin' the same! I'm a goddamn fool! But no more, I'm outta here!"

∽

Kyle sauntered down the balcony steps and headed towards the tool room, a grin on his smug face, feeling all the strands of his master plan finally coming together.

Elbie collected the few possessions he had from the workshop, fastened his tool belt around his waist and put his flask and the few dollars spare he had from his box in his pocket.

"Elbie, take this." Chloe reached into her jacket pocket and handed him a thick wad of money. "Call it your retirement bonus!"

Elbie held the money, then reached out to her, taking her into his arms in a tight embrace. "I hope you can find happiness. Shona would want you to be happy!" The tears were rolling down both their faces now.

"Thank you, Elbie. You're the father I *shoulda* had!" She grabbed his bag and held it close to him. "Now, go!" She sniffed and wiped her face with her sleeve.

They heard footsteps approaching the tool room and a very familiar voice singing happily to himself.

Chloe felt the panic slice through her.

"Elbie, go, NOW!" She heaved him towards the metal back door.

"Look after yourself, Miss Chloe!"

He disappeared through the door and raced over to his truck parked twenty feet away. Kyle appeared in the doorway, his smug smile fading as he saw Chloe standing there, the open back door blowing in the wind.

"Where's the old man?"

"I ain't seen him!" Chloe lied, hiding the diary in her inside jacket pocket.

He walked over to the open door and watched Elbie roar away fast.

"Arrrgggghhhh, FUCK!" Kyle banged his fist into the door, recoiling in agony as the metal rivets tore the skin off his knuckles. He barged past Chloe and ran to the nearest phone.

"EARL! The old man's headin' your way. Get in your truck and chase him off the fucking road if you have to!"

"Sorry boss, but that idiot little brother of mine still hasn't returned with the truck yet, after we sent him to finish the *last* job you gave us!"

Kyle slammed the phone down and, with one last murderous look at Chloe, he smoothed his jet black hair back into place and disappeared.

Putting her hand over her pocket, Chloe felt the edges of the diary. Completely exhausted, she thought of the one place she could go where she knew she would be safe.

Chapter 81

Chloe arrived at the Birds' farm late. She'd driven around for hours and hours, visiting every place she'd ever been with Shona, including her favorite place down by the riverbank, in the hope of finding some sign of where they had dumped her body. It broke her heart into even tinier pieces to know she was out there somewhere, cold and alone.

Driving up to the farmhouse, she saw something that sent a chill through her bones. The Bullens' dark green Ford pickup truck was parked outside, the tail hatch dangling loose.

Slamming on the brakes, Chloe jumped out of the car and ran up to the front door, praying that the murderous owners of the truck hadn't already done something terrible to Tom and Ruby too.

"Tom, Ruby! Open the door! Please!"

Chloe shifted her weight between her feet, waiting for the porch light to click on.

"Chloe! We've been trying to find you!" Tom extended his arm to guide her through the kitchen to the table.

"I saw that green truck. They murdered Shona. Where are they? I'll kill them! Oh, Tom! Shona's gone, she's gone!"

"Chloe, calm down! Please, for heaven's sake, take it easy!"

Tom tried to hold her as her body shook. As she lifted her head to take a breath, she saw a young man cowering behind Ruby.

"Miss Chloe, I'm so sorry for what I done, but I had to come here. I had to bring her home. Couldn't leave her lying out there in the cold, in that goddamn place all alone." Billy Bullen was standing there, patches of dry, dark blood staining his dirty white undershirt.

"*You* killed her? YOU? WHY?"

Chloe flew at Billy, who offered no defense as she rained down blows on him. Tom threw his strong arms around her, comforting her as best he could.

"Please...please try to calm down." Ruby held Chloe's raging face in her hands.

"I didn't wanna do it! They made me!"

Billy continued to snivel as Ruby held Chloe until her body felt limp in her arms. Carefully, she carried her to a chair at the kitchen table and soothed her distraught sobs until Chloe was calm enough to receive an explanation as to why the youngest Bullen brother had ended up on their doorstep that evening.

Chapter 82

S aturday evening, three nights later.
For the last three days and nights, Larry Bruce had hardly left his office. Pouring himself drink after drink, he sat silently in his leather chair, his dim desk lamp the only light in the room.

Out of the corner of his red eye, he noticed a flicker of movement in the darkness, near his open door.

"Who's that?" he slurred.

The figure stepped forward. Her face was pale, the dark circles hanging like hammocks underneath her tired eyes. She looked almost ethereal in the low light.

"Where the *hell* you been for the last few days?" Bruce demanded, a tiny fragment of concern in his drunken voice.

"Around," Chloe replied aloofly.

"What you doing here?"

"To find out if everything they say about you is true and to see once and for all if you've finally found the decency to admit to me, your *daughter*–" the word caught in her throat "–what a *murdering bastard* you are!"

"What the hell you talking about?" Bruce replied, adjusting his tie.

"Where d'you wanna start? Cuban? The Bullens–" She sat down in the chair in front of his desk. "–and Shona." Saying her name aloud still pierced Chloe's heart, but she owed it to her to find out the truth.

"Whoa–" He held his hands up. "I don't know what you think you know here, but–"

"OK, I'll tell you," Chloe interrupted matter-of-factly. "Three black guys a while back, you remember? The ones you set up with those wallets? D'you know what happened to them afterwards? The sheriff handed them straight to the Bullens! We can all guess what happened to them then, huh?"

"Why you so bothered, Chloe?"

"So, you admit to framing them? For *God's* sake, be honest for once in your fucking life."

Chloe didn't care anymore. Nothing would hurt her as much as what he'd already done.

"Of course I did. I ain't having that dolt Ellis bring in more coloreds every goddamn day. I wanted the message to get out they wouldn't last five minutes here. I called the boys, and they took care of it, so what?"

There wasn't a shred of remorse in Bruce's voice.

"And Cuban?"

"He was tougher, stupider than the others. When he attacked Kyle, he called up to me and yeah, I got the Bullens onto it. Can't have an out of control colored on the loose."

"Kyle attacked Shona first! Cuban was just defending her. Does that change your view now?"

"A nigger's still a nigger," he replied flatly.

"Now Shona."

She swallowed hard on the lump in her throat.

"What about Shona?"

"You knew, didn't you?"

"Shona led you astray. Before her, you were gon' have the control of the business, a wealthy man, a family–"

"I was MISERABLE before her!" Chloe shouted, the first bit of raw emotion she had been able to express in days. "You don't even know me, do you? How the *hell* can you be my father and not know *one goddamn thing* about me?"

"Shona Jackson was a waste of space. She was never gonna amount to anything and was trying to take you down with her. She was mentally unstable! I couldn't have her preying on my–"

"No, Larry. You let *me* tell you about Shona Jackson–"

~

Wednesday evening, three nights earlier.

Tom and Ruby led Chloe to the barn where Shona's bed was, followed by Billy Bullen who sniveled over what he had been forced to do. Opening the barn door, Tom flicked the light on. Looking over, Chloe saw her battered body lying on her bed. She broke out into fresh sobs when she saw the state they'd left her in.

~

Saturday evening.

Chloe leaned back in her chair, her voice eerily calm.

"Let me tell you about Shona Jackson, Larry. I pursued her, ME! She avoided me because of her feelings. When I was with her, she listened to me, really listened. Asked about my drawings, my ambitions, she even knew what my favorite color was. Even though I never actually told her, she just took the time to notice. I'd never laughed like I did when I was with her. But you...YOU set me up with a monster!"

Bruce sneered as he drained his glass.

"You know something, Larry? You're so big on protecting me, did you know Kyle raped me? Yeah, real good job you did protecting me! You know who'd make me feel better every time I was hurt? Shona. Then the *only* night we ever made love, you know who set that up? ME! When I found out what happened to her afterwards, I felt like I couldn't wake up another morning. All I wanted was to be with Shona. You say you were protecting me? Bullshit! You've hurt me more than anybody!"

Chloe glared at him.

"So, where did those animals bury the bodies?"

"I don't know. They don't tell me so it can't get traced back to me. That's why I pay them so goddamn well," he replied, remorseless.

"Not good enough. I want you to get them to tell me where they are," she demanded loudly.

Bruce shook his head. "Impossible."

"What about Jeffrey?"

"Ellis?"

"Why are you screwing him over? He's done nothing but try to help you. He made you an even richer man than you were before, but you go and blow it by betting his money away and hiring thugs to do your dirty work! I know all about the sheriff being on the payroll, and Sam Lewis. You pay him a lot of money to keep things out of the papers, don't you, Larry!"

"Keeping people quiet costs money, but you have no idea about business. Neither does Jeffrey."

"Everybody likes him. He's honest." Chloe replied.

"Honesty doesn't get you anywhere," Bruce said, pouring the last of his bottle of whiskey into his glass.

Chloe paused, his final statement ringing in her ears.

"You know what, Larry? I'm glad you finally admitted all that to me," she said, backing up to the doorway where she'd dropped her bag.

"Why's that?"

Chloe took a thick brown leather journal out of her bag. She walked forward and placed it on the edge of Bruce's desk, just out of his reach.

"Because it matches everything I read in Elbie's diary."

~

Wednesday evening.

"I'm so sorry. I'm so ashamed of myself. When they told me I had to shoot her–" Billy Bullen shook with guilt as he spoke.

Chloe swayed, wanting to rush over to Shona and lie next to her, but feared the ice-cold touch of her lifeless body. As thoughts of the future life they'd planned with each other circled her decimated mind, Billy Bullen continued.

~

Saturday evening.

"How did you get that diary?" Bruce's voice croaked.

Chloe stepped aside as another figure entered the room.

"The Bullens were arrested, Larry. It's all over."

"Who the hell are you?" Bruce growled.

"Sheriff Walters. Sheriff Landon's been *reassigned* with immediate effect. I've been drafted in to oversee this matter. I heard everything you said, sir, and I'm sorry, but it's enough for me to take you in."

"What the hell?" Bruce reached for his empty bottle.

"I wouldn't, Larry," the sheriff warned.

"This why you came back, Chloe? To set your own father up?" Bruce spat the words through his clenched teeth.

"No. I came here to tell you that the business is now solely in Ellis's name. I've sold my soon-to-be-inherited share to him. I don't want it. I never have. Couldn't you see that? I just wanted to be *free*! To draw, to ride, to live!" Chloe cried, her emotions spilling out now.

"What d'you mean *soon-to-be-inherited*? You get it when I die, not before! But I might just leave it to Kyle instead, how'd you like that idea?" he said cruelly.

"Not your decision anymore, Larry! You forfeited that right the second you were arrested. Didn't you read the small print on our contract? Or did you think I'd be stupid enough to leave out such an important detail?"

Bruce's heart sank when he recognized the voice of Jeffrey Ellis, who, seconds later, walked into his office. Behind him was his lawyer, holding a thick pile of papers tied up with red string.

"You can't do that!" Bruce roared, squirming as Sheriff Walters slapped his handcuffs on him.

"Oh, I think you'll find I can, Larry. As soon as Chloe came to see me, I had Dennis here go over our contract, and sure enough there it was. But how important is *don't get arrested for embezzlement, assault, fraud, bribery* and what else was it–" Ellis turned to Walters as he snapped his fingers theatrically, pretending to rack his brain. He was enjoying the moment.

"We have a pretty strong case for murder in the second degree, sir. Especially with the sheer amount of evidence we have now, thanks to this diary here," the sheriff replied, picking up Elbie's leather journal. "Full of wrongdoings all under your watch, Larry!" he added.

"This is fucking crazy. You can't do this." Bruce shook his head, but the reality of his predicament began to sink in.

"I'm promoting Ron Black to run this place. Life's too short!

I'm gon' spend my time at home now with Marjory," Ellis grinned.

Chloe stood in front of Bruce, coolly looking into his eyes.

"Oh, by the way, I have *one* more thing to tell you–"

∼

Wednesday evening.

"You saved me, Miss Chloe. I never forgot that. You coulda told my brothers you saw me that night at The Shelter, but you didn't. So, I couldn't do it, ma'am. I just couldn't take her away from you. I put my gun in the air and jus' fired at the sky!"

Chloe's head snapped to face Billy, in complete shock.

"She's *ALIVE*?" she breathed.

∼

Saturday evening.

"She's *ALIVE*?" Bruce was thunderstruck.

Chloe realized as Bruce was being led away that she still had one more question to ask him, before washing her hands of him for good. She looked him directly in the eye.

"Why, Larry? Why so much hatred for black people?"

"Why d'you keep callin' me that? You will address me as your father, Chloe!" Bruce demanded.

"No, Larry. That's not what you are to me now. Answer my question. Why the hatred all these years? What have they EVER done to you?"

Bruce could see in Chloe's eyes that there was no point fighting it anymore.

"Because that damn colored should've died in that machine, *not* your brother! I've always hated those damn stinking bastards. Then, after your brother died I couldn't stand to have 'em anywhere near me, reminding me of what I lost."

For the first time, Chloe saw genuine tears in her father's cold eyes.

"We *both* lost David, Larry. But that *damn stinkin' bastard* as you call him, ripped the shirt off his own back, made a tourniquet and stemmed the bleeding just long enough for me to get there and have those precious last minutes to say goodbye. You know why you didn't see him when you arrived? Because he ran off to get help!"

Larry Bruce stared blankly at her revelation. All these years he'd got it wrong. He had no words left for her as Sheriff Walters walked him swiftly out of the office.

~

Wednesday evening.

After a minute or two of staring at her, Chloe finally mustered up the strength to go over and sit on the end of Shona's bed, spotting the rocket postcard she'd bought her on the wall just above her head. Seeing the many puncture marks around its edges made Chloe ache, knowing that Shona must have looked lovingly at it practically every night before she went to sleep, then pinned it back up safely.

"Well, Billy, I guess you'd better stay here for now, till you get fixed up. Let me have your keys, and I'll put your truck in the hay barn in the field up top with Miss Chloe's car and throw a tarp over them both. That way your brothers won't see your truck in the driveway and find you till we figure out what we're gon' do," Tom said.

Billy nodded gratefully, knowing it made perfect sense.

"Let's leave things for tonight. Ruby here will get you something to eat."

Tom, Ruby and Billy gave Chloe her privacy as they bid her goodnight and left her alone in the barn with Shona.

Chloe couldn't take her eyes off Shona and what the vicious thugs had done to her. Her eyes were bruised and swollen, her lips cut and an angry, red graze covered most of the right side of her forehead. Ruby had tended to her wounds as best she could and placed thick blankets over her to keep her warm.

Crawling into the small space between Shona and the wall of the barn, Chloe tucked her shivering, bare legs under the blankets and snuggled down into Shona, her eyes red and raw, then draped her right arm gently over her motionless torso. Chloe's face lay next to hers, a fresh tear landing on Shona's grazed forehead. She made the smallest of movements as the salty tear stung her cut skin. Gasping, Chloe resisted the urge to shake Shona awake. But the injuries on her body were just too severe.

"I'm here, baby, shhh, I'm here. I'm here. Shhh, I'm not going anywhere. I'll be here when you wake up. Shhh...I love you, baby," she whispered in Shona's ear.

Chloe lay back down carefully, as if Shona were made of fragile glass. Breathing in her familiar scent, she nuzzled into her neck and fell into a deep sleep, hoping her presence and body heat would somehow help Shona to make it through the long, cold night ahead.

Saturday evening.

Jeffrey Ellis stood on the balcony outside Bruce's former office and smiled fondly at an exhausted Chloe as they were about to go their separate ways. The echo of Bruce's protesting yells still reverberated down the hallways of the canteen below.

"So, Miss Chloe, what will you do now?" he asked with genuine interest.

"Oh, I don't know. I hear California is mighty fine this time of year!"

Chapter 83

The following day, Chloe had made arrangements to pay someone a visit. The sheriff had called her that Sunday morning to tell her that they'd finally picked Kyle up, after catching him crossing the state border. She drove down to the station, determined to close one more door to her past. Taking a deep breath to prepare herself, she walked through the cell block.

"What the hell do you want? Finally realized you can't live without me? Get me out of here now! You're good for the bail money. That hotel you fucked your bitch in couldn't have been cheap!"

Even now, behind bars, Kyle's vitriol towards her was astounding. But she remained calm.

"No, I haven't. I've just come to tell you that the wedding's officially off. I ain't worth a dime to you now I've sold my share of the business back to Jeffrey Ellis. So, if you want it still, I guess you'll just have to marry him!"

Chloe was enjoying seeing the fury glaze over Kyle's stubbly face with him safely behind bars, never able to lay a finger on her again. He got up off the concrete seat in his cell and walked over to Chloe, quietly fuming as he leaned on the bars.

Unafraid, she looked him dead in the eye, her voice barely above a whisper.

"You make me sick, Kyle. I hope you rot in jail." She turned to walk away from him.

"Hey! You get back here right now! You can't do this to me! You can't leave me in here!"

"Oh, by the way," said Chloe, "your little friend, Billy Bullen?" She smiled. "He has *really* bad aim."

"What the hell you talkin' about?" His face blanched.

"Shona. She's alive." Her face was motionless.

Kyle rattled the bars of his cell, seething with rage.

"Bye, Kyle."

Chloe didn't look back as she walked away.

Two weeks later.

Unable to face speaking to her mother before she left, Chloe wrote a brief note to Antonia outlining where in California they would be staying and left an address. She was under strict instructions not to tell a soul. The risk of Bruce's associates seeking revenge on her and Shona was still too great. They spent their last night in Daynes at the Birds' farmhouse, safe in the knowledge that the next day, a search was being conducted of a patch of wasteland that Billy Bullen, in return for leniency, had told police was where the bodies were buried.

Chloe had spent the last few days rallying the people of the town to help with the search. Pretty much everyone she'd asked was willing to help, each remembering someone who had gone missing over the years. Every single one of the workers at Ellis and Bruce had promised to turn out that morning, out of respect for Shona, whose influence had touched them all as they were still reaping the rewards of the changes they were told she'd suggested for them. It made Chloe smile to know that they regarded her as a hero and in those few short months of working there she'd completely won them over, like she'd won Chloe over, by just being herself.

On the morning of the search, all the townsfolk walked together, blacks and whites putting their differences aside. Billy Bullen had marked out an area of interest on the map he had been given by Sheriff Walters. A promise of a lesser sentence had loosened his tongue, but Shona knew that deep down he wanted to help pay back in some way for what his brothers had taken from the town.

Arriving at the site, Chloe was completely astounded. Black faces were interspersed with white ones, the whole community coming together with one thing in common—they were sick of constantly being at war with each other. So many people had died because of it, and the town was tired. They were no longer at the mercy of the Bullen brothers, and the rest of the suspected Klan members had all mysteriously left town. Chloe's call to Joe at the local paper regarding a list of names she'd collated and asked him to publish in a week's time probably had a lot to do with their sudden disappearance, once Joe had put the word around that he had a copy of this list.

Chloe picked delicately through the dirt with her spade, looking up every now and again with a lump in her throat at the people around her who, at one time or another, had spoken hatred about the black community. These people were now working *with* them to search for the bodies.

She stood up and scanned the area. Across the site, she saw Shona attacking the dry mud with a pick-ax, holding her damaged ribs and grimacing as the pain of her exertion rumbled through her. Next to her was Billy Bullen, looking down at what Shona was determined to uncover.

Suddenly, the air shattered as Shona cried out.

"Quick! Over here!" she yelled. Chloe dropped her spade with a clatter and darted over, worried that she'd hurt herself.

Shona sank painfully to her knees and ripped clumps of earth out of the ground with her bare hands. Still weak from her injuries, her strength depleting rapidly, Billy Bullen crouched down next to her and carefully picked up what she had found.

"That's my boy, that's *him*! Oh, my *Woody*!"

Maria's voice echoed through the somber air as she ran to scoop up her boy in her arms, confirming his identity when she saw his damaged foot peel away from the earth surrounding him. Turning to Chloe, Maria's eyes glistened with tears.

"She found him for me, Miss Chloe. I got my boy back!" Maria gently carried her boy towards a second gurney that had been wheeled over to her. She kissed her boy's head and nodded as the white men acting as stretcher-bearers respectfully covered Woody's body.

Chloe's eyes stung with tears of pride at the sheer honor of knowing a woman so wonderful, so truly unique as Shona Jackson. Even though she had only been in Daynes a short time, her presence in the town, her reputation would live on for a very long time.

"Shona, over here!"

Another shout echoed across the field.

"What is it?" Shona ran over to where a small group of men were standing. They had removed their caps out of respect. Her eyes were drawn downwards to the large black hand they'd uncovered, the calloused fingers she recognised from the first time she'd met him...and the crucifix around his neck. Devastated, she sank to her knees.

"Oh, Cuban."

Chapter 84

It was finally time for Chloe and Shona to say goodbye to Tom and Ruby. After they had discovered Cuban's body along with the others, they'd laid him to rest by the Weaver, in Shona's favorite spot. They were all emotionally drained after the tumultuous events of the last few weeks.

"I wanted to give you something to say thank you." As they stood by her car, their bags all loaded up, Chloe took out a fat envelope and handed it to Ruby, who nearly burst into tears when she opened it.

"Oh, my dear, no. We can't accept this. You were already kind enough to give us the cow you bought at the auction. Now this is too much, Miss Chloe!" Ruby tried to hand back the money that was stuffed in the envelope, but Chloe gently pushed her hand away.

"No, I want you to have it. Use it for a couple of tickets to come pay us a visit when we get set up properly, maybe? Our forwarding address is in there too, but remember to keep it secret for now!" Chloe smiled as Ruby hugged her tightly.

"You take care of each other, you hear?" Tom said, waiting patiently to give them both a hug goodbye.

"We promise! There's a lot of lost time we got to make up

for!" Chloe laughed as she embraced him tightly. Then, with one final goodbye, both Chloe and Shona got into the car and drove off, watching in the rearview mirror as the Birds waved them away.

∼

Later that afternoon, a light tap on her door jolted the old lady from her nap. Struggling out of her high-backed armchair, she grabbed her walking stick and hobbled over to the door.

"Hello? Who is it?" her weak voice enquired, the door still firmly bolted.

"Dorothy, hi. It's me, Chloe—"

"Oh, hang on a second, dear." Dorothy struggled to wrap her arthritic fingers around the bolt on her door, but with one last heave, it crunched backward into its jacket. She opened the door.

"Thought I'd just stop by on my way through to tell you that I've found someone to fix your truck up, Dorothy."

Dorothy's eyes shone with sheer joy as she saw Shona emerge from behind Chloe, smiling that beautiful smile she had missed so much.

"Oh my goodness! Oh, my dear—"

"I missed you." Shona hugged Dorothy, wincing as the old lady squeezed her still-healing ribs just a little too firmly in her embrace, then slapped her on the back heartily.

"Oh, it's so good to see you, girls. You'll both stay, won't you? You ain't gotta rush off anywhere?" Dorothy's watery eyes were impossible to say no to.

Chloe looked at Shona, raising her eyebrow to tell her that whatever she decided was alright with her. Looking at Dorothy, Shona's bright blue eyes twinkled.

"Well, I guess we're gon' have to stay, Dorothy. I saw the state of that truck out there in your yard. I'm gon' need at least a coupla days straight to get all that rust off! Heck, I may be a genius, but I ain't no miracle worker!"

All three of them broke out into the happiest laughter any of them had heard in a long, long time.

∽

At the end of their few days with Dorothy, Chloe picked up her car keys and headed towards the front door. It was nearly 6 o'clock, and she and Shona had a long drive ahead of them to get to their hotel for the night in Arkansas.

"I'm real sorry we can't stay longer, but you remember from last time what it's like in this town. They can't know I'm here," Shona said sadly.

"And I've arranged for somebody to come visit you every day and bring your groceries over. You won't ever have to worry about bills again," Chloe said. "As soon as we get settled, you bet that we'll arrange for you to come visit us."

"Oh, I'd really like that. You take care of my girl, Miss Chloe–"

"I will, I promise I will. You take care of yourself, Dorothy."

The two of them climbed into her car, Chloe beeping the horn loudly as Shona waved at the old woman, who returned the favor by brandishing her wooden stick in the air with gusto.

∽

Half a mile up the road, Chloe slammed on the brakes, causing the car to skid to a juddering halt and Shona to fly forward in her seat.

"What the—! What's going on?" Shona yelped in surprise.

"Wait a goddamn minute," Chloe replied, deep in angry thought.

She jumped out of the car and stood beside it, her hands on her hips.

"What are you doing?" Shona laughed, perplexed at Chloe's strange behavior.

She received no answer, other than Chloe staring at the roof of her car. Four clicks later, Chloe gripped the soft material tightly and heaved the convertible roof down. Jumping back into the driver's seat, she smiled at Shona, who eyes were sparkling with marvel and pride.

"Am I gon' be *safe* with you drivin' this beast?" Shona said gripping her seat.

"Aww, you scared, honey?" Chloe reached over and ruffled Shona's hair.

"Um, maybe a little!"

"Why? Because I'm more James Dean than Doris Day?" she joked.

"OK, *now* I'm scared! But, I guess I should be safer in the car than on my horse, right?" Shona grinned.

Chloe rolled her eyes and laughed. It was going to take a while for her to live *that* one down.

"Alright then! Now step on the gas and fly this damn rocket to California." Shona threw her hands in the air excitedly, inhaling the sweet air deeply as she felt the breeze on her fingertips.

Chloe reached up to her head and slipped off the silk scarf she was wearing, tossing it theatrically onto the back seat. Giggling, she shook out her silky brown hair.

Stepping on the gas pedal, she shrieked with joy as she felt the cool summer evening air blow like a hurricane through each strand.

FEEDBACK

Thank you for reading 'Meet Me at 10'. We hope you enjoyed the book? Please now scan the QR code below to leave your feedback.
- Open the camera or the QR reader application on your smartphone.
- Point your camera at the QR code to scan the QR code.
- A notification will pop-up on screen.
- Click on the notification to open the website link

THE BEACH HOUSE

Liked *Meet Me At 10?*

Want to know what happened next?

Read your FREE sneak-peak chapters from book 3: *The Beach House* now to find out...

SOME SECRETS RETURN TO HAUNT YOU

THE BEACH HOUSE

THE SEQUEL TO MEET ME AT 10

VICKY JONES
AND
CLAIRE HACKNEY

PART 1: AUGUST 1958

CHAPTER 1

"Is it them?" Shona said. She whipped her neck around to look out of the back window and then back to look at Chloe whose knuckles were now white from her increased grip on the steering wheel.

"I think so," Chloe replied, her right foot pressing down on the gas pedal. Trying to keep composed, she kept her eyes fixed on the road, glancing up to her rearview mirror every few seconds. "I'd know that truck anywhere."

The dark green Ford pickup that had been following them for the last five miles on their way to the Mississippi border with Arkansas began to speed up.

"But that's impossible. They're murderers. The sheriff can't have let them out. And even if he had, would they *really* come all this way from Alabama?" Shona could feel her heart thumping as she wrapped her arms around the back of her seat and stared through the back window.

"We're the reason they lost their garage," Chloe replied, shaking her head with frustration. "But those Bullens have done so many favors for folks, I'd be surprised if strings *hadn't* been pulled. They've been in and out of jail so many times they're bound to know people." Chloe rammed the gas pedal in as far as it would go, causing the engine to roar even louder. "Come on, goddamn you!"

Shona looked down at her map. Locating Route 82, she ran her fingertip along the line. "This road goes on for thirty miles before a turnoff. We'll run out of gas before then if we're going at this pace. I knew we should have filled up when we last stopped." She looked back down at her map and frowned. "We've got what looks like a really long bridge to get across too. It's just up ahead. Less than a mile by my reckoning. There's nowhere to turn off until we get over it."

"A bridge?" Chloe said and gripped the wheel even tighter. She glanced up into the rearview mirror and licked her lips. "They're getting closer. Shona, I don't want to drive over a bridge. What if they try and ram us? We'll end up in the river." Her voice was shaking. Shona looked from side to side, through all of the windows, to see if there was any option for them to get off the road quickly, but neither side of the highway had any offshoots. It was featureless, save for a few trees and shrubs. Up ahead, she saw the steel jaws of a long gray cantilever bridge about to consume them.

"I got an idea," Shona said. "As soon as we hit the bridge, I want you to slow down."

"Slow down? Are you crazy?" Chloe replied, her brown eyes wide.

Shona's voice was eerily calm. "This engine is way more powerful than some pickup, but we're topped out right now. We need some lift." Shona nodded to the sign. "Here it is. The Benjamin G. Humphreys bridge. Chloe, do you trust me?"

"Of course I do."

"Then take your foot off the gas. Then, when I say so, floor it."

Chloe did as she was told. The Chevrolet began to slow down and, in turn, the green pickup crept closer, eating up the distance between them. Shona kept her eyes glued to the side mirror, waiting for the right moment. With their hearts in their mouths, the car began to cross the bridge, creeping more into the middle of the lane, just in case.

"Shona?" Chloe asked, her foot resting against the gas pedal.

"Now!" Shona ordered. They both recoiled with the force of the accelerating car. Thirty became fifty in moments, and the green pickup had no chance of keeping up. "That's it. We're nearly across the bridge. Don't slow down."

The tires thudded against every road joint, until they reached the sign welcoming them to Arkansas and thanking them for driving carefully.

"Look, there," Shona said. "A rest stop. We can pull in there. It's bound to have people there. They won't dare try anything then."

"Thank God," said Chloe, breathing a sigh of relief as she saw the sloping roof of the rest stop and its giant red and yellow sign. "Is the truck still following?"

"Yeah," Shona replied. She let a few moments pass by, the writing on the sign now readable. "Almost there. One, two, three. Now."

Chloe left it until the last possible moment before stomping on the brake and swinging the Chevrolet Deluxe skidding into the parking lot. Gravel and dust was churned up all around them, choking them momentarily. They both looked back up to the highway, waiting to see if the pickup would turn into the rest stop parking lot too. Seconds felt like hours as both Chloe and Shona stared. And waited.

"Please. Please, just drive past," Shona prayed quietly.

Chloe's hands, drenched in cold sweat, flexed around the steering wheel. Just as it looked as if the truck was slowing down to exit the highway, the male passenger leaned out of the window and made a lewd gesture towards Chloe. Whooping, he threw a beer can towards the Deluxe as the driver sped off along the road, passed the turnoff and into the distance.

"It wasn't them," Chloe said, resting her head heavily against the steering wheel, jumping when Shona lay a hand on the back of her neck. "Just some dumb punks."

"It's OK. We did the right thing. If it had been them then..." Shona tailed off, remembering that night she was almost murdered by Earl and Ernest Bullen. "We're safe, baby, no one is gonna chase us anymore. We got a new life now to look forward to. A new start. You OK?" Shona stroked the black string of Chloe's pink pebble necklace with her thumb, until after a few seconds she lifted her face from the steering wheel. It was wet with tears, her eyes red from the dust.

"That night, thinking you were dead, was the most terrified I'd ever been in my whole life. Even more scared than when Kyle..." She swallowed hard. "Did what he did to me."

"I know. But it's all OK now. Look at us. We're together. Those bastards are in jail, and Kyle? Well, he'll never see the light of day again, not with all the stuff the police had been dying to pin on him. They emptied the filing cabinet. We don't have to worry about anything other than enjoying our life together, Chloe. Just me and you. Forever. I promise. We're free now."

Shona leaned in, dying to kiss Chloe and comfort her further, but the car that pulled up near them made them both spring back into their seats.

"Well, not completely free. But there's a motel around the back there. Why don't we stay here tonight?" Shona flashed Chloe a smile that meant only one thing. Returning it, Chloe leaned over and grabbed her purse from the back seat.

"Back in a minute. I'll check us in."

"No, let *me*. You paid the last time, remember?" Shona insisted.

Chloe saw that smile again and blushed. "How could I forget? Our first night together."

"That's right. Well, it's my turn to treat you. I still got some money of my own. I'll be right back." Shona hopped out of the car and into the motel reception. Minutes later, she reappeared, jangling the room key.

Leaving the bigger bags they had in the trunk, they took what they needed for the night and headed to the motel room on the ground floor of the tired old block. Inside, the décor was pretty standard, the faded yellow wallpaper peeling at the corners. The two single beds were both draped in honey-colored comforters, the pillows looking less than plush. Between the two beds was a nightstand on which stood a chipped ceramic lamp complete with stained shade. At the far end of the room was a tiny bathroom, the mold-encrusted shower curtain just about visible through the sliding door. The room wasn't anywhere near as opulent as the Fortua had been, but this time it didn't matter.

Within seconds of the door closing behind them, they threw their overnight bags on the floor. Unable to resist any longer, Shona pushed Chloe up against the wall next to the door and began planting hot kisses on her neck, exactly in the spot where she knew it made her groan. Running her hands through Shona's hair, gripping it tightly, Chloe lifted her head up to meet her lips with her own. The force of her kiss made Shona stagger back, finally landing on one of the beds, with Chloe on top of her still kissing her. In one fluid movement, Shona rolled over so she was now lying on top. Pulling her lips away for a second, she swept her hand over Chloe's cheek and smiled at her, her blue eyes shining.

"God, you're so beautiful," she murmured. "There was so much I wanted to do that night. So much of you I wanted to explore. But I was so nervous, I didn't really know what I was doing."

Chloe gazed back at her, her hands still holding the back of her head, fingers stroking her messy blonde hair. "Are you nervous now?"

"No. Not anymore," Shona whispered back.

"Then what are you waiting for? Make love to me. The way you want to, the way you've always wanted to."

Shona didn't need to be told twice.

∼

Shona and Chloe checked out of the motel just before dawn. With the sound of the morning birdsong in the air, they packed up the car and set off on the highway towards their next destination. Chloe had unclipped and lowered the roof on the Deluxe, letting the wind blow through their hair as they sped along in the glorious heat of the late summer sun.

"So what are we telling people? About who we are?" Shona asked.

"Well, I did think we could tell people we were sisters." Chloe paused and glanced over to Shona, taking in her baby blonde hair and bright blue eyes. "But we look nothing like each other." She smiled.

"That might be our only option, though, in the circumstances." Shona smiled at Chloe's confused reaction, her eyes twinkling. "No one will buy the idea that we're just friends. I can't keep my hands off you."

"But you think it's OK for you to do that if you're my *sister*?" Chloe said as she raised an eyebrow.

Shona blushed. "Oh yeah. I guess I didn't think that one through, did I?"

Chloe laughed. "It's OK, I knew what you meant. But either way, we're gonna have to be careful in plain sight. Lucky for us there are a lot of war widows around, so no one will bat an eyelid if they see my sister living with me now.

They'll just think my *poor husband* is lying in bits somewhere on a battlefield. Never to be seen again." A smile formed at the corners of Chloe's mouth, her finally feeling free from Kyle's vicious clutches. "And we can't have none of that caper you got going on there," she joked, nodding down at Shona's wandering hand which was now brushing the inside of Chloe's thigh.

"Can you blame me? I got the most gorgeous girl in all the world next to me." Heeding Chloe's words, she lifted her hand away and lay back in her seat. "You smell that air? Every mile we drive we're getting closer to the ocean, I know it." She stared off into the horizon then breathed in a huge lungful of air, letting it out slowly.

Their journey took them through the plush greenery of Arkansas, the landscape noticeably changing to drier, dustier plains as they drove day and night, weaving their way onwards through Oklahoma, Texas, New Mexico, Arizona and finally across the border into California, via the bridge over the Colorado river.

"Welcome to California. The Land of Milk and Honey," Chloe said, a glimmer of excitement in her tired eyes. It was just after seven o'clock that Thursday morning and their long journey was almost at an end. With their final destination ever closer now, she turned onto the highway that led straight to the coast. In the fields on either side of the road were swathes of yellow poppies blowing gently in the light breeze, still going strong in the late summer warmth.

"Do you know where we're going?" Shona asked, looking at all the road signs they passed along the way.

Staring straight ahead, Chloe nodded, the tiniest smile at the corner of her mouth. "Yes. I know exactly the place," she replied.

Passing through Greenfield, then Salinas, the scent in the air seemed to change hour by hour as Shona lifted her nose and sniffed. The ocean was close; she could sense it. She closed her eyes and leaned her head back as the car ate up the miles.

"I wanted to surprise you with something. It's not far now," Chloe said, looking sideways at Shona, who was staring out of the window for her first longed-for glimpse of the ocean she'd craved to be near for so long.

Twenty minutes later, Chloe took a turnoff that began to lead down to a sandy path and there, at the end of it perfectly nestled next to the ocean, was a sight that made Shona gasp.

"What have you done?" she said, her mouth hanging open, her eyes wide.

"I made a few enquiries before we left Mississippi. I, well... I wanted you to have something special to come to after everything you've been through. I know this was your dream so..."

Chloe stopped the car and Shona, her legs feeling like jelly, climbed out of the car.

"All I need to do is go and see the realtor before they close at five and pay the deposit." Chloe reached out for Shona's hand. "It's ours, Shona. It's our new home."

Shona was in shock and put both hands up to her mouth. The beach house was an exact replica of the one where she'd spent a week back in 1956 with Dorothy down in Gulfport. It was almost identical to the postcard she'd bought as a memento of that week. Save for a lick of blue paint on the window frames and a touch-up of the white weatherboarding, it was just perfect.

Shona turned to Chloe, tears in her eyes, unable to believe what she was seeing. "How did you know?"

Chloe reached into her purse and took out the postcard of the beach house that had originally belonged to Shona, with numerous pinholes in each corner.

"When I saw Dorothy that first time, when I wanted to find out more about you, she let me stay the night in your old room. I saw the postcard pinned above your bed that you'd left.

Dorothy explained what happened with that Lucy girl, that she gave you her copy of the postcard to take with you. I somehow just knew it was important to you. When I left the next morning, I asked Dorothy if I could keep your postcard and she said 'yes', if I promised that one day I would make your dream a reality. So here we are."

Shona walked towards the beach house in a daze.

Chloe walked up behind her and whispered in her ear, "It's still early enough to go get the keys. You wanna stay in your new home tonight?"

"*Our* new home," Shona corrected. "Chloe, I don't know what to say. How can I ever show you just what this means to me?"

"Just make every day count. That's all I want, Shona. Just you and me, for always. In our forever home. Now, let's go get those keys."

CHAPTER 2

Sunnybrook was the name of the town only a mile up the road from the beach house. Just after they passed the welcome sign, they drove around the first corner of the town square, which was flanked on each side by small local businesses and the usual array of stores. After the town's garage came the local family butcher's, the drugstore and a small boutique hair salon. There was also a shoe repair shop, a candy store and a little bakery. At the end of that row was one of the roads leading out of town. Chloe continued to explore the town's amenities, pulling around the corner to the next side of the square where a smart-looking bar was situated.

"Looks like a nice place. Friendly. Named after the owner, it would seem. Bertie's," Shona said, reading the sign above the door of the bar.

The seating area underneath two blue and white striped awnings was populated by a small group of women laughing and fooling around. The deck area was immaculately scrubbed and presented, and there were small shrubs in planters at each edge of the front and umbrellas fixed to each bench seat. At the corner of that side of the square was the post office and next to that was a gorgeous little flower shop.

Nice, Chloe thought, remembering how much Shona loved pink roses.

Next door to the flower shop was the diner, then the grocery store. On the third corner of the square was the police station with only one patrol car parked outside, and the town's gas station adjacent to it. As Chloe did a second loop of the square, Shona pointed at the one place that had piqued her interest more than the others, the garage.

"Hey, you reckon there might be the chance of a job there?" Shona asked, her eyes keen.

"I dunno, what does that sign say?" They drove closer until Chloe could read it clearly. "Auction. Next Week. Hmm...well, maybe when the new owners open up?"

"Yeah, I guess," Shona replied, a little downcast. "How about that bar?" She pointed over to Bertie's. "Maybe I could get some work in there? Be a bit different to what I'm used to but I learn quick, so..."

Chloe laughed and gave her a cheeky smile. She refocused her eyes on the road, a thought crossing her mind as she drove around the town square. Spotting the realtors' office next to the flower shop, she pulled up in the nearest parking spot.

"I won't be a minute."

About twenty minutes later she reappeared holding a brown envelope and a big set of keys. Shona jumped in her seat like an excited puppy.

"For real? It's ours?" Shona grinned.

"Our new home. Bought outright. Cost almost all of the money I brought with us from my savings, but I don't care. No one can take it away from us."

Shona looked shocked. "You had *that* much money? In cash? In the car all this time?"

"I went to the bank before we set off, remember? My father used to put money in my account all the time for me, and there was my salary too that I hardly spent any of while I was with

Kyle. I had no friends to go out with. Well, apart from those few times we met up. But strawberry shakes aren't that expensive." Chloe smiled at the memory of her meetings with Shona in Ed's diner. Her face then hardened. "It's the least my father owes me after what he did. Oh, I know I could have been all proud and said I didn't want a penny from him, but I ain't stupid. That money is the key to our future, and it's mine by rights anyway. I see it as the inheritance I'll never get. And I can do so much more good with it than my father ever did. It buys us our dream, Shona. I asked the realtor to arrange for it to be furnished too. Nothing major, just the basics like a bed, couch, tables. Enough to get us started." Chloe's defiant expression melted into worry. "You ain't mad at me, are you?" She bit her lip. "I just wanted it to be perfect for you."

Shona waited for a few seconds of contemplation, before her face lit up. "No, of course I'm not mad. I'm too excited to be proud right now too. You call it inheritance from your father, but you know what I call it? I call it compensation. Come on, what are we waiting for? Get us back there!" Shona shrieked until Chloe turned the key in the ignition and floored the gas pedal, sending them roaring off back along the road they came in on.

"You OK?" Shona asked, her excitement to get home marred by concern for Chloe's strange silence on the way back to the beach house.

"Yeah, I'm fine," Chloe replied, fidgeting in her seat. "Just had a funny feeling pass over me a few minutes ago. It's nothing, probably just butterflies." She smiled and pulled into the front yard of the house. Before the car had even fully stopped, Shona jumped out and raced up to the porch steps.

Chloe, however, exited the car much more tentatively. Her face creased in confusion as she looked back down at her seat. Oblivious, Shona began bouncing around the veranda that bordered the perimeter of their new home, listing off the tasks she couldn't wait to start doing to fix up the house. As she reached the porch steps again after a full circuit, she looked over to Chloe, whose face had turned pale. The smile fading on her own face, Shona walked over and saw what Chloe was staring down at.

A small patch of scarlet blood had stained the white leather driving seat.

NOW SCAN THE QR CODE BELOW TO CONTINUE YOUR JOURNEY...

Open the camera or the QR reader application on your smartphone.
- Point your camera at the QR code to scan the QR code.
- A notification will pop-up on screen.
- Click on the notification to open the website link

JOIN IN!

If you would like to receive regular behind-the-scenes updates, get beta reading opportunities, enter giveaways and much, much more, simply visit the site below:

http://hackneyandjones.com

ACKNOWLEDGMENTS

This book has been a passion project, but we couldn't have done it without all our friends and family supporting and believing in us every step of the way.

Special mention to Sharon Atkinson for being so supportive in the writing group where it all started.

Many thanks to all of our beta readers, and for all the amazing support we've received from our **Hackney and Jones** Facebook group.

OUR TEAM

Virtual Assistant:
　Erin Hodgson
　writehandwomannz@gmail.com

Book Covers by:
　WooTKdesign
　wootkdesign@gmail.com

Edited by:
　Gary Smailes
　Bubblecow.com

Proofread by:
　Melanie Bell
　inspire.envisioning@gmail.com

www.ingramcontent.com/pod-product-compliance
Lightning Source LLC
Chambersburg PA
CBHW031545080526
44588CB00018B/2699